OPERATION PARAKRAM

OPERATION PARAKRAM

OPERATION PARAKRAM
The War Unfinished

**Lt. Gen. (Retd.) V.K. Sood
Pravin Sawhney**

SAGE Publications
New Delhi/Thousand Oaks/London

First published in 2003 by

Sage Publications India Pvt Ltd
B-42, Panchsheel Enclave
New Delhi 110 017

Sage Publications Inc
2455 Teller Road
Thousand Oaks, California 91320

Sage Publications Ltd
6 Bonhill Street
London EC2A 4PU

Published by Tejeshwar Singh for Sage Publications India Pvt Ltd, typeset by S.R. Enterprises in 10/12 Utopia and printed at Chaman Enterprises, New Delhi.

Library of Congress Cataloging-in-Publication Data

Sood, V.K.
      Operation Parakram: the war unfinished/V.K. Sood, Pravin Sawhney.
         p.   cm.
      Includes bibliographical references and index.
      1. Operation Parakram, India, 2001–2002. 2. India—Military relations—Pakistan. 3. Pakistan—Military relations—India. 4. India—Military policy. 5. India—Foreign relations—Pakistan. 6. Pakistan—Foreign relations—India. I. Sawhney, Pravin. II. Title.

DS480.853.S72   954.05'2—dc21   2003   2003005769

ISBN: 0-7619-9793-8 (US-Pb)   81-7829-246-7 (India-Pb)

Sage Production Team: Sam George, Ankush Saikia, Radha Dev Raj, Neeru Handa, Mathew P. J., Rajib Chatterjee, N. K. Negi and Santosh Rawat

Dedication

To the indomitable young officers and jawans of
the Indian Army, for their never-say-die spirit, their persever-
ance and their complete faith in their leadership, especially
in times of adversity. It is the duty of the nation
to ensure that they are never let down.

"Whenever there is a situation calling for (the) Army's help, the latter's role should be clearly defined to avoid confusion."

—General S. Padmanabhan
Chief of Army Staff
November 9, 2002

"National security is a matter of highest priority for my Government. After the December 13 attack on our Parliament by Pakistan-based terrorists, we were constrained to deploy our troops along the international border. This decision achieved its purpose by showing both our firmness and our self-restraint in dealing with our hostile neighbour."

—Dr A. P. J. Abdul Kalam
President's Address to Parliament
February 17, 2003

Contents

Preface

Even as the government called off Operation Parakram (meaning valour) on October 16, 2002, it was already thinking about its rebirth. The term "strategic relocation", used to describe the end of mobilisation, was indication enough that the government believed a war was still to be fought, but not immediately, which is why it was thought necessary to give the forces a long-overdue break. Once India developed cold feet after coming very close to war with Pakistan in June 2002, the 10-month-long Operation had started yielding diminishing results. It was simply not worth the mental, physical and financial havoc.

The morale of the troops was dipping precariously. All the peace-time activities of the army had come to a standstill for far too long. The army's schools of instructions had closed down, and all leave was either stopped or curtailed. There was excessive wear and tear of equipment which lay exposed to the vagaries of nature as the make-shift workshops in the field did not have the means to attend to equipment problems. And most importantly, there was a need for the political and military leadership to review the situation, learn lessons, and prepare for another time.

But first, a brief history of the events that enraged the government enough to order a general mobilisation of the army for war on December 18, 2001. On October 1, 2001, the Jaish-e-Mohammad carried out a fidayeen attack outside the Jammu and Kashmir Assembly killing 29 people. Even as the state Chief Minister Farooq Abdullah wept on national television, Prime Minister A. B. Vajpayee wrote a terse letter to the US President George W. Bush, claiming that India's patience was not unlimited, implying that unless the US reined in Pakistan, India would be forced to take matters into its own hands, which could cause a setback to the US-waged Operation Enduring Freedom in Afghanistan.

The threat was taken seriously, and Pakistan President Pervez Musharraf condemned the attack calling it an act of terrorism. But the Talibanised militants were not deterred by India's bold pronouncements. On December 13, 2001 they went a step further and attacked the Indian Parliament—it was then in session, though neither the Prime Minister nor the leader of the Opposition were in the House. The government deliberated and finally decided that written and verbal threats would not do anymore. Something concrete needed to be done to show people at home and the international community that India meant business. Finally, on December 18, 2001, Operation Parakram—essentially an army operation, as the air force and the navy can be mobilised at short notice—was launched.

Unfortunately, India is no US and Pakistan no Afghanistan. Hence, mobilisation, which implies that troops are launched into war in a matter of weeks, if not days, did not reach its logical conclusion as India continued to hope that the US would see its point of view and leash Pakistan. For some reason it ignored the fact that all nations have to fight their own wars, and that it could not be an exception to this rule. Driven by sheer naivete, India relied completely on the US in the belief that the "two democracies" had a common fight against international terrorism. It was presumed that after the tragic events of 9/11, the US would better understand India's decade-long fight against Pakistan-sponsored cross-border terrorism, and that the US-led world community would see terrorists through the glasses held by India and not distinguish between good (freedom fighters) and bad (murderers of the innocent) terrorists. Hence, it also believed that the US shared its concerns about Pakistan's proxy war in Jammu and Kashmir. Even while agreeing that nothing should be done to weaken the US-led war in Afghanistan, India hoped that its equally strong case against Pakistan would also be taken up soon by the international community. But its hopes were belied, as this did not happen.

As India was too caught up with its own vision of how the war against terrorism would unfold, it also failed to appreciate the growing role of Musharraf in the US scheme of things. It is no accident that the US interlocutor with Pakistan was Gen. Colin Powell. The two generals thrash out matters as only soldiers can, and came to the unambiguous give-and-take conclusions. The US secretary of state went on record saying that getting Musharraf on board against terrorism was his satisfying achievement. Though the Pakistani ruler did not put it so succinctly, it was clear that 9/11 changed his fortunes. And with a distinguished general as his inter-locutor, he could close a happy deal much faster than he expected.

However, all was not lost. Despite misreading the changing geo-political equations, India also learnt a few positive lessons from the army's mobilisation. For one, the army and the air force could do some serious collective training for war, an opportunity rarely available during peacetime. New military options were appreci-ated and tested. For example, the army practised to fight a suc-cessful war limited to the Line of Control (LoC). It also trained itself for a full-scale conventional war which could result in mean-ingful military objectives being met. Senior commanders believe that across-the-board training for a conventional war was pos-sible only because of the long mobilisation period. Such training would give more options to the military, thereby helping them retain an element of surprise in war.

Consequent to such training, the chinks in conventional armour were better understood. This resulted in India seeking to acquire weaponry on a scale not seen since the eighties under Prime Minis-ter Rajiv Gandhi. Setting aside the various reports of the Comptrol-ler and Auditor General which have found irregularities in defence procurements in the wake of the 1999 Kargil war, and scandals like the Tehelka exposé which have been a set-back to new acquisitions, the government decided to strengthen the armed forces.

That India is preparing to fight another day is evident from the fact that the government has pulled out all the plugs for defence purchases worth billions of dollars to be signed and procured in the third quarter of 2003. The expected deals will be of two types: the ostensible and the hidden. The former are needed to reinforce conventional strength for both regular and irregular war, and the latter are efforts to procure prohibitive technology needed for vari-ous indigenous missile projects. Russia, Israel, and hopefully France (in the same order), are the countries with whom this busi-ness would be done. India's topmost priority, however, would be to garner adequate quantities of spares, force multipliers for night-fighting and depth reconnaissance, and specialised ammunition. Should India and Pakistan go to war in the near future, which is likely, an embargo on arms and ammunition would be among the first actions taken by the international community.

Another significant issue that the government and the army is addressing at the moment is the importance of the irregular forces.

Musharraf is on record saying that in the event of a war, Pakistan would have used its irregular forces or jehadis to counter India's offensive. These would have played havoc with India's lines of internal communication, supply, and casualty evacuation systems during a war. As a result, to strengthen our own counter-insurgency operations, and to take an irregular war inside Pakistan-occupied-Kashmir, India has taken two important decisions. First, the Border Security Force (BSF) would gradually go back to its primary task of being the second line of defence.[1] The government has cleared the raisings of more Central Reserve Police Force to take over the BSF's present job in the border state. Besides providing unity of command, this move will help alleviate the many problems in the Unified Headquarters for counter-insurgency tasks in Jammu and Kashmir. One of the major problems with the smooth functioning of counter-insurgency operations has been the BSF's insistence that as the oldest paramilitary force, the Rashtriya Rifles (National Rifles), which is a regular army by another name, should function under its command and control. Second, the government has cleared the raising of more special forces for the army. These forces are likely to be trained and equipped by Israel.[2] It is axiomatic that these forces would be used to take covert battles across the LoC.

Even as India is strengthening its army's conventional prowess, there are palpable efforts to make nuclear deterrence credible. The 700-km range Agni-I was test fired twice—on January 25, 2002, and on January 9, 2003—and is reportedly ready for induction in the artillery. The government has contracted to lease four Russian TU-22 long range bombers, which are expected to be in service with the Indian air force soon. Alongside, the government has also announced the Nuclear Command Authority, and importantly, the operationalisation of India's nuclear arsenal. While more needs to be done, it certainly is better than nothing at all.

Senior political and military leaders are making a cogent case that Pakistan has failed to keep its promise of stopping cross-border terrorism. No one in India seriously believes that Musharraf

---

[1] "CRPF to replace BSF in J&K militancy fight", Ishar Wani, *The Asian Age*, February 3, 2003.
[2] "Special forces to counter insurgency", *The Times of India*, February 3, 2003.

would do so, or that the US would put Pakistan on the mat for its intransigence. For this reason, the army has done a "strategic relocation", and not a demobilisation on the border with Pakistan.

The army believes that a war with Pakistan cannot be ruled out, and hence the need for a speedy mobilisation. The government agrees with its military leadership that gunpowder be kept dry. There will be a need to order Operation Parakram-II in the near future. And this time it would be real.

Acknowledgement

The authors wish to thank Ghazala Wahab for contributing
the chapter on militancy, and for reading the manuscript
and offering useful suggestions.

After 9/11

A question which strikes people about Operation Parakram is whether there was a linkage between 9/11 and India's mobilisation for war. To appreciate this issue in the right perspective, it would be important to understand the mind-set of India's political leadership that governed its relations with the United States. It would also be desirable to learn why India continued to misread the changing strategic situation in the aftermath of 9/11 leading up to Operation Parakram.

To start from the beginning, India's May 1998 nuclear tests followed by Pakistan's tests generated a strong international response. Under the Chinese chairmanship, a special meeting of foreign ministers of the five permanent members of the United Nations Security Council was held on June 4, 1998. It prepared a communiqué which was reflected in the UN Security Council resolution 1172 of June 6, 1998. The highlights of the most formal expression of international condemnation for India and Pakistan were instructions to refrain from further nuclear tests; to refrain from weaponisation and deploying of nuclear weapons; to cease production of fissile material for nuclear weapons and to participate in negotiations for a treaty banning such production; to become parties to the Non Proliferation Treaty and the Comprehensive Test Ban Treaty unconditionally; and to resume stalled dialogue, specifically on Kashmir, mentioned as one of the root causes of tension between them. The resolution explicitly ruled out the recognition of India and Pakistan as nuclear weapon states, since this would violate the Non Proliferation Treaty, which has provision for only five nuclear weapon states.

Worse for India, the nuclear tests provided prospects of a new partnership between the United States and China to bring about stability in South Asia. US President Bill Clinton visited China in June 1998 and in the joint statement on South Asia both sides expressed their "shared interests in a peaceful and stable South Asia and in a strong global non-proliferation regime which has been put at risk by these tests". Both sides joined to strongly condemn the nuclear tests and reaffirm faith in UN resolution 1172. To India's chagrin, the US asked China to work for stability in South Asia. Both sides also renewed their commitment to press India and Pakistan to stop developing nuclear armaments.

Unnerved by the strong condemnation and fearing a growing US–China nexus against India, Prime Minister Atal Behari Vajpayee desperately wanted to mend relations with Washington. The deputy chairman of the planning commission and an articulate speaker, Jaswant Singh was roped in to commence a dialogue with the superpower. What followed were the famous ten rounds of talks in 1999 between Jaswant Singh and US Deputy Secretary of State, Strobe Talbott. When asked what was achieved by these talks, Jaswant Singh told a television channel:[1] Greater US support for a United Nations permanent seat for India, formation of a Joint Working Group on terrorism by both countries, President Clinton's India visit in March 2000, a better understanding by the US-led western nations of India's security concerns, an increased number of visits by foreign dignitaries since the passing of the UN resolution 1172, and better diplomatic and economic relations between US and India. (Later events would prove that he was wrong on most counts.) What he did not say was that his own stature had risen disproportionate to the office he held. The prime minister had grown accustomed to his foreign minister's advice more than the combined counsel of the Cabinet Committee on Security. As the turn of events would show, the nation had to pay dearly for this.

Meanwhile, initial anger and disbelief at India's nuclear tests led to a more sober assessment in the US that India needed to be engaged if UN resolution 1172 was to be realised. Talbott clarified the need to engage India after it gatecrashed into the nuclear club: "Having India and Pakistan stabilise their nuclear competition at

---

[1] Jaswant Singh on *New Delhi Television* on September 2, 2000.

the lowest possible level is both the starting point and the near-term objective of the US diplomatic effort."[2] The long term objective, he said was to ensure that India renounce its self-declared nuclear weapon status: "Until India and Pakistan disavow nuclear weapons and accept safeguards on all their nuclear activities, they will continue to forfeit the full recognition and benefits that accrue to members in good standing of the NPT."[3]

Considering Pakistan had repeatedly said that its nuclear and security policies are linked to what India does, the best course for Washington was to leash India through sweet talk, hugs, inane summit visits and photo opportunities with little substantive offerings. "The United States cannot concede, even by implication, that India and Pakistan have by their tests established themselves as nuclear-weapons states. Nor can it be seen to reward those who attempt to unravel the NPT", Talbott said.[4] It is hardly surprising that notwithstanding the declared sentiments of India and the US being "natural allies"—one being the largest and the other the strongest democracy—Washington, under President Clinton, did not back India's case for a permanent seat at the United Nations, did not lift technology and military sanctions imposed upon India after the tests, and did not permit sale of dual-use technologies to India either by itself or by third countries which have end-user obligations to the US. On the other hand, it pressed India to sign the Comprehensive Test Ban Treaty, go slow (read, stop) with missile testing and operationalisation, place a moratorium on fissile material production ahead of the Fissile Material Cut-off Treaty, and tighten export controls on sensitive materials and technologies even when India has not signed the NPT and the Missile Technology Control Regime.

To halt India's nuclear weaponisation and slow down its ballistic missile programme has been the core objective of US nonproliferation policy and the primary reason for its India fondness. Barring a few nuances, this bottom line has remained unaltered with the Bush administration as well. Testifying before the subcommittee of the Senate Appropriation Committee on May 15, 2001, the US Secretary of State, Gen. Colin Powell, said: "We really

---

[2] Talbott, Strobe (1999), *Foreign Affairs*, March–April, p. 119.
[3] *Ibid.*
[4] *Ibid.*, p. 120.

have to make sure that this nuclear genie doesn't get any further out of the bottle than it already is [nuclear tests by India and Pakistan]. And on a regular basis we consult them [India], we make sure they understand the seriousness with which we view the potential for something getting out of control in the region."[5]

India, however, hoped that relations with the US would improve further with the Bush administration. The latter had rubbished the CTBT, which led to an easing of pressure on India to sign the treaty. Unlike his predecessor, President Bush was committed to his Ballistic Missile Defense (BMD) plan. In the best traditions of "love all things American", India became the only country in the world to enthusiastically endorse President Bush's BMD plan, something which, leave aside its allies in Asia like Japan and South Korea, even tested friends like the United Kingdom had difficulty in embracing. Russia and China opposed it, and though Pakistan also opposed the Bush initiative, it was more to show solidarity with China than for any meaningful difference with the United States. Critics of the Bush initiative said that even a limited anti-missile shield that relied upon space-based sensors could trigger an arms race with the development of anti-satellite weapons to begin with, eventually leading to the militarisation of space itself.

According to many experts, India's gushing was premature, considering details of the plan were not available and the technology itself stood years away from being proven. Such comments did not dampen the spirits of the mandarins in the external affairs ministry. Stories were leaked to the media about India's growing closeness with the Bush team: that the United States was no longer breathing down India's neck on the CTBT issue; the sanctions imposed after the Shakti tests were under review by the Bush administration and could be lifted; and, importantly, India was privileged to receive US Deputy Secretary of State, Richard Armitage, who had travelled to explain the Bush BMD initiative to the Indian leadership. After all, Washington sends its envoys to only a few valued capitals to explain important decisions.

The Bush administration was not particular about India signing the CTBT—it did not matter either way. India could have conducted more nuclear tests even after signing the CTBT by taking cover under the clause of "supreme national security interest". It

---

[5] "US Sees Role in Solving Kashmir Row", *The Hindu*, May 16, 2001.

is well known that the Chinese nuclear weapons and missile cooperation with Pakistan has enhanced after India's May 1998 Shakti
tests. On the other hand, it is doubtful that India would jeopar-
dise a hopeful relationship with the United States by conducting
more tests.

The relationship remains hopeful because the contours of a new
polycentric world are emerging from the debris of the Cold War.
Few doubt that the United States as the pre-eminent power would
be in a position to shape the new world order. Moreover, the fact
that India and Pakistan have proven nuclear capabilities cannot be
ignored. Through its new security plan, the Bush administration
made a case that deep nuclear cuts, even if unilateral, are possible.
These would go a long way in assuring allies and new-found friends
like India that such measures are a better substitute than the arms
control regimes of the Cold War era, which were porous and have
rarely worked well. Such moves could also be interpreted as advancing disarmament, and thus would be good reasons for India to not
move towards nuclear armament.

India would be required, at best, to halt its nuclear weaponisation, and at worst to keep its weaponisation at a low level to assuage
domestic pressure. This would appear in tune with the unilateral
nuclear reductions by the United States. Regular engagement with
India would ensure that China's expected moves to challenge
Bush's BMD initiative do not unnerve it. For example, China may
choose to transfer ballistic missiles to countries where they may
pose a challenge to the US and its friends by complicating the
BMD. From India's viewpoint, one such country is Pakistan. Alternatively, China may develop its existing capabilities to make longer-range cruise missiles, especially in an anti-ship role. This would
be effective against ship-borne BMD, and would threaten India's
security. Or China may simply decide to make more nuclear warheads to saturate the BMD. In any case, nuclear and missile cooperation between Pakistan, China and North Korea has intensified.
China has become more aggressive in words and deeds in its relations with India. A signatory to the NPT and oft reneging on its
1996 pledge to abide by the MTCR (Missile Technology Control
Regime), China appears determined to teach India the harsh way
the consequence of its nuclear misadventure. The unpublicised
Strategic Defence Review has already cautioned the government:
"We [India] have to ensure that Pakistan does not continue to

match India in nuclear and missile technologies." The quid pro quo appears that in return for a United States hug and the hope of an independent role in its regional security plan, India would go slow with its nuclear weaponisation. The poser was whether such a deal was compatible with India's security interests. With hindsight, it was a mistake for India to have gone slow, on US urging, with its nuclear weaponisation and delivery systems programmes. By the turn of the century, Pakistan—which has never succumbed to US pressure even when bilateral relations were at their best in the eighties—had managed to steal a lead over India in strategic assets.

The story regarding the Indo-US Joint Working Group on terrorism was similar. India correctly believed that the US wanted Pakistan to stop cross-border terrorism in J&K. From India's perspective, the US played a positive role in restraining Pakistan during the 1999 Kargil war. It was the July 4, 1999, meeting between President Clinton and Premier Sharif in Washington which brought the war to a speedy end. The joint statement issued after this meeting, amongst other things, sought "concrete steps to be taken for the restoration of the Line of Control [by Pakistan]". Subsequently, during his visit to India in March 2000, President Clinton expanded on the theme in what came to be known as the US "four Rs" formula on J&K—the need to respect the LoC, to show restraint, to reject violence, and to restore the dialogue. Delhi was also elated about the fact that in comparison to four days in India, President Clinton spent barely four hours in Islamabad where the military ruler, Gen. Musharraf, was counselled to restore democracy at the earliest and to respect India's genuine concerns about terrorism.

Even as India was happy that the US shared its views of Pakistan as the epicentre of terrorism in J&K, efforts were made to hide the fact that the Taliban-inspired jehadis had entered the turbulent border state. On being repeatedly asked to table the prepared White Paper on terrorism in Parliament, Home Minister L. K. Advani said throughout the year 2000 that such a move would compromise the government's intelligence sources. With hindsight, it becomes evident that the government was hesitant to admit that the Taliban had entered J&K in the form of suicide squads. This was for two reasons: First, the government wanted to put the entire blame of cross-border terrorism on Pakistan by fanning the impression that Pakistan was fully in control of all terrorist outfits operating in J&K. Second, and more important, an admission by India that the Taliban were carving a role for them-selves in J&K would have been a blow to the bilateralism mantra enshrined in the Simla Agreement. It needs to be underscored that the J&K-specific jehadis' motivation, funding, training and arming with sophisticated weapons came from the Osama Bin Laden–Mullah Omar regime in Afghanistan, and not Pakistan as India would have the world believe.

It was only after the launch of the US-led Operation Enduring Freedom against the Taliban regime, when British Premier Tony Blair came calling to India in October 2001, that Prime Minister Vajpayee told him about the linkages between the 9/11 events and the December 1999 hijacking of the Indian aircraft IC-814. India admitted that if not Al Qaeda, Taliban-inspired jehadi organisa-tions had entered J&K. This was no news for the US or the UK. Fifteen terrorists out of the 19 that wrought havoc in the US on that fateful day were Al Qaeda-inspired Saudi nationals. The na-tionality of these die-hard terrorists was simply irrelevant; what mattered was their links with the Al Qaeda. Considering that the chairman of Al Qaeda, Osama Bin Laden, was living in Afghani-stan, the epicentre of the Al Qaeda–Taliban brand of terrorism was Afghanistan, which had to be eliminated. India hardly realised that the focus of the US war on terrorism would be at sharp variance with its viewpoint.

9/11 Changed the World

The unfortunate events of 9/11 electrified the Bush administra-tion. Nine days after 9/11, President George W. Bush delivered a terse message to the world: "Either you are with us, or you are with the terrorists." The Bush doctrine was loud and clear. Even as the US had singled out the war on terrorism as its top foreign policy priority, this unambiguous message to the world was about choos-ing between pro- and anti-US camps, without any demands what-soever. The US had declared war on the Al Qaeda and the Taliban regime in Afghanistan which harboured Osama. Geography, demog-raphy and closeness with the Taliban dictated that Pakistan should become the first country to make its choice regarding the war on terrorism. Instead it was India that offered unsolicited, unqualified assistance in double time to the US. There was hope in India that the US would soon declare Pakistan as a state sponsoring terrorism. India and the US had identical views on terrorism; Pakistan was already under a cloud for having trampled on democracy, something dearly held by both India and the US; and the world was not unaware that the Taliban were the creation of Pakistan. Leading Indian analysts joined the government in predicting that Pakistan had reached the end of its road. However, just the opposite happened.

Behind the scenes, the Bush team was determined not to repeat the mistake of the Soviet Red army, which had entered Afghanistan in 1979 and left ignominiously in 1991. The Bush military strategy was to support the Northern Alliance only as much as to ensure that Kabul did not fall soon, and to acquire basing rights for US special forces to operate in the north and south of Afghanistan. The US did not want to physically enter Afghanistan until the Taliban were decimated, and also did not wish to give a wholesome victory to the Northern Alliance which might not be to the liking of the post-Taliban dispensation in Afghanistan. Uzbekistan and Pakistan were the natural choices for basing the US special forces to operate in the north and south of Afghanistan. There was also the need to pacify Russian fears—they considered Uzbekistan as their "near abroad" and would have been alarmed at the physical presence of US troops closer to their home. The US reasoned that Pakistan, on the other hand, would be needed for a much larger purpose, as its demographic, ethnic and religious closeness to the majority Sunni Pashtuns in Afghanistan would come in handy to establish peace after the forceful removal of the Taliban. Gen. Powell was given the task of discussing matters with Pakistan and Uzbekistan, while President Bush took upon himself to talk with President Putin.

Once Bush told his secretary to do whatever was necessary, Powell and his deputy, Richard Armitage, prepared the following list detailing what Pakistan should do:[6]

1. Stop Al Qaeda operatives at the Pakistan border, intercept arms shipments through Pakistan and end all logistical support for Bin Laden.
2. Blanket over-flight and landing rights.
3. Provide access to Pakistan, naval bases, air bases and borders.

---

[6] Woodward, Bob (2002), *Bush At War*, New York: Simon & Schuster, p. 59.

4. Provide immediate intelligence and immigration information.
5. Condemn the September 11 attacks and "curb all domestic expressions of support for terrorism against the [United States], its friends and allies".
6. Cut off all shipments of fuel to the Taliban and stop Pakistani volunteers from going into Afghanistan to join the Taliban.
7. "Should the evidence strongly implicate Osama Bin Laden and the Al Qaeda network to Afghanistan and should Afghanistan and the Taliban continue to harbour him and his network, Pakistan will break diplomatic relations with the Taliban government, end support for the Taliban and assist us in the aforementioned ways to destroy Osama Bin Laden and his Al Qaeda network."

The US demand list was handed over to the Pakistan ISI Chief, Lt. Gen. Mahmoud, who happened to be in Washington. The latter was told to tell his boss that all demands were non-negotiable. Within hours, when Gen. Powell called Gen. Musharraf on the phone, he was surprised to hear that Pakistan had agreed to all its demands. Musharraf told Powell that he wholeheartedly supported the US-led war on international terrorism. The next day, President Bush told the visiting Japanese Prime Minister, Junichiro Koizumi: "In this new war, cutting off funding is just as important as dropping a bomb. Aid to Pakistan is just as important as landing troops."[7] Japan got the message loud and clear. So did the rest of the world. Gen. Musharraf had become Bush's closest friend outside the Western nations block. India was perhaps the only country which failed to note Gen. Musharraf's changed fortunes.

Within hours of receiving the US demands, President Pervez Musharraf had grasped the import of the Bush message and had decided to use it to his advantage by signing as "us" against international terrorists. It was the easiest decision for him to take as he, in any case, wanted to cut the Taliban leadership to size. Not only had it denied him strategic space in Afghanistan and started a Talibanisation of the Pakistan society, it also had thousands of sympathisers within the Pakistan Army and the ISI, and was running

---

[7] *Ibid.*, p. 138.

away with Musharraf's most precious prize—Jammu and Kashmir. Ever since the 1999 Kargil war, the Talibanised mujahids had overwhelmed the pro-Pakistan Hizbul cadres and were exerting tremendous pressure on the Hurriyat in J&K. Instead of Pakistan's political agenda—the right of self-determination—the Taliban's religious agenda of seeking the glorification of Islam was holding sway over the people in the turbulent state.

Musharraf's calculations were quick and shrewd. Irrespective of his carte-blanche embracing of the US, he, as Pakistan's army chief, would support the US-led Operation Enduring Freedom commensurate with Washington's support to Musharraf, the President of Pakistan. So overwhelmed was President Bush by Musharraf's open-armed response to fight alongside the US, that he told Powell: "President Musharraf is taking a tremendous risk. We need to make it worth his while. We should help him with a number of things, including nuclear security. Put together a package of support for Pakistan."[8]

Slowly as Musharraf won the trust of the US, his wish list also started unfolding: he wanted international legitimacy for himself and his brand of military democracy; he wanted massive doses of aid and writing off of huge debts to tide over Pakistan's financial crisis; he wanted that the US safeguard Pakistan's interests in post-Taliban Afghanistan; he wanted that the US understand his distinction between terrorism, which he condemned, and the so-called indigenous freedom struggle in J&K, which he supported wholeheartedly. The US agreed to Musharraf's piecemeal demands made in the most suppliant manner. A former pariah, Gen. Musharraf had become a hero in the US.

In sharp contrast to Musharraf, President Islam Karimov of Uzbekistan was not so clever. Though Karimov permitted the US to use his territory for search and rescue missions, he procrastinated when it came to allowing US special forces operations out of Uzbekistan. The search and rescue missions were needed to rescue any pilot whose aircraft got downed in enemy territory by hostile fire during the course of bombings in Afghanistan. Special operations, on the other hand, are offensive land operations. President Karimov had sought that the US "take action against his internal opposition, the extreme fundamentalist Islamic Movement of

---

[8] *Ibid.*, p. 82.

Uzbekistan"[9] before he allowed them use of his territory. The US was hesitant to do so as it could dilute the focus of Operation Enduring Freedom, and there was the possibility that every opposition figure in Uzbekistan be characterised as a terrorist, and consequently be subject to the US war on terrorism.

In India, no one cared to ask a simple question: If Musharraf was with "us", how could he be with the terrorists at the same time? By not appreciating that the definition of terrorism had changed for the US, India misread three crucial issues: the Bush administration was determined to fight international terrorism its own way, Musharraf would play an indispensable role in the US-led campaign on terror, and considering the campaign would be a long haul, close relations between the US and Pakistan would be strategic and not ephemeral in nature. Therefore, by the time the US launched Operation Enduring Freedom on October 7, 2001 against the Al Qaeda and the Taliban in Afghanistan, India had committed two mistakes.

First, it linked Pakistan-sponsored terrorism in J&K to global terrorism and thus allowed the US a greater role in J&K affairs. It should have occurred to India that Musharraf had cut a deal with the US—while he fought terror in Afghanistan, the US would appreciate that Kashmir is an indigenous struggle. For this reason, Gen. Powell, on a visit to Pakistan on October 7, 2001, said that the resolution of the Kashmir problem should be in accordance with the wishes of the Kashmiri people. The unsaid, yet unambiguous, message from the US was that it understood Musharraf's differentiation of terrorism and the so-called freedom struggle in Kashmir. With the writing clearly on the wall, India still hoped that the US, which had acknowledged Pakistan's terrorism in the 1999 Kargil war, would come down heavily on the Musharraf regime. Prime Minister Vajpayee was to later accept that Washington had become a "facilitator" between India and Pakistan on the Kashmir issue. Second, India blithely accepted Washington's suggestion that Operation Enduring Freedom was just the beginning of a long war against international terror. The United States was not asked if it considered the Pakistan-sponsored terrorism in Jammu and Kashmir a part of global terror.

India's clumsy understanding of the changed global strategic dynamics was evident when, within days of 9/11, Foreign Minister

---

[9] *Ibid.*, p. 129.

Jaswant Singh told a television channel that "Pakistan had imposed no conditions on the US for supporting the war against terrorism in Afghanistan. Any such bargaining will be tantamount to accepting terrorism and granting it legitimacy."[10] Jaswant Singh sought to label the entire Pakistani leadership as terrorists, with whom the US should not make deals. Worse, he took umbrage at the suggestion that the US would share a bed with Pakistan and not inform India (read, him) beforehand. This was naiveté personified, which remained a hallmark of India's security policy until Jaswant Singh left the external affairs ministry on July 1, 2002. Unfortunately, too much damage had been done by then. An obsessive faith in the US, which led to an inability to take decisions based upon national interests, had dented the government's credibility no end. Operation Parakram was one such casualty.

Even after Operation Parakram was ordered against Pakistan, India still had an opportunity to salvage the situation. Senior officials of the Bush administration were giving enough hints about their course of action. The global war on terrorism, they said, had broadened to become a war on both terrorism and weapons of mass destruction. In this context, Central Asia was too dangerous and too important to be ignored. It had fragile economies, unstable governments, rising religious fundamentalism, little democracy, and was blessed with oil and cursed with nuclear weapons (with Pakistan), which if not controlled could proliferate into the hands of terrorists. It was logical that the US would increase its foothold in the region to bring stability to an extremely volatile part of the world. The US, therefore, secured foothold rights in Uzbekistan and Kyrgyzstan, and arrived at an understanding with Russia and China that terrorism in their countries would be internal matters if they supported the US. Washington's focus was: "terrorist organisations, state sponsors of terrorism and non-state sponsors including terrorist funding organisations. Another focus was directed at weapons of mass destruction: organisations, states that harbour, sponsor, finance, sanction, or otherwise support those organisations or their state supporters to acquire or produce weapons of mass destruction".[11]

---

[10] Interview on *BBC World*, October 2, 2001.
[11] Woodward, Bob (2002), *Bush At War*, New York: Simon & Schuster, p. 189.

Given such a clear road map, it was presumptuous of India to believe that the US would put Musharraf on the mat for its sake. In private, the US told India that the Pakistan President did not want war with India and he was determined to take corrective measures. Even as India mobilised its troops for war, the US told India to await the announcement which Musharraf would make in his high-profile January 12, 2002 speech. Instead of a deep analysis of what Musharraf said, Foreign Minister Jaswant Singh welcomed the speech with circumspection. The speech ignored India's demands, and instead pledged support to the indigenous freedom struggle in J&K. Yet, India was willing to give time to Pakistan to show its honourable intent to curb cross-border terrorism. Bent upon not displeasing the US, India lost the opportunity to give a taste of its own medicine to Pakistan.

The US game plan was finally laid bare by President Bush. In his State-of-the-Union address to Congress on January 29, Bush pointed a direct finger at three countries—Iraq, Iran and North Korea—and termed them as "an axis of evil". Secretary Colin Powell went a step further and accused seven countries—Iran, Iraq, Syria, Libya, Cuba, North Korea and Sudan—as sponsors of international terrorism in the annual State Department report. It was obvious that steps against the three countries mentioned in the "axis of evil" would be taken up simultaneous to the war on Al Qaeda.

North Korea had not signed the Chemical Weapons Convention (CWC), and according to US estimates, it possessed large quantities of chemical weapons and their precursors, as well as nerve agents such as sarin. The rogue country deployed the 1,300 km No-Dong missile, and while it had declared a moratorium on missile testing until 2003, it was working on a Taepodong-2 missile that could potentially reach parts of the US with a nuclear warhead. Further, North Korea was caught in 1992 producing more plutonium than it had owned up to. Similarly, the credibility of the Saddam Hussein regime in Iraq had touched rock bottom. The US feared that despite sanctions, Iraq had repeatedly flouted the many UN resolutions made against it after the 1991 Gulf war. Iraq appeared determined to continue with a clandestine nuclear weapons programme, and had failed to disclose its stocks of chemical and biological weapons. It was clear from President Bush's address that the next immediate targets of the US would be Iraq and North Korea.

Iran, it appeared, would get a breather. Although Iran had signed the CWC in 1997, it had declared no weapon stocks or production facilities. According to the US, Iran still has large quantities of cyanogen chloride, phosgene, mustard gas, and some nerve agents that it was producing since the 1980s when it was at war with Iraq. The greatest concern, however, is over Iran's nuclear and missile ambitions. It already has the 1,300 km Shahab-3 medium range missile, which relies extensively on Russian and even Chinese help. However, considering the growing strategic importance of Iran, the US is hesitant to openly confront it. Later events were to prove that the US would remain focused on "the axis of evil" nations. India's security concerns were given mere lip service.

Meanwhile, all through Operation Parakram, the Indian leadership harped on the fact that the international community should declare Pakistan as a state sponsoring terrorism. Deputy Prime Minister Advani emphasised that terror states were far more dangerous than terrorist organisations.[12] The problem with these assertions was that they were not backed by any cogent military muscle, and the world community did not agree with India's assessment. The Russian President, Vladimir Putin, said on the eve of his visit to India on December 3, 2002: "President Musharraf has taken a number of resolute steps to combat terrorism. My position is that we should not put all the burden, all the blame on him [Musharraf] for negative developments, but we should, rather, try to stimulate him to continue his policy."[13] If like Russia, India had assessed the world (read, US) mood correctly in the aftermath of 9/11, Operation Parakram would have taken a different course.

---

[12] "Ostracise Terrorist States: Advani", *The Hindu*, December 2, 2002.
[13] "India, Pak Troops Withdrawal a Right Move: Putin", *The Hindu*, December 3, 2002.

2

Militancy in J&K: Moves and Counter-moves

In the summer of 1989, the air blowing from the Mughal Gardens of Srinagar carried more than the fragrance of flowers with it. It was heavy with the whiff of anticipation and the promise of independence. The murmurs were becoming louder by the day as more people joined the clamours of *azadi*. Terrorist activities in the Valley had almost doubled in one year. Yet, despite the nascent stage of violence, the movement spearheaded by outfits such as Jammu and Kashmir Liberation Front (JKLF), Ansar-ul-Islam, and Hizbullah Islamia Jamhooria, among others, was getting more popular support—both overt and covert. The political forces closeted in their insular edifices, however, could smell neither the rising dissension nor the seriousness of the changing mood of the greater population of Kashmir.

For chronological purposes, the year 1989 has been earmarked as the beginning of militancy in Kashmir. That single year saw at least 2,154 incidences of terrorist violence in the state, some as high-profile as the kidnapping of Rubaiya Sayeed, the daughter of the then Union home minister, Mufti Mohammed Sayeed. The year also saw a systematic emasculation of the state machinery in Jammu and Kashmir (J&K). Apart from targeting innocent civilians, the militants were increasingly taking on the J&K police, the Central Reserve Police Force (CRPF) and the Department of Intelligence Bureau (DIB) personnel.

The local populace of Kashmir was also coming out in the streets chanting the *azadi* slogan in support of the militants. The state government under Farooq Abdullah was either helpless or did not understand the gravity of the situation. It was no longer a law and order problem as government officials were dismissing it. In the absence of strong leadership at the top, the lower-rung civil and police officials were reluctant and often scared to take action.

The 1989 benchmark notwithstanding, dissension or clamour for independence in Kashmir is as old as the Instrument of Accession, which Maharaja Hari Singh signed on October 14, 1947. Despite the period of calm that followed, and also the wars which India fought with Pakistan over Kashmir, there have always been deep pockets of dissent in the state. India's original promise of holding a plebiscite to give the people a right to decide their future also kept the hopes of independence alive. So much so, that even a leader of the stature of Sheikh Abdullah—who was proud of his friendship with Nehru and rubbished Pakistan's claim on J&K on the basis of religion—toyed and even went public with the idea.

Fuelled by various extraneous and local factors, and compounded by Delhi's ad hoc and inconsistent policies, the 40-year-old dissension simply took a violent turn in the late eighties. However, this outburst was essentially political in nature. Despite Pakistan's efforts at lending it a religious shade, the militant movement in Kashmir remained indigenous and above religious differences. Kashmiris (read, Muslims of the Valley) were seeking independence from India because of their perceived grievances and not because they felt unsafe in a country with a Hindu majority.

The main reason for this was the very temperament of the Kashmiri people. Islam came to Kashmir through wandering minstrels and Sufis, and not by the power of the sword. The Muslims in this region hardly had any history of strife in the name of religion. They have always been tolerant people, simplistic in their faith and believing in the cult of Sufism. Even in 1947, when Pakistani raiders invaded Kashmir smug in the belief that the local population would support them on the basis of common religion, they were surprised to find the locals inimical to their designs. When Pakistan tried the same ploy 18 years later in 1965, it was yet again surprised by the lack of local support for its cause. The Pakistan Air Marshal Asghar Khan later explained the reason for Pakistan's daredevilry. He said, "It was assumed that widespread support existed within occupied Kashmir to make such a guerilla campaign a success."[1]

---

[1] Marwah, Ved (1995), *Uncivil Wars*, New Delhi: Harper Collins.

To this day, for an average Kashmiri, the idea of a merger with Pakistan is more abhorrent than staying with India.

Though there have always been pockets of religious extremism in Kashmir and a few madrasas have been teaching the intolerant faith, the majority, and terrorist outfits like the JKLF, largely remained indifferent to them. Even Jamaat-e-Islami had very few takers in Kashmir. The situation, however, started changing with the beginning of the eighties.

Sheikh Abdullah, who was considered the vital link between New Delhi and Kashmir, passed away in 1982. His son, the flamboyant Farooq Abdullah, inherited his father's mantle and proved his popularity by winning the 1983 elections. However, a term later, he squandered his legacy by entering into an alliance with the Congress for the 1987 elections. The polls were massively rigged, pushing many fence-sitters who contested and lost the elections, including the now notorious Syed Salahuddin, the chief of Hizbul Mujahideen, into militancy. Farooq Abdullah later regretted the unholy alliance as it put a permanent question mark on his credibility.

The 1987 debacle added to the rising discontentment among the local people. Though terrorist outfits (all indigenous) had started attacking and killing Kashmiri Pandits towards the end of 1989 in an effort to encourage their exodus from the Valley, the motive was political and economic, not religious. The Pandits of Kashmir were better educated than their Muslim counterparts and held better jobs, disproportionate to their population. Besides, they did not share the Muslim enthusiasm for independence from India. To the militants, they were stooges of the Indian government. Besides, it made sense to change the demography of the Valley. Another pointer to the non-religious profile of the insurgency was the fact that militants did not target other religious minorities. Sikhs were not touched at all in the early years. Unlike the Pandits, Sikhs were largely peasants or small-time businessmen. They wielded little political power, and therefore did not pose any threat to the separatist movement.

Terrorised by target killings, Pandits started moving out of the Valley by the beginning of the year 1990.[2] However, of all the civilians killed by the terrorists till 1994, the majority were Muslims. Had it been a religious movement, the figures would have been different.

---

[2] *Ibid.*

The Changing Profile

The nature of insurgency started changing once Pakistan hijacked the JKLF agenda under Prime Minister Benazir Bhutto. The rising levels of violence in Kashmir and the inability of the Indian government to control the problem gave Pakistan the opportunity it had been looking for since 1947. It began by supporting the JKLF by way of funds, arms and training. Camps were opened in Pakistan-occupied-Kashmir (PoK) and the JKLF chairman, Amanullah Khan, ran the movement from there. But even as Pakistan was supporting the JKLF, it floated a number of other indigenous outfits as early as 1989. Chief among these was the Hizbul Mujahideen. While the JKLF was fighting for independence, the Hizbul agenda was a merger with Pakistan. It made sense for Pakistan to weaken the JKLF and let the Hizbul run the campaign. The JKLF finally gave up the armed struggle in 1994, leaving the centre stage for Pakistan-dominated outfits led by the ISI-sponsored Hizbul Mujahideen.

As pro-Pakistan militants gained ascendancy in Kashmir, the nature of the movement started changing dramatically. Pakistan understood that the biggest sustainable force was religion, and hence it was necessary to wed freedom with religion. The internal situation in India also helped their cause. The demolition of the Babri Masjid and the communal carnage that followed in some parts of the country were used as fodder to foster communal intolerance. To further exploit the religious divide, terrorist activities were extended to the Doda district of Jammu by August 1992. Within a year, polarisation along religious lines was complete.

Though Kashmir topped the Pakistani agenda, it was abetting another war around this time. Ever since the withdrawal of Soviet troops from Afghanistan in 1989, Pakistan, with the tacit encouragement of the United States, was providing support (financial and military) and training to Afghan mujahideen. Before 1989, these mujahideen were supposed to fight the Soviets. However, after their retreat and the fall of Soviet-backed President Najibullah, the guns were trained on the Tajik-dominated Burhanuddin Rabbani government.

Gulbuddin Hikmetyar, with the support of the ISI, led the mujahideen (who were schooled in radical Islam in Pakistani madrasas) against the government of Rabbani. The ensuing civil war left nearly 10,000 dead. Even as the Pakistan-trained mujahideen

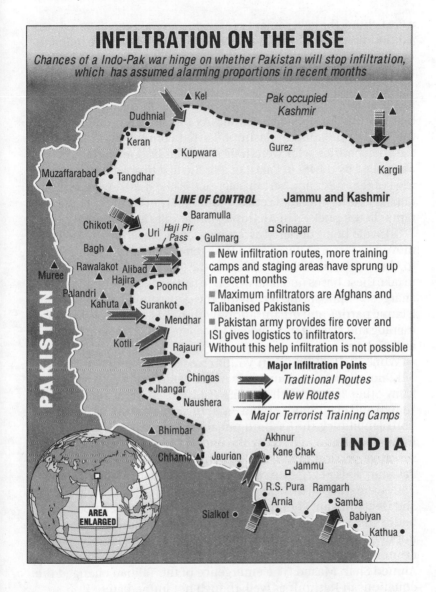

INFILTRATION ON THE RISE

Chances of a Indo-Pak war hinge on whether Pakistan will stop infiltration, which has assumed alarming proportions in recent months

▲ Kel

Pak occupied Kashmir ▲ ▲ ▲

Dudhnial

Keran

Kupwara

Gurez

Muzaffarabad ▲ Tangdhar

Kargil

LINE OF CONTROL   **Jammu and Kashmir**

● Baramulla

Chikoti ▲   Uri   *Haji Pir Pass*   ● Gulmarg

□ Srinagar

Bagh ▲

Muree ▲   Rawalakot   Alibad ▲
          ▲ Hajira
Palandri ▲   ● Poonch
       Kahuta ▲   Surankot
              ● Mendhar
        ▲ Kotli
              Rajauri

■ New infiltration routes, more training camps and staging areas have sprung up in recent months

■ Maximum infiltrators are Afghans and Talibanised Pakistanis

■ Pakistan army provides fire cover and ISI gives logistics to infiltrators. Without this help infiltration is not possible

Major Infiltration Points

➤ *Traditional Routes*

➤ *New Routes*

▲ *Major Terrorist Training Camps*

PAKISTAN

Chingas
● Jhangar
       ● Naushera

▲ Bhimbar

Akhnur

INDIA

Chhamb ▲ Jaurian   ● Kane Chak

□ Jammu

R.S. Pura Ramgarh

● Arnia   ● Samba

Sialkot ●   Babiyan

Kathua ●

AREA ENLARGED

were fighting the government in Afghanistan, Pakistan diverted over a thousand mujahideen into Kashmir in 1993. These were militants hardened by fighting against the Soviet army. This was the first time foreign mercenaries had entered the movement in Kashmir.

As the battle lines changed in Afghanistan, they changed in Kashmir too. The movement was no longer indigenous as it was being run from outside Kashmir. As the situation deteriorated, the local population in Kashmir started coming out in favour of the mercenaries who were hailed as Islamic warriors and were controlled by the ISI in Pakistan. For the first time since the beginning of the militancy, certain sections in the media were actually talking about "liberated zones" (completely in control of the militants) in the pockets of Anantnag, Baramulla and Srinagar.

To avoid being declared as a state sponsoring terrorism, Pakistan moved its terrorist bases from Pakistan-occupied-Kashmir (PoK) to Afghanistan in 1994. The ISI paid the Jalalabad Shura (warlords) to take these bases under its wings. To further wipe its hands off the charges of sponsoring terrorism, the government made various Islamic parties and organisations within Pakistan responsible for training and arming mujahideen who were to fight in both Kashmir and Afghanistan.

While in 1989 Kashmiri youth crossed the border to train in PoK, now they were doing so in Afghanistan along with mujahids from other countries, including Pakistan, Afghanistan, Algeria, Yemen and even Saudi Arabia. As a consequence of this privatisation of militancy, the Kashmir mujahids were exposed to militants from other nationalities. By the end of 1994, an even more conservative version of mujahideen emerged from the madrasas of Pakistan. This new group called itself the Taliban or the "students". They were steeped in the conservative school of Saudi Wahhabism and Deobandism. They were better trained and, more importantly, better motivated than the mujahideens of Hikmetyar who had not been able to make much headway against the Rabbani government in Kabul, which was backed by the Tajik commander Ahmed Shah Masud. The emergence of the Taliban changed the equations in Kashmir as well, though not immediately.

In the forefront of the militant activities in Kashmir were groups like Lashkar-e-Taiyyaba and Harkat-ul-Ansar that had a substantial number of foreign mujahids in their ranks. Though the majority still comprised the Kashmiris, they were now the hardened lot who had seen the battlefields of Afghanistan. Their respect for local traditions had waned after years of training abroad. And most importantly, they were not content to view the Kashmir issue in isolation anymore. The issue now encompassed the so-called Muslim brotherhood. However, the Indian government dismissed these as mercenary voices. Some of them were foreigners, no doubt, but they were not fighting for money—they were fighting for their religion. The word jehad was now being used quite frequently to describe the freedom movement.

A former Pakistan ISI chief, Lt. Gen. Hamid Gul, once had a dream which he voiced openly. He visualised a pan-Islamic force, somewhat along the lines of NATO, which would protect and ensure the rights of Muslims throughout the world. This force would recognise no borders and no international laws. It would fight wherever Muslim interests were threatened, be it East Europe, Central Asia, West Asia or even India.

What Pakistan could not achieve, the Taliban did within two years of their coming to power in most of Afghanistan. With the fall of Kabul in 1996, the whole of Afghanistan, with the exception of a few pockets in the north, was under the Taliban influence. They immediately started rebuilding Afghanistan according to their vision. And their vision was very simple—take the country back to medieval times, suspend all rights, make women as invisible as possible and rob the men of their minds. To achieve all this, it was important that an acceptable degree of terror be maintained. More importantly, the country had to remain in a state of constant war. Peace would demand development and some semblance of normal life, which were nowhere in the Taliban agenda.

Since the basic requirement for a war is the presence of an enemy, the Taliban made half the world its enemy. And where it fell short of enemies, it encouraged other people to fight, or rather, prepare for their battles from its territory. Under the Taliban, and in association with Osama Bin Laden of Saudi Arabia, Afghanistan became the first factory manufacturing terror in the world.[3] It gave space, funds, arms and training to anybody who had any grievances against anyone in the world.

---

[3] Rashid, Ahmed (2000), *Taliban: Islam, Oil and the New Great Game in Central Asia*, London: I. B. Tauris Publishers.

The Taliban was the product of Pakistan's ill-conceived foreign policy for Afghanistan. The ISI funded militant madrasas propounding Saudi Wahhabism in order to create a force to fight the Soviets in Afghanistan. Once that war was won, these illiterate Pashtuns who knew nothing except a contrived interpretation of the Quran and how to wield weapons were expected to return to the madrasas. Unfortunately, that did not happen. As the civil war in Afghanistan spiralled out of control, the Taliban emerged yet again to restore order.

Pakistan decided to wait and watch in the beginning. However, as the Taliban gained control of one region after the other in Afghanistan with lightning speed, it started supporting them in the hope that through them it would get strategic space in Afghanistan. Pakistan also believed that with a malleable Taliban, it would be able to quash the demand of merger of the Pashtun-dominated areas in North Pakistan with Afghanistan. However, all these hopes were belied. Taliban refused to recognise the Durand Line, and terrorists all over the world had a free run of the Pakistan–Afghanistan border. The biggest irony of all was that they started fomenting sectarian violence within Pakistan. A large number of junior ISI officials and Pakistan's Pashtun population started sympathising with them.

Pakistan could not upset the Taliban applecart for the simple reason that it was giving space to Pakistani groups operating in Kashmir.[4] However, what it did not realise was that these groups were being distanced from Pakistan and the ISI because of their exposure to mujahids from other countries. Moreover, many junior-level ISI operatives were also being swayed by the Taliban worldview. Pakistan probably realised what was happening, but could not strengthen its weakening link.

The Kargil war in 1999 saw the end of Pakistan's already marginal influence over the Taliban. What was called Operation Badr by Pakistan had a two-fold strategy. The first part involved the regular Pakistani soldiers in civilian clothes intruding into Indian territory in the Kargil sector to try to alter the Line of Control. These were assisted by the mujahids, who were now under the sway of the Taliban. At the same time, the Pakistan Army was to keep the border alive so that a large number of these mujahids could infiltrate

---
[4] *Ibid.*

into Kashmir. The US intelligence later disclosed that the Harkat-ul-Mujahideen and Lashkar-e-Taiyyaba were involved in the Kargil War.

However, once the first part of the strategy failed, Prime Minister Nawaz Sharif was compelled to call off the infiltration. But it was too late by then. The mujahids were no longer listening to Pakistan. When Nawaz Sharif's government fell and the Pakistan Army Chief Pervez Musharraf assumed power, he understood that his control over the mujahids was fast eroding. They were not only calling the shots in Kashmir, but also fomenting trouble in Pakistan. After all, if the Taliban model was the ideal then why shouldn't Pakistan embrace it as well?

The final blow to the Pakistan government's influence over the Talibanised mujahideen was when Harkat-ul-Mujahideen hijacked the Indian aircraft IC 814 in December 1999. The hostages were released following a week-long drama after Indian external affairs minister Jaswant Singh personally escorted Maulana Masood Azhar, Mushtaq Zargar and Ahmed Omar Shaikh to Kandahar. The Taliban minister for civil aviation was present on the tarmac to receive Masood Azhar. Upon his release, Masood Azhar founded a suicide bomber outfit Jaish-e-Mohammad while Mushtaq Zargar started Al-Umar. Like Harkat-ul-Mujahideen, both had close ties with the Taliban. Pakistan or General Musharraf had no control over them. General Musharraf, in fact, was now voicing the jehadi agenda.

Al Qaeda and the Taliban Wave

When the Taliban first came to power, their goals were limited to Afghanistan. They wanted to enforce on the Afghan people what they thought was the purest form of Islam. However, once they came in touch with Osama Bin Laden and his worldwide Al Qaeda ("The Base") network, their worldview changed. Bin Laden had a much higher goal—the ultimate goal of jehad. Bin Laden's foremost targets till now had been the House of Saud, the rulers of Saudi Arabia, and the United States. However, countries like India became smaller enemies because of Kashmir. Since terrorist outfits such as Harkat-ul-Mujahideen, Harkat-ul-Ansar, and Lashkar-e-Taiyyaba were training in Afghanistan, it became easier for Al Qaeda and the Taliban to identify with their cause as well. Hence began the process of Talibanisation of the Kashmiri militants.

Nationality was no longer important; ideology was—a Taliban could be Afghan, Indian, African, Chinese or even American.

Bin Laden convinced Mullah Omar to embrace the larger cause of Islam and provide sanctuary to all Islamic groups who were fighting so-called infidels in their countries. Omar's and Laden's definition of infidels also included some Muslim factions like Shias, and any Muslim ruler opposed to them. Bin Laden convinced Mullah Omar to give support and space to the Islamic Movement of Uzbekistan (IMU) led by Juma Namangani, which is fighting against the government of Islam Karimov in Uzbekistan.[5] Under Al Qaeda's influence and ideological training, IMU started recruiting dissidents from all over Central Asia, including the Muslim-dominated Xinjiang province of China. These dissidents or terrorists now have a free run of the entire region; they cross borders like shadows and talk of the great Islamic revolution that is to follow the jehad.

The Jehad

This is perhaps the most abused and misunderstood word in recent times. Most people think, incorrectly though, that jehad is the Islamic version of the Christian Crusades of the middle centuries. Prophet Mohammad had explained jehad as a continued struggle against one's own weaknesses to ensure that one does not stray from the path of faith. However, since the early Islamic years were marked by constant civil strife—first against the inimical forces in Arabia and later in the other parts of the Middle East—the definition of jehad was extended to include struggle against the forces which come in the way of religion.

However, the Prophet was very clear about the distinction between the two forms of jehad. The former was Jehad al Akbar or the greater jehad and the latter was Jehad al Akhtar or the lesser jehad. Even though Muslims in those days were impelled to fight the lesser jehad for the survival of their religion, it was never against civilians.

---

[5] Rashid, Ahmed (2002), *Jihad: The Rise of Militant Islam in Central Asia*, Hyderabad: Orient Longman.

Jehad al Akhtar could only be fought against proclaimed fighters. However, there was a provision for jehad against corrupt and unfaithful Muslim rulers as well. And it is this clause that has given excuses to people like Osama Bin Laden, Mullah Omar and Juma Namangani to carry out terrorist activities worldwide.

These outfits and their charismatic rulers have interpreted the Quran and the Sunnah to suit their own convenience. They have chosen to focus on words and symbols without their historical and social context. Moreover, in doing so, they have been leading millions of Muslim youth astray. The Al Qaeda has a worldwide network in nearly 34 countries, which, apart from the Middle East, includes the Xinjiang province in China, and countries like Bosnia, Indonesia, Philippines and Kenya. The Islamic Movement of Uzbekistan (IMU) run by Juma Namangani is active throughout the Central Asian Republics.

Cherie Blair, wife of British Prime Minister Tony Blair, made a comment on Palestinian suicide bombers that applies to Muslim militants worldwide. She said that when our young people feel they have no hope but to blow themselves up for some cause, there is something wrong somewhere. The majority of the Muslim world, particularly Central Asia, has a peculiar problem. The leadership is growing old, while the population is becoming young. Nearly 60 per cent of the people in most of these countries are under the age of 35. There is no economy, no education, no employment and consequently no future to speak of. In the absence of anything to look forward to, these restless, semi-educated youth become easy fodder for the machines of hatred. Even if they do not have an immediate enemy, they fight against distant and sometimes imagined enemies. Any Muslim's war becomes their war.

Jehad in Kashmir

Kashmir has increasingly become embroiled in this worldwide jehad. After the Kargil war, Mullah Omar declared his support for jehad in Kashmir. This was enough for militant elements everywhere in the world to embrace Kashmir as their cause. Post 1999, the war of independence which the ethnic Kashmiris believed they were fighting against India turned into a jehad as the movement was now being led by the Taliban. Pakistan started losing ground

rapidly as jehadi outfits like Lashkar-e-Taiyyaba, Jaish-e-Mohammad and Harkat-ul-Mujahideen—inspired, trained and provided
for by the Taliban and the Al Qaeda—took over the armed struggle
in Kashmir. Killings targeted at minorities—including the Sikhs—
increased, suicide bombers or fidayeen started hitting their targets
with greater success and, most importantly, the terrorists started
taking on the Indian Army with greater impunity.

Once upon a time, the Hizbul had made the JKLF redundant;
in post-1999 Kashmir, it was getting the same treatment from the
jehadi or the Talibanised outfits. Since it was being pushed to the
corner, and since General Musharraf found it increasingly difficult
to control the jehadis, the Hizbul declared a ceasefire in Kashmir
in 2000. However, this was soon retracted as friction appeared
within the Hizbul cadre. Syed Salahuddin, the Hizbul chief based
in Pakistan, derided the ceasefire moves made by its commander
Majid Dar in Kashmir.

Clearly, Syed Salahuddin could not ignore the jehadis, especially
since he was based in Pakistan. Between 1990 and 1994, Kashmiri
youth were queuing up to join the Hizbul; in 2000, they were going
the jehadi way. Compounding the situation was the changing attitude of the local populace. By the beginning of 2001, there were
increasing demands for according the dead jehadis a martyr's
burial. In 1994, the Hizbul was hailed as the liberating force; six
years down the line, the same respect or awe was being reserved
for the jehadis.

Despite the overt similarities between the condition of the JKLF
in 1994 and the Hizbul in 2001, the latter did not suffer a similar
fate for the simple reason that the Pakistan government backed
it. Besides, once it realised that it was getting marginalised by the
jehadis, it started towing their line, thereby ensuring its survival.

The End of History

Americans do not exaggerate when they claim that September 11,
2001 changed the world. However, they probably do not realise
exactly how it changed the equations in Kashmir. Operation Enduring Freedom was a windfall for President Musharraf in many ways.
Apart from the economic and social rehabilitation, Pakistan was
gradually able to bring Kashmir to the centre stage once again.

It served Pakistani interests to join the war against terrorism and wipe out the terrorism-churning machinery in Afghanistan. The Taliban, though a creation of Pakistan, had turned into a Frankenstein monster. Pakistan had hoped that with Taliban at the helm, it would acquire a strategic space inside Afghanistan. The Taliban ensured that the reverse became true. They refused to recognise the Durand Line and had their own agenda—Pakistani national interest did not figure anywhere in that. What India called Musharraf's about turn on Afghanistan was in fact a re-evaluation of a policy which did not yield the desired results.

As the Al Qaeda and the Taliban leadership went into hiding following the American attacks, the jehadi outfits active in Kashmir—Lashkar-e-Taiyyaba, Jaish-e-Mohammad, Al Omar, Hizbul Mujahideen—were rendered headless. The fountainhead from which they derived sustenance was no longer present. These outfits were expected to either go back to Afghanistan to fight the bigger battle or come under the umbrella of the ISI once again.

Most of the jehadi outfits did not reinvent themselves even after the American war with Afghanistan. The primary reason for this was that despite a change of guard in Afghanistan, the Taliban and the Al Qaeda leadership were still at large. From time to time, they issue a statement or release a cassette exhorting jehadis to continue their struggle.

The immediate fall-out of this was that the disarrayed jehadis became desperate. The first sign of this desperation was the suicide attack outside the Jammu and Kashmir Assembly on October 1, 2001, which killed 29 people. The Talibanised Jaish-e-Mohammad took responsibility for the attack which was condemned by everyone including Musharraf, who was now back to his old tune of supporting a freedom struggle in J&K. Hardly a year ago, he was talking of a jehad in Kashmir. The British foreign secretary, Jack Straw, linked the attack to Osama Bin Laden. Apart from that dastardly attack, there was a lull in the overall terrorist activities in the state. The jehadis were obviously groping in the dark.

Their desperation was again evident in the ill-conceived attack on the Indian Parliament on December 13. Pakistan again rushed to condemn the attack, as did the rest of the world. However, by this time the Indian leadership was obviously tired of waiting for the second phase of Operation Enduring Freedom to start, which the US promised would address Indian concerns (read, Kashmir).

The Indian government decided to take matters in its own hands and announced a general mobilisation of its troops, the biggest ever in Indian history. There was immense pressure on Pakistan to rein in the jehadis, but Musharraf was at pains to explain that he did not control them. In his address on January 12, 2002, directed towards both his compatriots and the West, he reiterated his commitment to fight terrorism. He declared that he would not allow any organisation to run a terrorist movement from Pakistani soil. He also banned a number of jehadi and Islamic organisations, some of which were fomenting sectarian trouble within Pakistan. Among the banned outfits operating in Kashmir were Jaish-e-Mohammad and Lashkar-e-Taiyyaba. Their offices were sealed and the leadership rounded up.

Interestingly, the Hizbul was not banned. The general lull in terrorist activities continued in Kashmir, though sporadic killings did not cease. Despite the troop mobilisation, the possibilities of war had receded. It appeared that India was looking for a face-saving formula to demobilise its troops. It continued to harp on Pakistan handing over 20 criminals on India's list, including underworld don Dawood Ibrahim, an accused in the Mumbai bomb blast case. Also on the list were a few old Khalistan hands. Pakistan continued to ignore these demands.

On the Kashmir front, the mobilisation seemed to have achieved practically nothing. With the onset of spring—the time when infiltration starts—there was a marginal increase in violence, but that was almost along expected lines. In May 2002, the suicide bombers started attacking various army camps in places like Rajouri, Jammu and Udhampur. The most audacious of these was the attack on the Kaluchak camp near Jammu. In a pre-dawn attack, the fidayeen killed 32 people—mostly the women and children of army personnel.

Once again, India and Pakistan were on the brink of war. Musharraf condemned the attack and again threw his weight behind the anti-terror campaign run by the US. He assured the world that nothing was happening at the Line of Control. Though he did not say it in so many words, the fact was that the jehadis were already inside Kashmir and they were not listening to Musharraf. In an interview with the American channel PBS, the US Deputy Secretary of State, Richard Armitage, said, "There are jehadists that are outside the control of all Pakistani authority. There are also jehadists that were already existent in Kashmir. They didn't need to cross the Line of Control to cause trouble" (Reported in *The Hindu*). These jehadis were not yet ready to fall in line with Musharraf's freedom fighters. They were still hopeful that the flagging jehad would be resuscitated.

Even as the West was working overtime to avert a war between India and Pakistan (there was at least a weekly visitor from either the US or the UK to the sub-continent), Musharraf was fine-tuning his long-term plans for Kashmir. His first priority, obviously, was to cleanse Pakistani society of the Taliban elements. The jehadis on the run in Pakistan had started attacking targets, mainly Western, within the country. The most dramatic of these was the attack on the US consulate in Karachi. Musharraf's second priority was to come up with a programme which would not only serve his national interest in Kashmir, but also ensure that in the changed world order Pakistan would not be called a state sponsoring terrorism. Hence, he was at pains to explain, time and again, that there was an indigenous freedom struggle going on in Kashmir, which Pakistan supported.

In an interview to the US magazine *Newsweek* in July 2002, he said, "First of all, I don't call it cross-border terrorism. There is a freedom struggle going on in Kashmir. What I said is that there is no movement across the Line of Control." In the same interview, he added, "On Afghanistan we changed our policy. We saw the environment and thought that we should join the coalition.... But Kashmir is our national interest."

Militancy has come full circle in Kashmir today. In 1994, the JKLF was sidelined, training camps were shifted from Pakistan to Afghanistan and the process of "jehadification" had begun. By 2001, the Hizbul was sidelined and the Talibanised jehadis were holding sway in Kashmir, looking up to Mullah Omar and Osama Bin Laden for inspiration, moral support and material sustenance. In July 2002, Mullah Omar was on the run and Pakistan once again appeared to be the only benefactor of the freedom fighters. They could no longer afford to be jehadis. The training camps that were earlier moved to Afghanistan now shifted back to Pakistan-occupied-Kashmir (PoK). A report in an Indian newspaper mentioned the existence of at least three active training camps in PoK.

Musharraf stated that the happenings inside PoK should be left to Pakistan. Moreover, Mushtaq Ahmed Zargar, the commander of Al Omar, said in an interview to a Pakistani newspaper, "Pakistan continues to give us political, moral and diplomatic support. General Musharraf has said that they will fully support Kashmiris on these fronts. Pakistan is justified in saying that it would not allow terrorism originating from its soil. But our movement is not terrorism...and we are not doing any such thing from Pakistani borders." Clearly, the third chapter of Kashmir militancy has begun. And this time, Pakistan would be loathe to concede ground to anyone.

A New Phase

Pakistan informed the global community that it cannot hold the Kashmiri militants in leash indefinitely, and therefore India needs to initiate a dialogue with Pakistan at the earliest. However, what it did not say was more important. The freeze on militants would continue as long as it takes Pakistan to streamline its new policy on Kashmir. Hence Musharraf and the ISI were working overtime to isolate the pro-Taliban militant outfits. The two primary Talibanised outfits, Jaish-e-Mohammad and Lashkar-e-Taiyyaba, were disbanded and their leaders, Masood Azhar and Hafiz Saeed, were detained and arrested respectively. The third group, Al Omar, run by Mushtaq Zargar, decided to relinquish its jehadi agenda and started towing Musharraf's line.[6]

The militants who agreed to reinvent themselves were put at the disposal of either Hizbul Mujahideen or Al Omar. According to the newspaper reports coming from Pakistan, the idea was to make the Kashmir movement more organised and cohesive. In the early phase of the movement, Pakistan thought it wise to create a number of smaller outfits to deflect attention. However, now it appeared that it had started thinking that for a sustainable agitation with the respectability of a freedom struggle, it was important to create a single cohesive body, with an inbuilt political front. Further, it was imperative that such a body remain Kashmiri in nature and not appear to be based in Pakistan.

Rumours were afloat in PoK about a new militant group, Kashmir Liberation Army (KLA), to be headed probably by Mushtaq Zargar. All the other groups were likely to come under its umbrella.

---

[6] A report in the Pakistani newspaper *Herald*, quoted in "Kashmir is an Indian Struggle", *The Indian Express*, September 3, 2002.

Though KLA would enjoy Pakistan's tacit support, inclusive of weapons and funds, for appearances sake it would be a completely indigenous and independent body. The allegations that Pakistani nationals are operating in Kashmir would have been met by the reasoning that they were originally Kashmiris who fled Kashmir to escape Indian aggression. According to Mushtaq Zargar, "Whoever is fighting in Kashmir is a Kashmiri. The fact that those who fled from Kashmir in 1947 due to Indian repression and settled in Pakistan are now taking part in the freedom struggle along with their oppressed brethren does not impair the cause."[7]

Meanwhile, the jehadi elements in Kashmir—a substantial number—started flexing their muscles once again. The home ministry reports said that around 300 militants have infiltrated the Valley from across the border recently. This was in addition to those already present there. Though Lashkar-e-Taiyyaba and Jaish-e-Mohammad were banned in Pakistan and the US, they have been active in Kashmir and were still not willing to tow the Pakistani or Hizbul line. The Lashkar created four factions and divided the Kashmiri operations between them. Al Madina, which also includes a section of Al Omar and Hizbul, was active in Srinagar and the adjoining area. The Babul Hind Force focuses on Anantnag district in south Kashmir. Azam Jehad, which targets the security forces, was active in the Doda and Udhampur districts of Jammu. Another group, Al Mansooriyan, was meant to target civilians in and around Jammu. The same report also said that this level of coordination between different militant outfits had not been seen before.

The fact that the jehadi outfits are still refusing to fall in line with Pakistani policy implies that their source of sustenance, both physical and moral, has not dried up. If they feel that they can still fight the Indian security forces on their own, then obviously the American war against terrorism has not been entirely successful. If Mullah Omar, most of the top Taliban leadership and Osama Bin Laden are still at large, there is little possibility that this so-called jehad will end in the near future. There are reports already that in the absence of Osama Bin Laden, his son has risen in the ranks and is now directing the worldwide jehad.

---

[7] In an interview to the Pakistani newspaper *Herald*, quoted in "Kashmir is an Indian Struggle", *The Indian Express*, September 3, 2002.

Whatever the future of jehad in Kashmir may be, the insurgency was poised to enter a violent new phase in 2003 in spite of innumerable government initiatives. Newspaper reports in India indicated that nearly 400 security personnel and 1,000 civilians died in terrorist violence during 2002. And this, when the Indian Army was mobilised and Pakistan had assured the world that nothing was happening on the Line of Control.

Through the summer, there were a number of instances of infiltration—some of which were foiled and some successful. Interestingly, there were also reports about Musharraf training a new breed of young militants in PoK who would be the future freedom fighters. A report from the Indian home ministry indicated that a fresh movement of Kashmiri youth from Kashmir to PoK had begun. These young boys were being taken across the border by the militants in small batches of 10 to 15.

President Musharraf has already told the West that the freeze on militancy—India believes that there was never a complete freeze—will not continue indefinitely unless India initiates a dialogue. Pakistan was obviously waiting to complete the electoral process before increasing the tempo in Kashmir. As if on cue, Hafiz Saeed was released on November 19, 2002, and Masood Azhar on December 30, 2002. While Saeed started issuing threats to the Indian government, Azhar has left for an unknown destination. There is no doubt that the tempo will increase. And this time, the initiative would rest with the Pakistan-trained and rechristened freedom fighters. In this fight, nationality would be an important factor. So there may be Afghanistan-hardened militants, but they would be of Kashmir origin—at least officially.

The Indian Response

India's response to the changing profile of terrorism in Kashmir has been sporadic and reactive. Initially, when the insurgency broke out in the Valley in 1989, India treated it as a law and order problem. The state police, and the paramilitary forces which were rushed to the Valley, came down heavily on the people. The more people took to the streets, the more civilian heads were crushed with a vengeance. In a few months, the state administrative machinery had broken down completely. There were daily demonstrations in the Valley, and the police, instead of doing its job, switched sides and started eulogising the power of the militant's gun. The years 1990 to 1992 witnessed the biggest deployment yet of army in internal security operations in the Valley. While credit should go to the Army Chief, Gen. S. F. Rodrigues, for overpowering militancy in the Valley towards the end of 1992, he unfortunately thought of the army's role as "aid to civil power". This denied the army the opportunity to formulate an aggressive operational policy in the formative stages when the uprising was limited to the Valley.

Moreover, the army's morale took a beating when Gen. Rodrigues was criticised by the political leadership for saying that "good governance is the army's responsibility as well". George Fernandes—who later became the defence minister—sought the general's resignation in Parliament. The honest general only said that the army had helped overcome terrorism in the state of Punjab, and was now doing the same in the Valley. It was no secret that the political and administrative leadership had packed its bags and left Punjab in the eighties for the army to salvage the situation. The political leadership misinterpreted the general's remarks and concluded that the army's top brass were seeking a larger role in running the country.

This incident, which was blown out of proportion by politicians, had its impact on India-Pakistan diplomacy as well. In February 1992, militants of the Jammu and Kashmir Liberation Front (JKLF) based in Pakistan-occupied-Kashmir (PoK) had threatened to cross the Line of Control (LoC) in Kashmir to show open solidarity with their cadres in the Valley. India warned Pakistan that if it did not stop them the situation could go out of control. Understanding India's seriousness, Pakistan stopped the JKLF cadres, but accused India of moving troops into forward locations to attack PoK. At this point, Gen. Rodrigues, after getting clearance from the Defence Minister, Sharad Pawar, invited the Pakistan army chief, Gen. Asif Nawaz Janjua, to visit India. The visit did not materialise mainly because the Pakistani leadership estimated that it would weaken the militancy in the Valley. On India's part, the unsavoury incident in the Parliament, which happened soon after the proposed JKLF march, had dampened Gen. Rodrigues' spirits. The army thereafter took little initiative for the rest of his term as chief.

Gen. Rodrigues' successor, Gen. B. C. Joshi, sought to raise the morale of the army. Even before taking office, he publicly identified militancy in the Valley and asserted that it would be a long-drawn challenge to overcome it. One of the first things he did on assuming charge on July 1, 1993 was to inform the Prime Minister that the army's use for internal security duties would imperil national security. He suggested that the army be allowed to go back and train for its primary task at the border. He offered to raise more Rashtriya Rifle (RR) units in quick time for internal security operations. Even while Prime Minister P. V. Narasimha Rao concurred with his army chief, there was a clash of swords between Gen. Joshi and the state Governor, Gen. K. V. Krishna Rao—a former army chief—who had assumed office on March 12, 1993.

Governor Rao accepted his job only after the Prime Minister had agreed to his priorities, which were to curb militancy at the earliest, and then conduct assembly elections in the state. According to Governor Rao: "In essence, my view was that Kashmir was mismanaged over a period of time, and that militancy had to be put down before anything else could become functional in the state. Once militancy was controlled, efforts should be made to revive the assembly, which still had two years to go, and after a suitable period, try and hold elections—views that I set down in my letter to him [Prime Minister Rao] as a follow-up to our discussion."[8]

After discussions with the local army commander, Governor Rao sought two divisions worth of additional army troops and twelve BSF battalions urgently to establish an effective counter-insurgency grid for the Valley. Gen. Joshi expressed his inability to do so, but promised to raise more RR units. The prime minister, instead of resolving the issue, thought best not to take sides, and let matters drift. Problems were further compounded by the appointment of Rajesh Pilot, a junior minister in the home ministry, as minister-in-charge of Kashmir affairs in January 1993. On the one hand, the army chief and the state governor publicly declared that they were answerable to the prime minister alone. On the other, the media had a field day reporting differences between Pilot and his senior minister, S. B. Chavan, over Kashmir affairs. Prime Minister Rao was simply not the man for the moment.

Around this time, Pakistan added to India's problems with a change in strategy. Foreign mercenaries who were well armed,

---

[8] Rao, K. V. Krishna (2001), *In the Service of the Nation*, New Delhi: Viking, p. 428.

trained and had fought in the Afghan war were inducted into the Valley. These hardened terrorists were skilled in the use of rocket-propelled grenades and improvised explosive devices, which were responsible for the maximum number of casualties. The terrorists inside the country were now a mix of foreign mercenaries and pro-Pakistan Hizbul Mujahideen, the former still in small numbers, who were bold enough to challenge the army in tactical battles. The terrorists also expanded their area of operations to the Doda district of Jammu division. Given the even mix of Hindu and Muslim population in the towns of Doda, Kishtwar and Bhadarwah of Doda district, the situation was ripe for terrorists to inflame communal passions.

Against this backdrop, Gen. Joshi was busy with the raising of RR units and working on proactive means to combat terrorism; Governor Rao was determined to suppress terrorism at the earliest with the army, paramilitary forces and police that were available to him, and hold elections as soon as possible; the home ministry was busy sorting out differences between its two ministers; the external affairs ministry was occupied countering Pakistan's charges of human rights violations by Indian security personnel; and the Prime Minister's office had little ideas of its own. There was no cohesive thinking on how to fight terrorism; everyone was working in isolation. It was evident that whatever Governor Rao and Gen. Joshi were to do would have an impact on counter-terrorism operations in the following years.

Rashtriya Rifles

First raised in 1990 under the government Composition Table Part-II, the RR is a non-field force at par with the Territorial Army, the National Cadet Corps and various paramilitary forces. At the time of its inception, this was a good move as the government did not want to increase the strength of the regular army and it hoped that retired soldiers would gradually join the RR. The move was meant to both provide lateral employment to soldiers who superannuate young, and keep the army's annual allocation on pay and allowances in check. It was argued that the RR force so raised would be better trained and motivated than paramilitary forces for counter-insurgency (CI) operations.

Unfortunately, things changed with the beginning of the insurgency in Kashmir in 1990. The retired soldiers did not join the RR and, in December 1993, Gen. Joshi ordered the raising of 30 battalions and associated headquarters (about 40,000 troops) of RR in a record time of one year—and that too, from within the army resources. This was done to ward off international criticism instigated by Pakistan that India had increased its regular army strength in Kashmir, leading to an escalation in human rights violations. The other reason for this move was Gen. Joshi's plans to hit the terrorist bases in PoK, which necessitated that the regular army revert to its operational role on the LoC.

Despite assurances to the army chief by Prime Minister Rao himself, the home ministry, responsible for all paramilitary forces, refused to fund the RR until it weaned away from the defence ministry and came under its total control. This created a piquant situation: the RR, which was a regular army by another name, could not be under the home ministry. At the same time, it could not be what it actually was—a regular army—due to the lack of funds.

Things continued to drift with a heavy cost for CI operations at two levels. First, the Unified Headquarters (UH), which was formed in Kashmir in 1993 to ensure that all CI forces—various paramilitary forces, state police and the RR—work together, did just the opposite. The Border Security Force (BSF), as the oldest paramilitary force, argued that the RR should come under its command. The RR, on the other hand, found the BSF and the Central Reserve Police Force incompetent. The two forces and their respective ministries could just not work together. This made the Unified Headquarters a non-starter, where CI forces worked against rather than with one another.

If this was not enough, the RR manifested a host of internal problems, to the glee of militants and their Pakistani sponsors. A force which was culled together from various units and had a frequent turnover of troops lacked cohesion, motivation, a regimental spirit, and élan, good communications and weaponry. There were several reported and many more unreported instances of soldiers running amok. Cases of soldiers inflicting self-injuries to be eased out of the Valley were not uncommon. A few resorted to suicide as the stress became unbearable. The commanding officers of most RR units had no communication at all with their troops.

There was a discernible decrease in discipline and patience. Round-the-clock vigilance, lack of sleep, and an all-pervading psychological fear was taking its toll on the troops. Added to this was the shortage of young officers who could lead men by example from the front and infuse them with confidence. It was a Herculean effort for the army high command to bring about an acceptable normalcy and stability in the RR units a little before the 1999 Kargil war.

At the time of the Kargil war, the RR had a total of 36 battalions under two CI force headquarters (each equivalent to an army division headquarters)—"Victor" for the districts of Anantnag, Pulwama and Badgam, and "Delta" for Doda district. The Overall Force Headquarters (OFH) under an officer of the rank of Lt. Gen. was, and remains at the time of writing, the weakest link in the RR because it was an administrative rather than an operational headquarters. The operational control of the RR was with the local corps commanders in Kashmir.

The CI grids were disturbed during the Kargil war when regular troops supporting the RR were moved to the war theatre and the two corps commanders—15 and 16 based in Srinagar and Nagrota—relinquished their CI responsibilities. The commander, OFH, was moved from Delhi to Srinagar in June 1999 to assume command of the RR, and he replaced the corps commanders as the security advisor to the chief minister for CI duties. Unfortunately, even while the nation was fighting a war with Pakistan in Kargil, differences between the RR and other paramilitary forces in the UH did not diminish.

After the war, the CI situation deteriorated for various reasons. As the commander of the OFH was unacceptable to the chief minister, he was sent back to Delhi. The local corps commanders reverted back to their additional CI tasks. Regular troops like the 8 Mountain division, which had been involved in CI duties in Srinagar and were moved to Kargil for the war, were placed permanently under the newly raised 14 corps headquarters in Leh. This created a grave imbalance in the CI grids at a time when Talibanised jehadis had started infiltrating into the state. The government ordered the raising of two additional CI force headquarters—"Kilo" for Kupwara and "Romeo" for Rajouri were raised in September 1999 and January 2000 respectively. The earlier internal problems of the RR manifested themselves once again, and there was little cooperation between the RR, paramilitary forces and the police. The stakes now were much higher as the Talibanised jehadis were different from the foreign mercenaries and indigenous militants.

The events of 9/11 brought some initial reprieve from terrorism in Kashmir. But it did not last long. Operation Parakram—the mobilisation of the army against Pakistan since December 2001— once again wrought trouble for the RR. The army had occupied its forward defences and its reserves were ordered to be ready at short notice for offensive operations. This meant that all regular troops involved in CI ops were withdrawn. Besides, there was a greater need to protect the hinterland from terrorist attacks in the event of a war. The army therefore raised another RR force headquarters called Uniform force for the Udhampur area of Jammu division from within its own overstretched resources.

The present strength of the RR force is over 70,000 troops, divided into five force headquarters—Kilo for Kupwara, Victor for the Valley, Delta for Doda, Romeo for Rajouri and Uniform for Udhampur. With the persistent overall shortage of young officers, and considering that the cream of the army holds the frontline, the RR unavoidably gets a stepmotherly treatment in terms of men, material and financial resources. Even worse, the status of this CI force— whether it is part of the regular army or a paramilitary force— remains undecided. Moreover, its mandate to exist is being enhanced incrementally by the government, with its present term to expire on March 31, 2004. To sum up, the RR, whose strength is over and above that of the regular army, remains an orphaned child being tossed between the defence and home ministries.

The answer probably lies in the government deciding both the status and mandate of the RR at the earliest. This would make the defunct Unified Headquarters alive and useful. Considering that the RR is a force created from the army, it can only be amalgamated as a combat arm of the regular army. Once this is done, there would be little reason for paramilitary forces in Kashmir to not come under the command of the RR. This would ease the dual tasking of the local corps commanders whose primary job remains on the LoC. The two corps commanders could then hand over their CI ops duties to the Director-General of the RR, who could become the sole security advisor to the chief minister of the state.

The second benefit would be that the RR would get independent funding, which at present is a measly amount. It is bizarre that a 75,000-strong professional force should be dependent on the army's annual allocation, which itself is meagre. The RR could then have its own administrative, operational and training infrastructure, like a regimental centre, pay office, etc. Most of all, the Psychological Operations (psy ops) unit, which would also provide psychologists to advise commanders in CI combat, could be formed. The need of the hour is to reassure the RR troops before there is a morale breakdown, which, if it comes to pass, would be a national shame.

Unified Headquarters (UH)

The brainchild of Governor Rao, the UH was formed on May 14, 1993. According to Governor Rao:[9]

What was set up was a Unified Headquarters and not a Unified Command, as erroneously referred to by some people. The unified concept comprised setting up a unified headquarters under the advisor (home) at the highest level in the state in order to coordinate between the security forces, intelligence agencies and civil departments concerned. At the field level, the two corps headquarters, in addition to their normal operational role of defence against external aggression, were to be responsible for anti-militancy operations in the state, with the exception of Srinagar city. Under the corps, the divisions were to be responsible for anti-militancy operations in their territorial jurisdiction, and all paramilitary forces meant for anti-militancy operations were to be under the operational control of the divisional commanders.

It was never realised that the nemesis of UH lay within its own concept. The paramilitary forces were most hesitant to work under the operational control of the army because the ethos, training, motivation, discipline, style of functioning, and chain of command of the two forces were poles apart and impossible to bridge. The problem was further compounded when the paramilitary forces were required to work with the RR, which was practically the same as the regular army. Both indulged in one-upmanship and worked at cross purposes rather than with one another.

---

[9] *Ibid.*, p. 448.

Matters within the UH top leadership were not smooth either. It was difficult for a corps commander, for instance, to share intelligence and operational matters with a civil bureaucrat, considering that regular troops were also involved in CI ops alongside the RR. Moreover, a corps commander could not be expected to take operational orders from a governor, even when the latter happened to be a former army chief. For these reasons, the UH has remained stunted in growth. This is evident from the fact that foreign dignitaries are usually given two briefings on terrorism in the state—one at the UH and the other at the local corps headquarters.

What Governor Rao did not do probably needs to be done now. After the status and mandate of the RR has been decided, all paramilitary forces on CI duties in the state should be placed under the command and control of the RR. The UH, therefore, should be re-named Unified Command (UC). These twin political decisions regarding the UC and RR would help resuscitate the UH, which is fast losing its relevance. At a still higher level, the government needs to consider the recommendations of the Committee on Border Management, one of the four task forces formed after the Kargil war.[10]

The Committee made two recommendations regarding paramilitary forces. The first was the one-force-one-border principle, which has been accepted by the government. The second recommendation refers to the need for all Central Paramilitary Forces (CPMF) to come under one ministry. The three forces actually involved in guarding the border—the BSF, the Assam Rifles, and the Indo-Tibetan Border Force—should be designated as Border Guarding Forces (BGF) and categorised as CPMF. Further, the CPMF should be under the defence ministry alone. All other forces under the home ministry, like the Central Reserve Police Force, should be designated as Central Police Organisations (CPO). In essence, this implies that over a period of time, the BSF would need to revert to its original role of border guarding, and come under the defence ministry. Until this happens, all paramilitary forces, including the BSF, should be under the command of the army/RR for counter-terrorism duties in Kashmir.

This will not be an easy task. For example, as soon as the government announced in December 2001 that Operation Parakram

---

[10] Lt. Gen. Sood, a co-author, was a member of the Border Management Committee.

was a mobilisation for war, according to the Union Book on War all paramilitary forces—even those involved in CI operations in the hinterland—automatically came under the command of the army. One of the adverse fall-outs of this long mobilisation has been that paramilitary forces are exerting political and bureaucratic pressure to revert to their peacetime chain of command. The good thing, however, is that for once the functioning of the UH has improved manifold.

Reactive Counter-Terrorism

Despite claims by political leaders, India has never exercised a proactive counter-terrorism option in Kashmir. The army has been ordered to maintain a strictly defensive posture along the LoC. This implies a static holding of defences and a few troops being made available for mobile interdiction of infiltrating columns in the immediate hinterland. Indian experts have lauded this posture as a measure to avoid war. The result has been that at the operational level, the initiative has passed completely into the hands of the insurgents and their Pakistani patrons. The latter dictate the rates of engagement, infiltration, and areas to be activated and to what purpose, including methods of initiation.

Senior army commanders had argued since 1990 that since no insurgency which enjoys an inviolate sanctuary has ever been defeated, India must shift its strategy from combating the elusive insurgent to hitting their sanctuaries, routes of ingress, observation posts that facilitate infiltration and logistics bases. Loss of these would mean slow but sure strangulation of insurgents. Gen. Joshi was the first chief to advocate a proactive counter-terrorism option to the government. The situation in 1993, it could be argued, favoured such an approach. Most terrorist sanctuaries were in PoK and the Northern Areas, as Pakistan had still not shifted them to Afghanistan; the foreign mercenaries had yet not arrived on the scene; the indigenous terrorists were not bold enough to challenge the army; the Pakistan-backed All-Party Hurriyat Conference had not been formed; India could have got away with its offensive strategy as both India and Pakistan were not declared nuclear weapon states; and Kargil, which sanctified the inviolability of the LoC, had not happened. However, Prime Minister Rao, known for his non-confrontationist attitude, dismissed the army's suggestions.

Gen. Joshi's successors, Generals Shankar Roychowdhury and V. P. Malik, did not share his enthusiasm for proactive measures to combat terrorism. Gen. Roychowdhury, however, was the first army chief to say that the external security of the nation was linked to its internal security, implying that the army would need to play a big role in counter-terrorism operations in addition to its primary job. It was an undeclared war by proxy which had been unleashed by Pakistan, he commented. Surprisingly, Gen. Roychowdhury, who understood the dimension of the proxy war by Pakistan, did not share his predecessor's ideas about using media as a force-multiplier. At a time when India should have pursued a vigorous counter-terrorism policy, it did just the opposite and let matters drift. The army did not make use of the media, and started losing the propaganda war unleashed by Pakistan. Successive weak governments were also hesitant to disturb the status quo with Pakistan. The focus of the army and the government shifted to counting the number of terrorists killed and arms captured. A completely defensive mindset within the army cost it dear: it was caught unawares in Kargil, and the troops came under tremendous pressure when the Talibanised jehadis entered Kashmir after the 1999 Kargil war.

On being asked how the government proposed to combat the increasing numbers of Talibanised mujahids after the Kargil war, the Home Minister, L. K. Advani, kept repeating his three-pronged mantra to bring normalcy to the state: talks with "misguided" militants, more development work, and a proactive (read, defensive) posture by security forces to check violence. The measures adopted include additional BSF and CRPF units, border fencing—especially in the Jammu division—reducing gaps between border posts, use of helicopter gunships by CI forces, construction of a few border roads, recruitment of more Special Police Officers—mostly renegade and surrendered militants—and creation of more Village Defence Committees (VDC) in the border areas of the Jammu division. The VDC comprises five to six civilians, mostly ex-servicemen, each armed with outdated 303 rifles and about 100 rounds of ammunition. For obvious reasons, these are confined to Jammu, and are seen by the state government and the home ministry as a substitute for additional paramilitary or police forces. The utility of the VDC has, at best, been marginal.

Things continued to drift, until December 13, 2001 (12/13) when terrorists belonging to Lashkar-e-Taiyyaba attacked the Parliament. India launched Operation Parakram without much thought on how to deal effectively with terrorists already in the state. Even as the world focus shifted to Pakistan-aided infiltration on the LoC, Talibanised mujahids continued creating mayhem inside the state with impunity. India said that these mujahids were under the control of Pakistan's ISI. Such assertions were unfortunately seen as niggardly pronouncements, considering that Pakistan itself was under assault by these elements.

India was apparently getting beaten by its own game. Our leaders insisted that the Talibanised mujahids belonging to the Lashkar-e-Taiyyaba and Jaish-e-Mohammad who were responsible for wanton terrorist attacks—the J&K state assembly building, Indian Parliament, the Kaluchak camp, the Rajiv Nagar killings, and the attack on the Amarnath yatra pilgrims—were under orders of the ISI. The pro-Pakistan Hizbul Mujahideen, with whom India had opened back-door negotiation channels, was not put on notice. This issue negated India's case against Pakistan, considering that President Musharraf had already banned the Talibanised mujahids and these outfits were responsible for terrorist violence in Pakistan as well.

For domestic consumption, the government kept hinting about a change in strategy to fight these Talibanised terrorists, which, of course, was never disclosed. Once India announced the holding of assembly elections in the state in September–October 2002, it became clear that the proposed new strategy was old wine in a new bottle: pumping in more security forces to fight rising terrorist violence. The CI grids were displaced once again: the army and the RR were moved to rural areas, and additional paramilitary forces were sent to the state. For India, the anti-terror campaign had come full circle. For terrorists, it was business as usual.

Summary

- Pakistan created the Taliban, but after the latter captured Kabul in 1996, they did not care much for Islamabad.
- Consequent to Pakistan's defeat in the 1999 Kargil war, the Talibanised mujahids tightened their grip over militancy in J&K.
- 9/11 provided Musharraf with the god-sent opportunity to force the Talibanised mujahids to reinvent themselves and serve Pakistan's cause (i.e., a merger of J&K with Pakistan).

- India has all along lacked a proactive line of thought to combat terrorism.
- There is an urgent need to review the Rashtriya Rifles and Unified Headquarters for optimal counter-insurgency operations.

3

Operation Parakram: The War Half-started

Operation Parakram was unusual in many ways. Never before had a war between India and Pakistan been an announced one. The Indian Army Chief, Gen. S. Padmanabhan, announced to the media on January 11, 2002 that the mobilisation for war was complete and the armed forces were waiting for the political nod. Never before had the Army remained mobilised for 10 long months. Never before had there been an open debate about the very motive of a mobilisation—were there any purposes other than war? And never before had an army chief, who was also the chairman of the Chiefs of Staff committee, said at the official termination of the operation that "whenever there is a situation calling for Army's help, the latter's role should be clearly defined to avoid confusion."[1]

Sure enough, the Defence Minister, George Fernandes, did not quite agree with the army chief. Replying to questions in the Parliament on November 20, 2002, Fernandes said that the intended objectives of the 10-month long forward mobilisation were achieved with "great distinction". According to the minister:

- The mobilisation exerted immense pressure on Pakistan and forced Gen. Pervez Musharraf to denounce support to jihad through his January 12 and May 27 speeches.

[Thanks are due to Vir Singh, K.K. Mehrotra and Ramneek Singh of the Cartographics News Service (KBK) for preparing the sketches used in this chapter.]

[1] "Troops Deployment Made Pak Change Tack: Army Chief", *The Times of India*, November 9, 2002.

- Pakistan was forced to ban a few terrorist organisations, close down some terrorist camps in PoK and arrest a few leaders.
- The mobilisation focused the attention of the international community on Pakistan as a state sponsoring terrorism.
- Elections in J&K were successfully conducted.
- Infiltration in the year 2002 came down to 53 per cent of the figures of the corresponding period of the previous year.
- The experience gained during the mobilisation enabled the Army to reassess and revalidate its operational plans and procedures.

In his address to his nation the very day Fernandes was speaking in the Indian Parliament, President Pervez Musharraf outlined his biggest foreign policy achievement: his government had upheld the honour and dignity of Pakistan by not succumbing to Indian pressure, and Pakistan had succeeded in highlighting the Kashmir cause to the international community. Meanwhile, the Indian Prime Minister, A. B. Vajpayee, admitted that India was close to a war with Pakistan on two occasions—in January after the December 13 terrorist attack on the Parliament, and in June after the May 14 attack on families of soldiers in Kaluchak, Jammu. Importantly, Vajpayee publicly regretted not going to war with Pakistan after December 13, admitting that it was a mistake.

Amidst the cacophony of claims and counterclaims, what becomes absolutely evident is that India was closest to a war—just a few hours away—in the beginning of January, probably around January 5 or 6. By January 11, 2002, when Gen. Padmanabhan addressed the media, the Indian political leadership had long changed its mind. If India was serious about attacking Pakistan, there was no need for the army chief to declare war readiness. His meet-the-media event, which obviously had clearance from the highest quarters, was meant to pre-empt Musharraf's much-publicised January 12 address to the nation. Even as the world was waiting with bated breath and high expectations to hear what Pakistan's ruler had to say in his new role as the US ally fighting international terrorism, India wanted to give the impression that its mobilisation was responsible for Musharraf's deliverance. From that time onwards, the Indian government and analysts were busy attributing gains to the prolonged mobilisation.

It would be instructive to briefly reconstruct the sequence of events relating to Operation Parakram between December 13, 2001

and January 11, 2002. The December 13 terrorist attack on the
Indian Parliament, then in session, trigged off a series of events.
When five terrorists armed with AK-47 rifles and hand grenades
starting firing at about 11:40 am on that fateful day, except for the
Prime Minister and the leader of Opposition, most of the political
leaders were trapped inside the Parliament building. In the ensuing gun battle between the terrorists and policemen, the former
were gunned down without harm to any Member of Parliament.
Within hours of the unexpected assault, Vajpayee told a shocked
nation that "the attack was not on the Parliament, but on the entire
nation. We have been fighting terrorism for the last two decades
and the do-or-die battle is in the final stages". Read in conjunction with his earlier letter to President Bush in the aftermath of
the terrorist attack on the J&K state assembly on October 1, 2001,
where he had unambiguously stated that India's patience was not
unlimited, the Prime Minister's message to the nation and the
world spelt finality.

On December 14, the Delhi Police confirmed that the Pakistan-
based Lashkar-e-Taiyyaba (LeT) and Jaish-e-Mohammad (JeM)
were behind the attack. The Indian foreign secretary, Chokila Iyer,
called the Pakistan High Commissioner in Delhi, Ashraf Jahangir
Qazi, the same day and handed over a set of three demands—
Pakistan should stop all activities of LeT and JeM, their leadership
should be taken into custody, and their financial assets should be
frozen and access to them be denied. The next day, Vajpayee issued
a fresh warning to Pakistan to stop sending terrorists into J&K, and
hinted at military action in PoK if Musharraf did not heed India's
ultimatum. Pakistan's reply was swift. Musharraf rejected India's
demand for action against the terrorist groups, claiming that the
proof was inadequate. Moreover, he warned India that any military action would be met with instant retaliation.

On December 17, Musharraf held a meeting with his corps commanders at General Headquarters in Lahore to review the dete-
riorating situation with India. The same day, Vajpayee chaired a
meeting of the Cabinet Committee on Security (CCS) in Delhi, which
was attended by the three service chiefs—the Army Chief, Gen. S.
Padmanabhan; the Air Force Chief, Air Chief Marshal A. Y. Tipnis;
and the Navy Chief, Admiral Sushil Kumar—amongst others. The
CCS took stock of the situation and reviewed the steps taken by
the government since December 13. Apparently, no decision was
taken at the meeting.

The next day was momentous. Heavy mortar and artillery shelling by Pakistan was reported on the Line of Control (LoC) in Naushera and Rajouri districts in J&K, which caused many residents of these areas to flee for their lives. The Indian troops retaliated and destroyed more than six Pakistani bunkers close to the LoC. According to informed army sources, the prime minister called the three service chiefs and told them to prepare for a war with Pakistan. On being asked by Gen. Padmanabhan what the government expected from the war, Vajpayee is understood to have said: woh baad mein bataayenge (that will be told later). Such was the beginning of Operation Parakram, where neither were the political objectives for war defined, nor did the military leadership press too hard to find them. Even though this sounds incredible, the army leadership at this stage was not unhappy about it. Ever since the end of the 1999 Kargil war—called Operation Vijay by India and Badr by Pakistan—the army had known the unavoidability of Operation Parakram. The prime minister's nod to the armed forces was the expected culmination of a persuasion by the army which began in the aftermath of the Kargil war.

Pakistan planned the Kargil war in two parts. In part one, regular Pakistani troops in civilian clothes belonging to its Northern Light Infantry were to make deep intrusions and occupy Indian territory in the sparsely patrolled higher reaches of the Kargil sector in J&K. The Talibanised mujahids—who were inspired and supported by the Taliban regime in Afghanistan—were to ferry logistics, help prepare forward defences and stock ammunition for the vanguard of the regular forces. Part two of the plan was the infiltration of large numbers of these extreme mujahids into J&K to form the actual vanguard. Regular troops were to keep the LoC alive with fire, keep the Indian Army engaged, and provide cover to mujahid infiltration. While part one of what Pakistan called Operation Badr failed and eventually culminated in the removal of Prime Minister Nawaz Sharif by Gen. Musharraf in October 1999, part two of the operation continued with a vengeance. This was partly eased with the removal of the Taliban regime from Afghanistan two years later in November 2001.

After the failure of part one of Operation Badr, Musharraf was forced to abide by the jehadi agenda, which he did not control completely. In the two years that the Talibanised mujahids belonging to the LeT and JeM held sway in J&K, the Indian Army remained under pressure like never before. Like the Liberation Tigers of Tamil Eelam (LTTE) in Sri Lanka, these terrorists were highly motivated and a determined lot who would unhesitatingly embrace suicide. The mujahid fidayeen (suicide squads) attacks started to increase dramatically in J&K. The fidayeen attacked the high-security Indian Army 15 Corps headquarters, a paramilitary (BSF) headquarters, a Rashtriya Rifles sector headquarters, and a special police protection headquarters, all in the Valley. Even the historic Red Fort in Delhi, which housed army units, was not spared. They routinely attacked and ambushed army and paramilitary forces in pitched tactical battles. The rate of attrition among soldiers and policemen increased considerably with the end of 1999.

By the beginning of 2000, the lower-level formations of the army in the Northern command, which is responsible for the state of J&K, was restive. Even as the government's counter-insurgency strategies proved ineffective, a few morale-raising tips came from the lower army formations deployed on the LoC. In a tacit understanding, while the senior army brass in J&K winked, the units adopted a calibrated offensive action across the LoC to engage the Pakistan Army and sanitise areas of infiltration. For example, on January 22, 2000, fighting in the Chammb sector left 16 Pakistani soldiers dead with fewer Indian casualties. While both sides blamed each other for the fight, the truth was that India, in strength, attacked a Pakistani post and overran it. Five dead Pakistani soldiers were dragged back by Indian troops. Later, under the full glare of publicity, they were handed over to the Pakistani sector commander. Similar instances occurred in Akhnoor, Mendhar, Kotli, Naushera and Pallanwala between January and April 2000. It was payback time at the LoC.

Formation commanders on the LoC started justifying the need for such action on the grounds that Pakistan must face local military defeats. It was argued in private that body bags going home under the glare of cameras would compel the Pakistan Army to rethink its proxy war in J&K. The regions to the south of the Pir Panjal range, especially Akhnoor, Mendhar, Bimber Gali, Poonch and Pallanwala, became the focal points of India's local, calibrated offensive action. Local artillery commanders argued that in addition to punitive raids by the infantry and special forces on Pakistani posts, more Bofors regiments need to be inducted into J&K. Further, heavy pounding of Pakistani positions in areas where infiltration occurred would be a morale booster for Indian troops. Instead of discouraging such actions, the army headquarters let the Northern command handle things their way. To make sure that the nation understood things, the Army Chief, Gen. V. P. Malik said in July 2000 that chances of a war with Pakistan were high. His assessment was based on the thinking that Pakistan may, in anger, retaliate in strength, which could result in a full-scale limited war in J&K.

However, Pakistan's mind was not on the escalation of war. It was content with its strategy of supporting terrorism inside J&K. Having lost considerable clout to the Talibanised mujahids after Nawaz Sharif called off part one of Operation Badr, Musharraf could not take the risk of losing a full-scale war with India. This would have further emboldened the Talibanised mujahids and could have led to his ouster from power. The best strategy for Musharraf was to seek an accommodation with the Taliban-inspired jehadis in J&K and give a tit-for-tat reply to India's local attacks on the LoC. Consequently, the LoC became more live, and both sides sought to improve their tactical positions even if that meant a slight disturbance of LoC. For India, the Northern command started setting the pace of things to come with Pakistan. Instead of dictating things, the army headquarters wholeheartedly supported actions suggested by its Northern command.

The aftermath of Black Tuesday (9/11) provided India with an opportunity to bridle Pakistan's cross-border terrorism in J & K. The jehadis struck at the J&K Assembly building on October 1, 2001. Even as Prime Minister Vajpayee sent the no-nonsense missive to Washington, and the J&K Chief Minister, Farooq Abdullah, demanded that the Indian military undertake hot pursuit inside PoK, it was evident that the pressure for all this came from the army. It reasoned with the political leadership not to let go of such an opportunity to teach Pakistan a lesson. India would need to fight its own war rather than wait for the US-led nations to leash Musharraf. And what better opportunity than when Pakistan was tied down with the US-led Operation Enduring Freedom in Afghanistan and the US had shown the lead by seeking to oust the Taliban regime. With Operation Enduring Freedom firmly under way, the biggest military threat to Musharraf did not come from the Taliban forces facing Pakistan, the domestic anti-American outcries—especially in the Pashtun belt along the Durand Line—or the divided clergy whipping up religious fervour. Pakistan could well manage its domestic affairs and the western front. Musharraf's main worry was the eastern front facing India. His two corps, 11 and 12 Corps at Peshawar and Quetta, were tied down as the result of the American war and would not be readily available should India launch limited operations across the LoC in J&K. Pakistan's 7 and 9 Infantry Divisions of 11 Corps had their operational role in the hilly region of J&K. Further, the Pakistan Air Force was not really comparable in strength and readiness to the Indian Air Force.

The army suggested that India strike at militant bases in PoK, conduct raids on Pakistani pickets close to the LoC that were supporting infiltration and use the air force on the Indian side of the LoC. The Northern command was of the opinion that no additional troops were needed for these tasks. According to the army, such proactive measures would help raise the morale of Indian troops, put Pakistan on the defensive and force it to make difficult choices, and help sever the growing ties between the people of Kashmir and the Talibanised mujahids. India would, however, need to keep all three defence services on alert if Pakistan decided to up the ante. The political leadership, divided on the military option, finally chose to reject the army's advice. Ahead of US Secretary of State Gen. Colin Powell's visit to India on October 14, 2001, Foreign Minister Jaswant Singh announced that India would do nothing to put Pakistan under military pressure.

The Ghost of Kargil

Around this time, a government-backed debate on the probability of a limited conventional war with Pakistan had gained momentum. The key people who supported the likelihood of a limited conventional war were former army chief, Gen. V. P. Malik, who fought the 1999 Kargil war for India, the government-funded Institute for Defence Studies and Analysis (IDSA), and the Defence Minister, George Fernandes himself. As the genesis of the debate lay in the conduct and lessons of the Kargil war, it is necessary to recapitulate the highlights of the war.

Operation Badr was unique in that it was the first joint operation between the Pakistan Army and the Talibanised mujahids in J&K. The entire operation was conceptualised and planned in complete secrecy. Initially, the plan was confined to the army chief; the chief of general staff; the director general military operations; GOC 10 Corps, Rawalpindi, which is also responsible for the division-plus size of Force Command Northern Area (FCNA) and GOC, FCNA. Once planned and approved by Nawaz Sharif, the 62 Infantry Brigade under the FCNA, which was responsible for operations in the Kargil sector, and the Talibanised mujahids were brought into the picture. Throughout the winter, nominated regular troops of the Northern Light Infantry (NLI), Chitral and Bijaur Scouts, and selected Special Service Group (SSG) commandos carried out extensive training in high-altitude warfare. A logistics and operational base for the operations was established at Olthingthang. The northern areas were placed under Pakistan Army rule to deny access to the media and facilitate optimal exploitation of resources.

During the period from October 1998 to March 1999, when the Zoji La pass (which separates Kashmir Valley from the Ladakh region of J&K) on the Srinagar–Kargil–Leh highway was closed and the upper reaches of the entire Kargil district were snow-bound, the Pakistan Army was engaged in making extensive preparations for the intrusions planned for the following summer. Roads and mule tracks were extended up to the LoC on the Pakistani side. Administrative bases were established close to Pakistani posts on the LoC. Heavy weapons, ammunition, rations and other essential supplies were stockpiled, telephone cables were laid, and material for the construction of sangars (a defensive fortification constructed by piling up rocks in areas where it is difficult to dig down) was moved forward. In some areas, artillery field guns and mortars were dismantled and moved forward to gun positions close to the LoC to enable them to interdict NH 1A. Additional artillery units were inducted from Pakistan's 11 Corps at Peshawar. Eight to ten new helipads were constructed to support the planned operations.

The choice of Northern Light Infantry troops for Operation Badr was a masterstroke by Pakistan. These battalions, besides having the capabilities of an infantry battalion, also specialised in commando operations, snow warfare and anti-heliborne operations. Interestingly, they were listed as a paramilitary force and not as regular army in respected publications from organisations such as the London-based International Institute for Strategic Studies. After the failure of Operation Badr, these troops were finally inducted into the Pakistan regular army as the sixth infantry regiment on

Pakistan's Independence Day, August 14, 1999, by Musharraf. As 90 per cent of NLI troops belong to Gilgit and Baltistan regions and are predominantly Shias, it helped to both maintain secrecy about Operation Badr and ensure minimum backlash from the misadventure. Pakistan's contention that it had not employed its regular army in Kargil was based upon these facts.

The Pakistan Army's designs in the Kargil sector took India's military strategists completely by surprise. The first reports of the intrusions came to an army unit in Kargil sector from the local people on May 6, 1999. Two reconnaissance patrols that were expeditiously dispatched to investigate suffered heavy casualties. On May 9, 1999, Pakistan artillery achieved a direct hit on the ammunition dump in Kargil and it went up in smoke. Extensive patrolling immediately followed over the next few days. The initial assessment was that the icy mountaintops were occupied by lightly armed mujahids. Uncoordinated assaults were launched without proper artillery support to quickly evict the intruders so as to avoid a national uproar. Among the battalions hurled at the enemy in this manner were the 1 Naga and 8 Sikh battalions. The troops were taken completely by surprise and came under withering fire from heavy automatics, 120 mm artillery mortars, and even rapid-firing air defence guns employed in the direct firing role, and suffered many casualties.

While the first intrusions by Pakistan across the LoC were detected, GOC, 15 Corps, Lt. Gen. Kishan Pal told a Unified Headquarters meeting dealing with counter-insurgency operations in Srinagar on May 14 that the "situation was local and would be dealt with locally". Years of counter-insurgency operations had blunted both the generals and troops for conventional operations. The seriousness of the situation was realised when the Indian Air Force finally joined the operation on May 26. In the crucial period before this, units ordered to evict the intruders suffered very heavy casualties and, after the war, as many as 48 officers and all ranks from these units were to face courts of inquiry on charges ranging from command failure to cowardice and desertion. In hindsight, Pakistan had accurately assessed the initial response of Indian troops disoriented by counter-insurgency operations.

The realisation came only when it was too late that India had been taken in by Pakistan's elaborate electronic deception plan. The realistic Pushto (an Afghan language) conversations about the

movements of the so-called mujahid fighters, defensive preparations, and logistics support picked up by Indian electronic warfare
units were played on tape recorders and broadcast on walkie-talkie
sets. Subsequently, close contact with the intruders revealed that
they were Pakistani soldiers from NLI battalions. It was found that
there was not a single mujahid among the intruders. Only then
did the seriousness of the intrusions dawn on the Indian army.

The primary objective of India's military campaign was to conclude military operations against Pakistani forces as early as possible without enlarging the scope of the ongoing conflict. This was
achieved on July 26, 1999, when the last of the Pakistani intruders
was successfully evicted from the Indian side of the LoC. The 121
Independent (I) Infantry Brigade, with its headquarters at Kargil,
was responsible for operations in the Kargil sector. The brigade
group formed part of 3 Infantry Division at Leh. This division was
responsible for operations in Ladakh, including the 140-km-long
LoC in Kargil district up to NJ 9842 along the 110-km-long Actual
Ground Position Line (AGPL) at Siachen Glacier and the Line of
Actual Control against China. With only four infantry battalions
in its order of battle, the defensive dispositions of 121 (I) Infantry
Brigade on the LoC included several large gaps. There were similar gaps in the same areas on the Pakistan side of the LoC as well.
It is axiomatic that no army can physically hold every metre of
territory along the country's borders either in peacetime or in war;
further, it is not a military necessity. While the tactically important features are physically held, the gaps are denied to the enemy
through obstacles such as land-mines and are actively patrolled
when a threat is discerned.

Detailed plans were then made by the Indian army headquarters and approved by the government to evict the Pakistani intruders from the Indian side of the LoC as early as possible and with
the least possible casualties. India also effected certain precau-
tionary defensive deployments of field formations to ensure that
Pakistan was denied the opportunity to launch an offensive elsewhere along the LoC and international border. The Indian government stipulated that the LoC was not to be crossed, so as to
avoid escalation to a larger conflict. Meanwhile, Indian battalions
continued to launch assaults to evict the Pakistani intruders, suffering heavy casualties as attack plans were based on incomplete
information and the extent of defensive preparations carried out

by the Pakistanis was not fully appreciated. During the initial stages, artillery support was inadequate due to the fact that normally only a few artillery units—one field regiment (105 mm), one mortar regiment (120 mm) and one medium battery (130 mm)—were available in the Kargil sector. The first few battalions to be launched into action had been hastily inducted from the Kashmir Valley, where they were engaged in counter-insurgency operations and were not acclimatised to high-altitude warfare. They also lacked high-altitude clothing and specialised mountain-fighting equipment.

It was appreciated that the recapture of each of the ridgelines from the well-entrenched Pakistani regular forces would be an extremely difficult military operation. Infantry assaults would have to be undertaken along narrow super-high-altitude approaches under scorching fire from several directions. It is a well-known military maxim that the mountains favour the defender. An attacker assaulting uphill is at an immense disadvantage. The Indian army headquarters realised that the maximum available firepower would have to be requisitioned, including that of the IAF, to soften enemy positions by way of coordinated preparatory bombardment to reduce the combat potential of the enemy's posts and break his will to fight. And this was a prerequisite for infantry battalions to launch physical assaults to regain each position. Cabinet approval for air strikes against the enemy positions within Indian territory was sought and obtained. The first wave of air-to-ground strikes by Fighter Ground Attack aircraft of the IAF on May 26, 1999, was a significant event in Operation Vijay. Pakistan was taken completely by surprise at this unexpected Indian response. Pakistan, of course, dubbed it an overreaction against the so-called "Kashmiri freedom fighters" and continued to deny the involvement of regular army personnel.

The Indian military strategy was to contain-evict-deny, i.e., to immediately contain and limit the intrusions up to the areas already affected, then prepare for and evict the Pakistani soldiers from the Indian side of the LoC, and, finally, enhance surveillance, patrolling and deployment, where necessary, to ensure that the Pakistan Army is denied an opportunity to launch such a venture again. Though the army leadership went along with the government in not opening up another front to avoid escalating the conflict, the army moved several field formations into J&K to be prepared for just such an eventuality if it became necessary.

The following aspects of the Kargil war would be instructive in understanding the relevance of a limited conventional war:

- Three operational issues tilted the Kargil war in India's favour: use of the air force on the Indian side of the LoC, creation of an overwhelming superiority of land forces in the localised war area, and employment of massive concentrations of artillery, also in a direct firing role, which wrought a devastating effect on the enemy. As the Pakistan Air Force did not enter the war, the Indian Air Force enjoyed air supremacy over their side of the LoC in the Kargil sector. In technical terms, even the Pakistan Army did not participate in Operation Badr. The NLI troops were listed as paramilitary forces which, unlike in the case of India, are directly under the control of General Headquarters in both war and peace, and are commanded by regular army officers. In a manner of speaking, the Kargil war was peculiar: it was fought on Indian territory by the Indian Army and Air Force against Pakistani paramilitary forces, a few special forces, and the Talibanised mujahids.

- Kargil was probably the first crisis situation or war between India and Pakistan where a threat of nuclear weapons played a role. For instance, during the war, a vigorous debate was on in the country regarding the need to cross the LoC in order to bring the intrusions to a quick end with minimum casualties. Many senior defence analysts strongly recommended that the restraint imposed on the army and the air force by the government must be lifted and a free hand should be given to the defence chiefs to conduct operations. A small minority continued to advocate restraint for two reasons: First, an enlargement of war would diffuse the aim of evicting intruders from Indian soil. Second, the good will of the US-led world community, which did not favour re-drawing of borders with force, would be lost. However, the government withstood all pressures to cross the LoC and clarified that if such a course of action became militarily necessary, the Cabinet Committee on Security would consider it. In reality, Prime Minister Vajpayee was known to have seriously considered a Pakistani nuclear strike had India escalated the war. It is another matter that the Indian military did not think in a similar fashion.

- It is debatable whether the Pakistan Army would have conceded defeat so soon if Nawaz Sharif had not capitulated to US pressure. The Indian military assessment was that the war would have continued longer than it actually did to completely evict intruders from Indian soil.

- During the 49-day air campaign, the IAF flew 550 strike missions, 150 reconnaissance missions and over 500 escort flights. The IAF also flew 2,185 helicopter sorties, logging 925 flying hours, for casualty evacuation and air transport operations. Though some of the pilots spotted Pakistan Air Force (PAF) fighter aircraft, including F-16s, on their radar screens, the PAF studiously avoided raising the ante and the IAF continued to enjoy local air superiority throughout the Kargil conflict. During the air campaign, the IAF gained the ability to improvise new bombing techniques and methods of attack. This willingness and ability to innovate paid handsome dividends. The sustained air strikes came as a surprise to Pakistani military planners who had not vectored such a determined Indian response into their calculations. The air strikes had an extremely detrimental psychological impact on the enemy troops who found themselves powerless to retaliate against the death and destruction being rained down on them from a distance. However, it must be stated that several army commanders expressed their reservations about the effectiveness of the air strikes. On certain occasions, formation commanders had firmly stated that they wanted the air force to stay away from their areas. Some bombs were even reported to have landed on Indian troops. It was clear that the IAF lacked suitable dedicated ground attack aircraft, especially for strikes in the mountains, and its pilots were not concentrating on practising ground strikes as much as they ought to. The IAF also did not possess precision-guided munitions in adequate quantities.

Gen. Malik arrived at the following conclusion in the aftermath of the Kargil war:

In the changed Indo-Pak strategic environment, there is a likeli-
hood of limited wars than an all out war. A limited war implies
limited political and military objectives, not hurting exces-
sively at any one time, limited in time, space and force levels.
A synergised politico-military diplomatic approach is essential
from the very beginning. The escalatory ladder can be climbed
in a carefully controlled ascent wherein politico-diplomatic
factors would play an important part. Military operations,
diplomacy and domestic environment would have to be orches-
trated with fine judgement for a decisive outcome.[2]

Jasjit Singh, a former fighter pilot and director of IDSA, saw a
greater role for the air force in a limited war:

Air power will assume increasing importance in the coming
years, especially in limited conventional wars. During the Cold
War, air power was the primary vehicle for strategic nuclear
deterrence to avert war. In the years ahead, air (and missile)
power will be the central tool for conventional deterrence, as well
as controlled punitive strike for coercive diplomacy.... Esca-
lation by counter-attacking in areas other than the Kargil sec-
tor, as was advocated by many senior retired officers at that
time, would most likely have resulted in heightened fears of a
nuclear exchange and a combination of pressure by the inter-
national community and domestic public opinion would
have resulted in cease-fire.... [The answer, therefore, lay in the]
use of combat air power to attack sensitive targets across the
LoC. This would indicate a resolve to escalate if the adversary
was not willing to withdraw and India was forced to continue
fighting from a position of disadvantage. There would still be
a risk that the war would expand to full scale war. But it would
be more likely that a calibrated air strike would extract an air
power response only.[3]

Notwithstanding the debate on a limited conventional war, it
was left to Operation Parakram to test its relevance.

---

[2] "Indo-Pak Security Relations: Kargil and After", *The Indian Express*, June
21, 2002.
[3] Singh, Jasjit (2000), "Dynamics of Limited War", Paper at the IDSA Seminar, January 5–6.

Operation Parakram

Operation Parakram was ordered without giving any political directive to the armed forces about the target to be achieved. Considering it was a bottom's-up operation—implying that the tone of what was to be accomplished was set by the Northern command—the armed forces did not press the political leadership initially to give the objectives of Operation Parakram in writing. In numerous briefings to the top political leadership including the prime minister, the armed forces, especially the army, had made elaborate presentations explaining the need for proactive action across the LoC to check infiltration. While agreeing with the military leadership, the political leadership wanted to first exhaust diplomatic and other non-military options before embarking on what is the final argument of kings—a war.

Operation Parakram was initiated with the intention of waging a possibly full-scale war to support India's offensive action in J&K. Explained in two simple steps, the government first gave the go-ahead to the military to cross the LoC with multiple thrusts to occupy territory in PoK, thereby inhibiting infiltration. As a senior serving general put it, the aim was to inflict on Pakistan a hundred cuts rather than one amputation in the form of, say, cutting the country in two, which is neither militarily possible nor desirable. Options were kept open to attack and either occupy or improve Indian tactical positions in certain areas of high military significance in PoK—for example, the Bugina Bulge, the Lipa Valley or the Hazlpir Pass. The problem with these areas was that an entire division (10,000 troops) was needed to wrest them from Pakistan, and it could be a long-drawn affair, as fighting in the mountains was an arduous proposition. Second, should Pakistan find the pressure unbearable in PoK and decide to enlarge the war beyond J&K, its efforts would be checkmated by India's Operation Parakram. In the initial stages, therefore, India's military aims were limited to J&K. The focus was on inhibiting the proxy war using the two-part strategy outlined by the Army and accepted by the government.

In operational terms, given Pakistan's elongated geographical advantage, it operates completely on interior lines and can mobilise its holding formations to move into battle locations within a maximum time of 96 hours. Its mobile offensive reserves—armoured formations—can be concentrated simultaneously. The Indian

LIMITED WAR PLANNED FOR JANUARY 2002

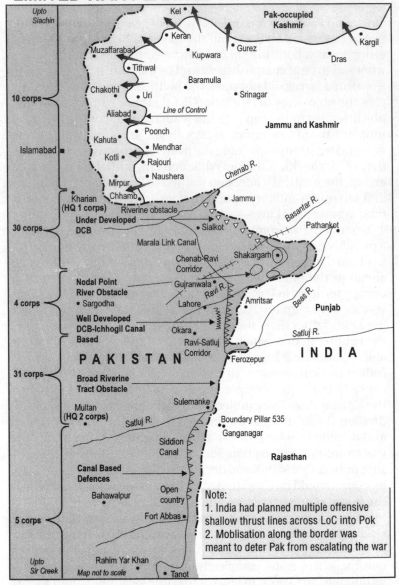

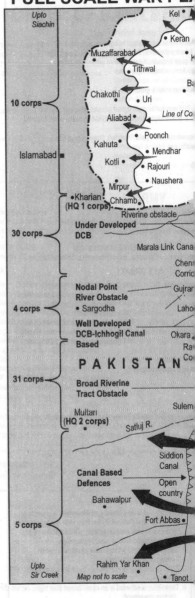

FULL SCALE WAR PLA

Upto Siachin

Kel

Keran

Muzaffarabad

Tithwal

Chakothi • Uri

10 corps

Aliabad • Line of Co

Islamabad Kahuta • Poonch

Kotli • Mendhar

Rajouri

Mirpur

•Kharian Chhamb Naushera
(HQ 1 corps)

Riverine obstacle

Under Developed DCB

30 corps

Marala Link Cana

Chen
Corrid

Nodal Point River Obstacle   Gujrar

• Sargodha

4 corps   Laho

Well Developed DCB-Ichhogil Canal Based   Okara

Ra

PAKISTAN   Co

31 corps   **Broad Riverine Tract Obstacle**

Multan   Sulem
(HQ 2 corps)   Satluj R.

Siddion
Canal

Canal Based Defences   Open
country

Bahawalpur

Fort Abbas •

5 corps

Upto
Sir Creek   Rahim Yar Khan

Map not to scale   • Tanot

Pakistan Army
Under 9 corps HQs ar
2 armoured divisions a
6 independent armoure
brigades, 7 engineer br
Under Air Defence Co
8 Air defence artillery b
Pakistan Air Force
393 combat aircraft in 7
1 maritime strike and 1
Pakistan Navy
1 fleet HQ, Principle su
inshore/offshore 7
Naval Air
Combat 4, Armed Hept

Strike F
1 corps
2 corps

(Centered a

1 Corps (Strike formatio
Mangla/Kharian)
6 Armoured division (Kh
17 Infantry division (Kha
37 Infantry division (Guj
8 (Independent) armour
41 (Independent) artiller
1 corps artillery brigade
101 Air defence brigade
One engineer brigade
One army aviation wing
Signal unit
Electronic Warfare unit
Anti tank guided missile
Notes: ■ HQs 30 corps
undertaken after a phas
■ The second grouping

12 Infantry Division *
(Murree)

4 Pok   2 Infantry
brigades   brigades

GHQ RESERVES (To
10 SSG battalions,
8 battalions for irregular ta
32 Commandos (Janbaz)
24 wings of frontier corps
25 Mujahid battalions,
Northern Light Infantry ba

NNED FOR JUNE 2002

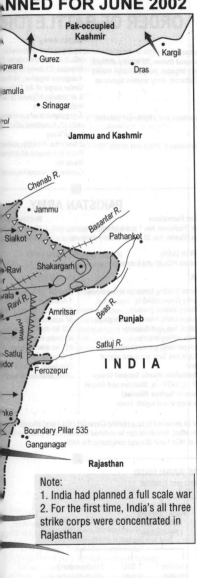

Pak-occupied Kashmir

• Gurez
• Kargil
• Dras

pwara

amulla

• Srinagar

rol

Jammu and Kashmir

Chenab R.

• Jammu

Basantar R.

Sialkot

Pathankot

-Ravi

Shakargarh •

r

wala

Ravi R.

Amritsar

Beas R.

Punjab

Satluj R.

-Satluj

dor

Ferozepur

INDIA

nke

Boundary Pillar 535
Ganganagar

Rajasthan

Note:
1. India had planned a full scale war
2. For the first time, India's all three
strike corps were concentrated in
Rajasthan

Army is also capable of mobilising its holding formations in the same time frame (96 hours). The armoured formations and its accompanying logistics build-up, however, would take between seven to 10 days to concentrate for war. This is because India operates on exterior lines of communication, as its strike formations are based deep inside the country. In the envisaged short and intense war scenario between India and Pakistan, this would be a major operational advantage for Pakistan, which it has already dovetailed into its "offensive-defence" military doctrine, thereby implying that offence is the best form of defence. India's Operation Parakram was conducted to deny this advantage to the Pakistan Army.

Parakram was different from Operation Vijay in six respects. First, unlike in Vijay, the Indian Army and Air Force were to cross the LoC and take the war inside PoK. There was little doubt that once India crossed the LoC or used its Air Force across the LoC, Pakistan would join the war immediately with all its might. The only issue was how much Pakistan desired to restrict the war to J&K while hoping that international pressure would force India into a ceasefire at the earliest. In operational terms, if both sides so desired, it would have been possible to restrict the war to within J&K for a few days—at the most a week—before it became an all-out war.

Second, while disagreeing with George Fernandes' and Gen. Malik's concept of a limited conventional war, the military leadership had grasped the two limitations inherent in an all-out war with Pakistan: (a) India's war objectives would necessarily have to be limited because Pakistan maintained an operational-level parity in conventional forces, and (b) the war could well be short depending upon when India or Pakistan succumbed to world pressure to end war. For these reasons, India had to prepare for a short and swift all-out war which would achieve worthwhile aims. Keeping these limitations in mind, the military aims and accompanying strategy changed substantially with time as the army and the air force fine-tuned their drills. By June, when the second brush with Pakistan appeared imminent, India's military aims had become more ambitious.

Third, unlike in Operation Vijay where a few defensive and strike formations were mobilised to discourage Pakistan from leading an offensive inside Indian territory, in Parakram, mobilisation was total. After a careful assessment, up to three mountain divisions

were moved from the eastern sector facing China to the western
sector for a war with Pakistan. These divisions, which have a dual-
taking role—against both China and Pakistan—had never been
switched before for two reasons. India feared that China would
open up a military front simultaneous to an India-Pakistan war to
relieve the pressure on Pakistan. This time around, it was assessed
that in the obtained geo-strategic environment, China would not
support Pakistan openly. Moreover, Pakistan possessed nuclear
weapons to safeguard its vital interests. The second reason was that
these dual-role formations required eight to 10 weeks of reorientation training to be converted into viable infantry divisions. A
tactical battle for defence on linear obstacles was so intricate and
finely drawn that a mountain division without reorientation training could not hope to perform well. The mountain divisions would
need to re-equip with anti-tank weapons from a company to the
division level. They would require a divisional medium regiment,
divisional locating batteries and divisional armour regiments.
Moreover, the war-wastage rates of all weapons, ammunition and
equipment did not cater to the re-equipment of mountain divisions into viable infantry divisions. There will also be the need for
comprehensive shooting by all weapons for recalibration.

The answer, therefore, lay in using these mountain formations
to support operations in the Jammu and southern Kashmir sectors. In fact, given the sensitivity of this area, both armies guard
the LoC with infantry divisions that are oversized—having up to six
brigades instead of the usual three—mountain divisions. Pakistan's
10 Corps has oversized 12, 19 and 23 divisions and the Headquarters Force Command Northern Area which looks after Siachen.
Similarly, India's 15 Corps has heavy 19 and 28 divisions, and 16
Corps has massive 25 and 10 divisions. The Indian divisions in
J&K, unlike the Pakistani forces, have the dual task of manning
the LoC and checking the movement of insurgents into the state.

Fourth, war-wastage reserves were taken out of depots and
moved to forward locations to replace damaged equipment. Quick
cannibalisation and improvisations were made to ensure that
maximum equipment was war-worthy. Fifth, the US was reconciled
to an all-out war between India and Pakistan this time because
the desired conditions for peace could not be met. Finally, according to the Union Book on War, all paramilitary forces were brought
under the operational control of the army. Unlike what happened in

Vijay, the Director General Rashtriya Rifles (DGRR) was not moved to Srinagar. At that time, the 15 and 16 Corps commanders in J&K, who doubled as security advisors to the chief minister on counter-insurgency operations, had gone to their primary task on the LoC. During Operation Vijay, it was hoped that the DGRR, as the new security advisor, would be acceptable to the paramilitary forces in the Unified Headquarters in Srinagar. Unfortunately, the Chief Minister, Farooq Abdullah, and the heads of paramilitary forces did not extend the required help and resources to the DGRR. Therefore, it was decided that while the peacetime arrangement of the Unified Headquarters would not be disturbed, all uniformed personnel in J&K would operate under the army, controlled by the Northern Command Headquarters in Udhampur.

Once the mobilisation was complete in about two weeks, units and formations commenced familiarisation and fine-tuning of operational drills. Extensive anti-personnel and anti-tank mines were laid all along the border. Many villagers close to the border, especially in Punjab, fled their homes. Crops were damaged and a total of Rs 300 crore was paid to the farmers as compensation by the central government.

Meanwhile, Pakistan also started reinforcing troops and moving high-calibre weapons close to the LoC. It was reported that Pakistan had activated its medium-range ballistic missiles for use with conventional warheads. In the first week of January, China reportedly shipped two squadrons worth (40 aircraft) of brand new F-7MG fighter aircraft to beef up the Pakistan Air Force. Pakistan's concern was the movement of its 11 and 12 Corps—parts of which were involved in the US-led Operation Enduring Freedom in Afghanistan—to the eastern front facing India. The Pakistan Army had taken control of its Jacobabad, Dera Ghazi Khan, Panjgur, Pasni and Gwadar airports as the US troops were landing in Pakistan.

While on the one hand Pakistan was making a strong case that a war with India would limit its assistance to Operation Enduring Freedom, on the other, its counter-mobilisation betrayed its intentions of not escalating the war with India. Up to 60 per cent of the Pakistan Army and Air Force was deployed north of the Shakargarh bulge. Pakistan had strengthened PoK with layers of defensive formations to thwart Indian offensives across the LoC. Its overall military strategy appeared to be to defend the LoC wholeheartedly. Only if the war prolonged in J&K, and the US-led world community failed to tame India at the earliest, was Pakistan expected to expand the scope of the war.

The first indication that India had changed its mind on the imminent war came on the night of January 5 or 6, 2002. As one of the three offensive corps—the others being 1 and 21 Corps—2 Corps was poised opposite Pakistan's Fort Abbas in the Rajasthan sector. India's only 40 artillery division which had he 333 Prithvi missile group was part of 2 Corps. There was some confusion within the advancing elements of 2 Corps. A few armoured elements had moved close to the border. The guns were moving into their forward hides when the military police asked them to stop their advance all of a sudden. A shrewd commanding officer who had no previous knowledge of such orders was certain that the military police person who asked his unit's elements to halt was a Pakistani spy. The next thing the unit knew was that the advance was to be commenced, but in the reverse direction. Something had gone wrong.

On Pakistan's urging, the US satellites had taken photographs of India's offensive forces precariously close to the border, ready to launch. When presented with such proof, instead of explaining it away as the usual army drills, the Indian political leadership directed the army to take appropriate action. The 2 Corps commander, Lt. Gen. Kapil Vij was immediately replaced by Lt. Gen. B. S. Thakur, chief of staff at the Army Training Command in Simla. The media got wind of this unfortunate incident on January 20 when the Defence Minister, George Fernandes, was on a visit to the US. Analysts zeroed in on the fact that Lt. Gen. Vij had been made a scapegoat. The corps commander could not have moved his elements without the knowledge of his immediate superior, Lt. Gen. S. S. Sangra. The political leadership, unfortunately, had done a somersault.

From then until June, the army was focused on how to regain the element of surprise. The initial military aim to occupy territory in PoK to inhibit infiltration no longer looked attractive because Pakistan had taken adequate countermeasures to meet India's threat. The army reasoned that the attrition rate would be high and nothing substantive would be gained. To understand the army's changed thinking, a glance at some basic facts is essential. India has three offensive strike corps—1, 2 and 21. Pakistan, on the other hand, has two strike corps—1 and 2. Pakistan's Army Reserve North (ARN) centres around 1 Corps based in Mangla/Kharian, and has two holding corps under it—30 Corps in Gujranwala and 4 Corps in Lahore. Its Army Reserve South (ARS) comprises of 2 Corps based in Multan and has two holding corps—31 Corps in Bahawalpur and 5 Corps in Karachi. There are unconfirmed and possibly exaggerated reports in the western media that Pakistan has a division's worth of independent armour around Karachi.

Between January and June, the Indian Army had enough time for training the three divisions moved from the east facing China. It was decided to employ these formations in the Jammu corridor, which is considered militarily vulnerable. Since Pakistan's 1 Corps has traditionally been used in the Shakargarh bulge, which falls in a politically sensitive area, India's 1 Corps has remained there to counter any Pakistani offensive. In short, India's 1 Corps is meant to counter Pakistan's 1 Corps in the Jammu and northern Punjab region, while India's 2 and 21 Corps threaten Pakistan's 2 Corps in the Rajasthan sector.

India decided to utilise its three-fold military advantage: its three strike corps as against Pakistan's two, the IAF's edge over the PAF, and the fact that the mountain divisions moved from the Chinese front were operationally reoriented and ready for war. Sometime during these months, 1 Corps, which had a traditional role in Jammu, was moved to Rajasthan. The Indian Army had all its three strike corps poised in the Thar desert. The military thinking was that once the balloon went up, instead of seeking multiple thrusts in PoK, the army could cross the border boldly into the Thar desert. Sooner rather than later, Pakistan would move its ARS to check the Indian advance. Considering that India had all three strike corps in Rajasthan, Pakistan would have little option but to move its ARN also southwards to meet the growing Indian threat. An ensuring attrition battle would end to India's advantage.

In the event of a war, the strategy would have been manoeuvre and attrition combined in the desert, in consonance with the army doctrine which states: "The Indian Army believes in fighting the war in enemy territory. If forced into a war, the aim of our offensive(s) would be to apply a sledgehammer blow to the enemy." This strategy would have given India two advantages: Pakistan's military centre of gravity, its two strike corps, would have been destroyed in details, and land captured in the Thar would have yielded some advantage on the negotiating table after the war. Therefore, the earlier military aim of Operation Parakram stood modified.

The May 14 terrorist attack on soldiers' families in Kaluchak once again sounded war drums. Gen. Padmanabhan, on a visit to Nepal, said that the time had come for India to act. The armed forces had done enough training and were ready for war. The government, in consultation with the armed forces, set the date for action at around June 15, 2002. Once the leave of all armed forces personnel was cancelled, the media got wind of what was in store. The June 15 deadline was made keeping in mind the forthcoming monsoons in another 15 days, which, according to experts, would restrict India's options for war in the mountains in J&K and Punjab. Analysts of all hues went to town painting the most plausible war scenario: either a salami slice (multiple cuts along the LoC) by Indian forces, or a deep thrust reaching Skardu—Pakistan's 62 brigade headquarters responsible for most of the infiltration across the LoC. Long after Operation Parakram was called off by India, the media remained as ignorant as ever of the army's bold plans for war in June—the plans were so audacious that they had never been war-gamed before. For example, the *India Today* weekly (December 21, 2002 issue) had reported in its cover story what the analysts were saying all along. According to the magazine, India's offensive 1 Corps would engage Pakistan's Army Reserve North around the southern Kashmir and Jammu area in an attrition battle. The "real offensive would be in PoK by strike formations moved from the east and tasked to capture strategic points used by Pakistan to push in terrorists". Nothing was further from the truth. A few people like Gen. Malik cautioned that Indian forces should strike at a time of their own choosing, and not immediately, as the element of surprise was lost.

No one figured out why the US and many others nations had issued an evacuation advisory to its citizens in India and Pakistan this time around, something which was not done in January. Unlike most media pundits, the US and Pakistan got wind of the fact that India had moved its 1 Corps between its 2 and 21 Corps in Rajasthan. It was not difficult for them to realise that the main battle would be fought in the Thar. Unlike in January, the Indian armed forces were prepared and determined in June to seize the initiative and launch major offensives in the desert sector on an unprecedented scale. The US feared that a full-scale war could escalate into a nuclear exchange if India's offensive managed to go deep inside Pakistan. Meanwhile, Pakistan test fired two nuclear-capable ballistic missiles in May. This was meant as a warning to India to apply brakes on its most ambitious plan ever. Therefore, tremendous pressure was successfully put on the Indian leadership, and India was once again tamed by June 10.

In hindsight, three observations could be made about India's plans in June: First, the army did not believe in the concept of a limited conventional war. Two, the army believed that Pakistan would not use its nukes early in a war. Most importantly, it appears that the Indian political leadership was deterred by Pakistan's nukes more than Pakistan was by India's putative nuclear second-strike capability.

For the Indian Army, Operation Parakram was as good as over. It was clear that such preparation and high morale as existed for the June war would not be available in the near future. From then on, it was the beginning of troubles for the army, as continued mobilisation was giving diminishing returns. The army leadership kept repeatedly impressing upon the government that demobilisation should be ordered at the earliest, as the morale of the troops was dipping. While extra care was taken by the senior personnel to redress the grievances of troops, there were instances of soldiers running amok because of frustration due to the long mobilisation. It was not possible for any army, however professional, to remain on alert indefinitely without a defined purpose. Any amount of adjustment and resource availability in the field could not equate with the cosiness of peacetime locations and normal activities. There was also the need to commence peacetime activities; all training institutes and centres had been closed since December 2001. Further, the troops had neglected their family obligations for too long. The worst affected were young officers with small children. Having worked so hard to uphold the morale of troops for war, these officers were the backbone of the army. Even during peacetime, not more than 14 per cent of the soldiers got family accommodation; it was the young officers who needed leave most to attend to their families. Moreover, the army chief himself was keen that the troops return to barracks with or without accomplishing the mission before he retired by the end of year. The only mission he knew that could come out of Operation Parakram was a war with Pakistan. After June 15, he realised that the Indian leadership simply did not have the stomach to take a war inside Pakistan.

The army sights were henceforth focused on how to start peace-time activities even while waiting for a nod from the government to demobilise. It started considering the leave applications of troops and officers. Up to 15 percent unit strength on leave was allowed, and 35 days leave was permitted. The first priority for leave went to troops in J&K that had a treble task: on the LoC, mobile patrolling along the LoC to curb infiltration, and counter-insurgency tasks in the form of Rashtriya Rifles forces. Training institutes and schools of instruction were instructed to open up gradually. The rotation of troops, which had been arduous since the beginning of the insurgency in J&K in 1990, also commenced. Various formation headquarters were slowly told to move back to permanent locations to restart planning normal activities. For example, headquarters southern and western command gradually started pulling back from operational areas.

Around this time, when the army was working on maintaining the morale of troops, there was a certain laxity in operational vigil. Finding an Indian post temporarily vacated in the Machhal area north-east of Kupwara, Pakistani troops occupied it in mid July. Called Loonda post or Point 3260, approximately 800 metres inside Indian territory, it provided good observation of the Pakistani town of Kel. This town was notorious as a major staging post for infiltration into India. Once it became known that Pakistan had occupied the post, the army, in a sensible move, sought the use of air power to soften the target before a recapture using land forces. The IAF used two Mirage fighters in the operation and helped the army recapture the post on August 2. As there is continuous rivalry and one-upmanship between the air force and the army, it was only a matter of time before the media came to know of the operation. Called Kargil-II by the media, it embarrassed the government to no end. Instead of taking the hint that Operation Parakram had outlived its purpose, the government attempted to keep a lid on the incident. It was time for India to demobilise its army.

The army's repeated entreaties finally bore results. Considering that Pakistan was not helping India find an honourable reason to demobilise forces, assistance was sought from the National Security Advisory Board (NSAB), the unofficial and lowest tier of the National Security Council. Consisting of retired bureaucrats, army personnel and university professors, the NSAB had been assembled once before in its three-year existence under the Vajpayee government. At the height of the Kargil war in June 1999, the main debate was whether the army should cross the LoC or not. The army was keen that the option to cross the LoC, if the need arose, be made available. Aware that exercising the option would mean a full-scale war, the government wanted to NSAB to endorse the same. The other achievements of the NSAB have been a draft nuclear doctrine, from which the government distanced itself within hours of its being made public in July 2000. The suggested doctrine was found too ambitious by the US. Another task given to the NSAB was to write the strategic defence review, which awaits release.

The NSAB assembled in Delhi on October 16, 2002. The main presentation was made by the former army chief, Gen. V. P. Malik. His three main points were that the mobilisation had achieved the desired objectives, the element of surprise, which was of great military value, was lost, and that continued mobilisation would have a detrimental effect on the morale of the troops. Within hours of the meeting, the government announced that Operation Parakram was over. Instead of demobilisation, the army was told to undertake a "strategic relocation". The latter was more of a necessity, as the rolling stock for sending troops back to the barracks would take a few months to be ready. It was decided to first send the strike elements with heavy equipment to permanent locations. Next, the holding formations were to go back. Before leaving, these formations were required to lift or destroy thousands of mines laid by them ahead of their defences. Moreover, if Pakistan misbehaved, these troops would be available to discourage any misadventure. The government announced that the troops in J&K would not be reduced. While it was certain that the troops pulled out from the Chinese front would not go back in a hurry, the accretion in force levels in J&K implied that the government had not given up the option of raids inside PoK; this is what was suggested by the Army after the terrorist attack on the J&K assembly on October 1, 2001—a suggestion which eventually snowballed into Operation Parakram.

Defence Minister George Fernandes told the Parliament on October 20, 2002, that Operation Parakram had cost the nation Rs 8,000 crore, excluding the Rs 300-crore compensation paid to people in the border states where troops were deployed. A total of 130 lives were lost in the 10-month long mobilisation. What he did not disclose was the colossal damage done to the equipment which lay in the open facing the vagaries of nature. It will indeed take a long time before the army gets a grip on the extent of damage incurred with regard to equipment and ammunition. Estimates show that it could take up to six months for the army to get its equipment in a war-worthy state.

According to the military leadership, Operation Parakram did two good things. It provided an excellent opportunity for troops to train themselves in operational locations. The troops like nothing more than to undertake their professional training and not fatigue by maintaining golf courses, which, unfortunately, has become commonplace in peacetime locations. The army and the air force were able to put their heads together to evolve and practice new drills needed for the war in mountains and deserts. The other benefit from the long mobilisation was the frequent interaction between the political and military leadership. The CCS, headed by the prime minister, sought military advice on a regular basis, and in most cases agreed with it. Thus, there was a better understanding of each other's perspective.

The Virtues of Mobilisation

Realising that the government would not go to war, and did not know how to order troops back to the barracks without losing face, the Indian defence analysts went into overdrive. New virtues were found in continued mobilisation and what had already been achieved. Sample these: Some argued Operation Parakram had proved that Indian political-military pressure had significantly increased the costs to Pakistan for its mythical policy of the low-cost option of pursuing terrorism under the nuclear umbrella.[4] While presenting the annual budget for the year ending June 30, 2002, Pakistan's Finance Minister, Shaukat Aziz, stated that "Islamabad has had to spend Rs 2,000 crore extra during the last six months because of India's mobilisation and threat to exercise the option of using military force. This raised Pakistan's military expenditure by 0.6 per cent of the GDP in six months." According to these analysts, "India's aim must be clear: Pakistan's permanent reversal of

---

[4] "High price of low cost terror", Jasjit Singh, *The Indian Express*, June 17, 2002.

cross-border terrorism. Therefore, India should keep up the military pressure even if some relaxation of the alert status is introduced." Reports in the western media that Pakistan was diverting funds and even equipment received from the US and other nations for fighting international terrorism to its eastern-front stand-off with India were ignored. China's wholehearted support to Pakistan by supplying equipment and products on an emergency basis was also overlooked. Even worse, these analysts betrayed a complete lack of understanding of what mobilisation meant for the army. In the context of the subcontinent, mobilisation implied that troops in complete battle gear moved to their operational areas and were launched within days into war. There was little provision for a prolonged stay in forward concentration areas, which, if carried out, could have led to psychological costs at the least.

Another implausible argument for Operation Parakram was given by a leading defence analyst, K. Subrahmanyam, who spoke about containing Pakistan militarily.[5] According to him, "If the armed forces are clearly informed that this deployment is for containment and not at this stage a preparation for hostilities, they would adjust themselves and take all necessary steps to reduce the hardships to the troops. A unilateral announcement of de-escalation in deployment will reduce our leverage vis-à-vis the international community and Pakistan and come in the way of a containment strategy." Also the architect of coercive diplomacy as the biggest gain of Operation Parakram, Subrahmanyam and many others believed that President Musharraf's January 12 and May 27 announcements were the result of India's military pressure. The truth was that the heat of Operation Parakram was felt more in the US and other world capitals than in Islamabad. The US was worried that a war between India and Pakistan could easily escalate into a nuclear exchange. Coercion would have worked on Pakistan if the Indian military threat had been plausible and overwhelming in Islamabad's perception. At no stage did Pakistan feel compelled to meet the Indian demands.

Defence Minister George Fernandes suggested that there was nothing unusual about the prolonged mobilisation, and compared it to the NATO forces during the Cold War. No one questioned

---

[5] "Containing Pakistan", by K. Subrahmanyam, *The Times of India*, October 15, 2002.

him on the fact that NATO forces had built air-conditioned build-ings in forward areas and made a provision for their families to stay in these locations. The Indian Army, on the other hand, moved into defences which had no such comforts. There were many reports about how troops had to cope with water shortage in deserts dur-ing the summer months when temperatures soared beyond 50 degrees Celsius. The other gains of Operation Parakram mentioned by Fernandes are of a political and diplomatic nature, which will be dealt with in the next chapter.

Summary

- Operation Parakram was a mobilisation for war alone. No other motive was given by the government to the military leadership.
- The genesis of Operation Parakram lay in the aftermath of Opera-tion Vijay, the 1999 Kargil war with Pakistan.
- Operation Parakram was a bottom's-up operation conceived by the army's Northern command, and was accepted by the army headquarters. The political leadership did not issue any written directive to the armed forces about what it wanted to achieve through the war.
- The military aims of Operation Parakram changed over time. In January, it was undertaken for offensive action in J&K, with the option of preparing for full-scale war if Pakistan chose to esca-late the conflict outside the state. In June, Operation Parakram was aimed to both launch deep thrusts in the Rajasthan sector and destroy Pakistan's offensive formations in detail.
- Operation Parakram rubbished the concept of a limited con-ventional war, especially one which was limited in space and force levels.
- Operation Parakram should have been terminated in June.

4

Operation Parakram: Coercive Diplomacy

The Vajpayee government ought to be held responsible for two serious setbacks to national security. First, it conducted the 1998 nuclear tests without giving much thought to the consequences. Second, it ordered Operation Parakram before it could muster the political courage to take it to its logical conclusion. On the first issue, the government maintained that national security had been strengthened, when just the opposite seemed to have happened. There remain a number of unanswered questions regarding the operational aspects of nuclear weapons—the state of nuclear readiness, command and control, delivery systems, etc.—and, most importantly, the involvement of the military leadership in the nuclear weapons policy loop. For all practical purposes, Pakistan appears to have benefited more from the nuclear tests once India decided that it would not displease the US. By toning down its nuclear weapons policy after the tests, India sought to improve relations with the superpower at the cost of national security.

This had an adverse impact on Operation Parakram. India's political leadership was not certain whether Pakistan was deterred as much by its putative nuclear arsenal as it was by Pakistan's. India, therefore, attempted to make a virtue out of necessity and hoped that Pakistan would be deterred through the circuitous route of the US. This strategy worked to a certain limit. The benefits, however, got nullified as India overextended this approach. By the time Operation Parakram was finally called off, it had long become counterproductive. On the one hand, President Musharraf's personnel stature had risen amongst his army commanders and the jehadis for daring India's military mobilisation. On the other hand, the US had become more than a mere facilitator between India and Pakistan.

India had only two options to extract maximum benefit from the US-led war on terror after 9/11. It could have emulated the US example and taken Operation Parakram to its logical conclusion even before the terrorist attack on the J&K state assembly building on October 1, 2001. Or it could have decided to talk with Pakistan after the latter jumped on the US bandwagon to combat terrorism. India did neither, thereby letting the US and Pakistan decide the course of action. Operation Parakram, therefore, was steered more by Washington and Islamabad than Delhi. This was the only important reason why despite the enthusiasm of the Indian armed forces to hand a military defeat to Pakistan, Operation Parakram would be remembered as the war gone wrong. All suggested benefits of Operation Parakram, like coercive diplomacy, were incidental and in some cases not even cost-effective.

India had psychologically foreclosed the option to take advantage of 9/11 and militarily settle scores with Pakistan much before Operation Parakram became a reality. The contrived chance meeting between President Bush and Foreign Minister Jaswant Singh at the White House in April 2001 was considered a big honour by India. Thereafter, to disregard US advice was not considered proper. Jaswant Singh was meeting with US National Security Advisor Condoleezza Rice when the president walked in and took the Indian foreign minister to his Oval office for a 40-minute chat. According to the White House spokesperson, Bush condemned the terrorist attacks in Kashmir, and asserted that terrorism must end everywhere, including Kashmir. India was satisfied with the vague assurance even as no road map for tackling terrorism in J&K was spelt out by the Bush administration.

After 9/11, sensing India's concerns, the US once again rolled out the red carpet for Jaswant Singh when he visited Washington in October 2001 and for Vajpayee the following month. While Jaswant Singh was still in the US, terrorists struck at the J&K assembly building on October 1. Prime Minister Vajpayee sent a missive to the US president after the terrorist attack, which he took seriously. The Indian premier said that his country's patience was not unlimited. Within days, the British Prime Minister, Tony Blair, and Gen. Powell arrived in Pakistan and India to do a fine balancing act to ensure that things did not spin out of control. Blair proved a more astute politician, well versed in the complexities of the region, than the US secretary of state. While condemning the terrorist attack in Srinagar, Blair was careful not to blame Pakistan for the dastardly act. He advised India to exercise patience and let Operation Enduring Freedom—the war in Afghanistan against the Taliban—continue unhindered. Terrorism in Kashmir, he hinted, would be taken up in phase two after the ouster of the Mullah Omar regime in Afghanistan.

Meanwhile, Pakistan condemned the terrorist attack of October 1 in Srinagar as well. By doing so, Musharraf made a distinction between terrorism which he condemned, and the so-called freedom struggle in J&K which he supported wholeheartedly. This was the first time since the Agra summit in July 2001 that Musharraf felt relieved of the jehadi pressure which had increased manifold since Pakistan's defeat in the 1999 Kargil war with India. At the Agra summit, Musharraf was compelled to exhort the jehadis in J&K, knowing well that Pakistan's agenda and theirs was entirely different: Pakistan wanted J&K, while the jehadis sought the glorification of Islam. For this reason, ever since coming to power in October 1999, Musharraf repeatedly warned India that the window of opportunity for talks between India and Pakistan was fast receding. He obviously had the growing jehadi clout in J&K in mind. With Operation Enduring Freedom underway in Afghanistan, Musharraf was determined to regain his lost clout from the Taliban-inspired jehadis in Kashmir.

For the next six months, until the May 14 terrorist attack at Kaluchak in Jammu, the US, the UK and Pakistan would refer to jehadis as terrorists, and India would fail to understand that its position was different from theirs. India was itself partly responsible for this dilemma. It was during Blair's visit to Delhi on October 5, 2001, that Vajpayee linked 9/11 for the first time with the hijacking of the Indian aircraft IC-814 to Kandahar, and asserted that Jaish-e-Mohammad operated in tandem with Bin Laden's Al Qaeda. Since it was universally accepted that JeM operated from Pakistani soil and the hijackers of IC-814 were Pakistani nationals, India wanted to make the point that Pakistan was running with the hare and hunting with the hound—it had signed to fight terrorism alongside the US, but was the epicentre of terrorism itself.

The US and the UK appreciated Pakistan's viewpoint better. While acknowledging its cardinal role in creating the Taliban and arranging for Bin Laden to befriend the Taliban chief, Mullah Omar, the superpower was of the opinion that the Pakistan government had finally disassociated itself from the jehadis. The latter were responsible for the Talibanisation of Pakistani society and were slowly infiltrating the ranks of the Pakistan army. The epicentre of terrorism was, therefore, the Taliban-run Afghanistan, and not Pakistan as India proclaimed. Unfortunately, India could not air its views loudly and publicly as it would have found it difficult to explain to Indians why it blamed Pakistan for the hijacking of IC-814 when it was the Taliban who masterminded it. Why were jehadis belonging to JeM, LeT and Harkat-ul-Mujahideen being called Pakistan-supported terrorists when they were inspired by Al Qaeda? By merely letting them operate from Pakistani soil, could one infer that the Pakistan government was supporting these terrorist outfits? Conversely, Pakistan itself was a victim of these jehadis who were creating mayhem in Pakistan with domestic fundamentalist support. The Taliban, after all, were motivated and inspired by the jehadi ideology which had its epicentre in Afghanistan where Bin Laden had been living since 1996. The jehadi nationality was of little consequence. The more there were terrorists from different nationalities, the more was the opportunity for the glorification of Al Qaeda and increased leverage vis-à-vis Muslim regimes combating these jehadis.

This was the central difference between India's perception and that of the US-led coalition. India said that Pakistan created and nurtured the Taliban, which was true. However, the US believed that the war on terror was against Bin Laden's Al Qaeda which has an extensive network and roots in the Muslim world. The Taliban were a small entity who joined the Al Qaeda after Bin Laden, the chairman of Al Qaeda, chose Kandahar as his base. The point that India missed or chose to ignore was that Pakistan shared geographical boundaries and demographical features with Afghanistan, and it would be impossible to bring any semblance of normality in post-Taliban Afghanistan, where warlordism would abound, without Islamabad's assistance. The US had the experience of the eighties to back this belief, because without Pakistan's help at that time, the Red Army would not have been defeated. Further, it is the conviction of the Bush administration even today that stability in Afghanistan and the Central Asian republics is impossible without keeping Pakistan's strategic interests in mind.

By supporting Operation Enduring Freedom, Pakistan desired to achieve two objectives: to get back the strategic space in Afghanistan which was snatched by the Taliban, and to garner the silent endorsement of the US that it would not push Musharraf too hard on terrorism in J&K, as that would make his position tenuous within the Pakistan army. Leaving space for tactical alterations, this was the basic understanding between US and Pakistan on J&K. Not entirely oblivious of this deal, India unfortunately hoped that Pakistan's central role in the war on terror would be temporary, and that the US would put Islamabad on the mat soon.

Even as Prime Minister Blair professed to have understood India's concerns, Gen. Powell, who visited India on October 16, 2001, after a brief stopover in Islamabad, had a different agenda. His task was to keep Gen. Musharraf on board in the war against terror, and to keep India engaged with various allurements. While Musharraf's decision to sign on the side of the US was not a difficult one, his worry was his own army which, since the time of the late Gen. Zia-ul-Haq in the eighties, had been infiltrated with fundamentalist sympathisers. The threat to Musharraf's life had increased from within the army ranks itself. It was left to Gen. Powell to demonstrate that Musharraf's decision was a good one for both Pakistan and its army. Addressing the media in Islamabad a day before he came to Delhi, Gen. Powell said that the Kashmir issue was central to the Indo-Pak dispute, and stressed that the issue be resolved bilaterally taking the wishes of the people of Kashmir into account. That was what the Pakistan army wanted to hear, but not what would endear the US to India. Therefore, a crisis management exercise was done by the US state department for India's benefit to emphasise that what Gen. Powell said was not what he had meant. Too eager to bail out the US, India readily accepted the US explanation that Gen. Powell had said Kashmir was an important and not the central issue in the Indo-Pak dispute.

The fact that the UN Security Council resolution 1172 of June 6, 1998, passed after the nuclear tests by India and Pakistan, had unequivocally mentioned the Kashmir dispute as the main cause of tension between India and Pakistan was glossed over. Also brushed aside by India was the mention by Gen. Powell that both sides should meet the aspirations of the people of Kashmir. The issue of involving the people of Kashmir for the resolution of the Kashmir issue was to become the US policy on Kashmir since then.

What Gen. Powell offered in India was President Bush's commitment to give a higher priority to transform Indo-US relations, to consult India continuously on the post-Taliban scenario in Afghanistan, and to jointly fight terrorism, including the terror directed against India. Compared to what the US gave Pakistan for fighting international terrorism, India only received ample doses of hope.

However, India appeared content with the slender hope of a strategic relationship with the US, until the terrorist attack on the Indian Parliament on December 13, 2001, which changed the ground situation. Speaking in Parliament the next day, Vajpayee declared that enough was enough. Now India had to embark on an *aar-paar ki ladayee* (a war to the finish), the premier thundered. India ordered Operation Parakram, and it was time for Prime Minister Blair and Secretary of State Gen. Powell to visit the region once again. The US and Pakistan were certain that India meant business. Pakistan pressed the US to stop India's military adventure as that would severely affect the war in Afghanistan. Instead of assisting the US troops to hunt for the top Taliban and Al Qaeda leadership reportedly hiding in the mountainous range along the Pakistan–Afghanistan border, the Pakistan army would be constrained to focus on its eastern front against India. This was India's finest hour: Pakistan and the US were coerced—for the first and last time—by India's military mobilisation. Both had a lot to lose. Already under domestic fundamentalist pressure for helping the US against the Taliban, Musharraf would have had to contend with the opening of the military front by India. The US, on the other hand, faced two adverse possibilities. Its war against the Taliban would have suffered a setback, and the possibility of a nuclear war between India and Pakistan loomed large. There was palpable panic in the US and Pakistan at India's sudden military move.

India should have utilised this opportunity by making a single, focused and realisable demand in exchange for an end to Operation Parakram. India's singular demand should have been that Pakistan stop infiltration across the LoC forthwith. Even if the jehadis were not completely under Musharraf's control, the Pakistan Army had total control over its side of the LoC. The latter could completely stop infiltration if it so desired. At this juncture, the US would probably have pressed Musharraf hard to ensure that Operation Enduring Freedom did not fall into jeopardy. India could then have utilised the cessation of infiltration, though temporary, with intensified counter-insurgency operations against the jehadis in the state. Next, it would have been time for bilateral talks between India and Pakistan over Kashmir, and missile and nuclear issues, besides others matters as agreed in the "composite dialogue" formula.

India, instead, let the opportunity pass by diluting its demands and asking what was impossible for Musharraf to give. The defence and external affairs ministry wanted cross-border terrorism to end. The home ministry prepared a list of 21 criminals—later revised to 20—wanted for various heinous crimes in India and suspected to be living in Pakistan, to be handed to Delhi for trial. As the home ministry was headed by the senior-most minister, L. K. Advani, the demand for 20 criminals became uppermost. Therefore, when Prime Minister Blair met with the Indian leadership in Delhi on January 5, 2002, he was not at all prepared to react to India's demand. A nation, after all, could not go to war just because the adversary refused to hand over 20 wanted criminals. Side-stepping India's queer demand, Blair signed the "New Delhi Declaration" with Prime Minister Vajpayee, and declared that the US-led world community would fight terrorism.

India, however, was not satisfied. It wanted Musharraf to take concrete action on its demand of 20 criminals and stop cross-border terrorism forthwith. The US swung into action at this stage. It asked Musharraf to give a road map to meet India's demand, and asked India to de-escalate tensions with Pakistan concurrently. Even as India called off its military march inside PoK, all eyes were set on Musharraf's January 12 speech. The US assured India that Pakistan had agreed to meet India's concerns. In his much-awaited speech, the Pakistan president banned five terrorist organisations under the Anti-Terrorism Act of 1997—Lashkar-e-Taiyyaba and Jaish-e-Mohammad, which were earlier declared as terrorist organisations by the US after the Indian premier had presented their linkages with the Al Qaeda to Prime Minister Blair, and three sectarian outfits indulging in violence within Pakistan, namely, the Sipah-i-Sahaba, Tehreek-i-Jafria and Tehreek-i-Nifaz-e-Shariat Mohammad. The existing madrasas in Pakistan were ordered to register with the government and a ban was put on starting new ones. Musharraf further said that no organisation would be allowed to indulge in terrorism in Kashmir from Pakistan's soil and areas under its control. While affirming his government's resolve to provide moral and political support to the freedom struggle in Kashmir, he made it clear that any Pakistani national in India's list of 20 wanted criminals would not be handed over. Finally, Musharraf asked for US mediation to kick-start an Indo-Pak dialogue on Kashmir.

In essence, Musharraf's speech was about reversing Talibani-sation in Pakistan society. Regarding India's concerns, Pakistan apparently asked the banned LeT and JeM to close shop in Pakistan, and shift base to PoK under changed names. Musharraf left no doubts that he made a distinction between terrorism and freedom struggle. However, India was not totally disappointed. Foreign Minister Jaswant Singh said that India would wait to see Musharraf's words translate into deeds on the ground. Thus, the war was averted on specious assurances.

It was left to Gen. Powell to decipher what had happened. Arriving in Delhi on January 17, the focus of his visit was on the steps to be taken to de-escalate tension and to discuss India's list of 20 criminals. Powell told the media in Delhi that India was sending more details on the 20 criminals to Pakistan. Thus began the mud-slinging match between India and Pakistan on the issue of wanted criminals. Even as Pakistan threatened to send its own list of 20 wanted criminals being sheltered in India, Musharraf made it clear that he was willing to take appropriate action against non-Pakistani nationals in India's wanted list. Pakistani nationals, he said, would be dealt with under Pakistani laws. Nothing, however, came out of the whole exercise. Regarding de-escalation of tensions, Jaswant Singh told the visiting dignitary that India would first wait for infiltration to decrease on the LoC before extending an olive branch to Pakistan.

This was only a lull before the storm, as terrorists struck at an army camp in Kaluchak on May 14. On the eve of the visit of US Assistant Secretary of State, Christina Rocca, to the subcontinent aimed at bringing urgency in India and Pakistan to defuse mutual tensions, three terrorists belonging to the LeT killed 30 defenceless family members, mostly women and children, of army personnel living in an army camp in Kaluchak, Jammu. To make matters worse, terrorists masquerading as army men attacked three more army and paramilitary camps in the next four days. The army chief, Gen. Padmanabhan, who was on a visit to Kathmandu, sounded the clarion call by saying that the time for action had come. The government took the attack on army families seriously and did not wish any longer to duck the pressure from the army to go to

war with Pakistan. The government, in close consultation with the
opposition parties, set out to deliberate what action needed to be
taken. In a unanimous resolution, the Parliament backed the government to take action as it deemed appropriate.

Prime Minister Vajpayee visited the frontline in Kupwara in the
Valley on May 22 and told soldiers to prepare for a decisive battle.
The leaves of soldiers were cut short and India was once again ready
for war. However, so was Musharraf. President Bush and Gen.
Powell were on the phone with Musharraf and the Indian leadership to see how the war could be avoided. This time around, India's
terms for peace were precise: Pakistan must end infiltration, and
dismantle the terrorist camps and support infrastructure (which
sounded more like a demand to abolish the ISI) permanently. It
was a tall order to extract from Musharraf. The last thing he would
do was come down heavily on jehadis, who he was slowly wean-
ing away from the Al Qaeda and bringing under his control. He
was to brag later to the *Washington Post* that "hundreds of people
are itching to fight India on its side of Kashmir",[1] implying that he
would reinvent the jehadis and use them in a war to sabotage the
Indian Army's internal lines of communication in J&K.

Even as Gen. Powell faced the near impossible task of bringing
India and Pakistan back from the brink of war, the chemistry
between the two soldiers eventually paid off. Apparently an understanding was reached between Gen. Powell and Musharraf: Pakistan
would stop infiltration across the LoC for a while. In return, the
US would get India to start talks with Pakistan on Kashmir. Depending on how the talks went—if India would talk seriously on the
core issue of Kashmir—Pakistan would continue to regulate the
flow of infiltration. Even if India was oblivious of such a deal, New
Delhi was more than eager not to go to war with Pakistan for two
reasons. First, being aware of India's military plans to start an all-
out war, the political leadership was worried about Pakistan's
nuclear weapons. Second, and more importantly, the prime minister was keen to refrain from annoying the US because, if he did,
India's carefully crafted relationship with the US after the nadir of
the 1998 nuclear tests would suffer a major setback. According to
the advice given by the external affairs minister to the Cabinet
Committee on Security, this would benefit Pakistan, which, despite

---

[1] "Bridging the Great Divide", *The Economist*, June 1, 2002, p. 31.

its unrelenting cross-border terrorism, would be seen as a messenger of peace. Therefore, when Gen. Powell told India that Musharraf had assured him India's demands would be met, New Delhi was immensely pleased. The war was once again called off.

When the war clouds receded, Musharraf was back with a bang. Pakistan test fired a series of nuclear-capable ballistic missiles and, instead of offering words of conciliation, Musharraf's much-awaited television address on May 27 did just the opposite. He asserted that "nothing was happening on the LoC", and lambasted India's Hindu fundamentalists for attacking Muslims in Gujarat. India kept quiet hoping that the US would tame Musharraf and get him to show results on the ground. The British and US dignitaries flew into the region once again. Their mission this time was to help India independently verify that the infiltration level on the LoC was decreasing. The British Foreign Secretary, Jack Straw, the US Deputy Secretary of State, Richard Armitage, and the Defence Secretary, Donald Rumsfeld, arrived in quick succession in June, touching base in Pakistan and India.

Musharraf snubbed the British foreign secretary by refusing to meet him in Islamabad because he had earlier said in London that cross-border terrorism in J&K must end. Jaswant Singh told Straw in Delhi that a bilateral mechanism for joint patrolling with Pakistan for verification of infiltration across the LoC could be adopted. Within a week of Straw's leaving, Armitage arrived in Delhi on June 16 from Islamabad and publicly declared that Musharraf had given him an assurance that cross-border terrorism would end permanently and terrorist training camps in PoK would be shut down. Buoyed by the news, India announced three conciliatory measures. The naval ships on high alert along the western seaboard were told to come back to their stations; career diplomat, Harsh Kumar Bhasin, was earmarked for posting to Islamabad as the high commissioner; and restrictions on Pakistani aircraft over Indian airspace were lifted. Considering that India had linked any peace moves to a visible drop in infiltration on the ground, these measures were perceived as taken under US pressure. Even worse, Armitage had taken an assurance from India that it would demobilise its army after the assembly elections in J&K due in September. From then onwards, at every opportunity, US dignitaries visiting India reminded the government of its promise to send the troops back to the barracks by October.

Pushed against the diplomatic wall, India declared that the mobilisation would help keep Pakistan's nefarious designs in check during the four-week-long assembly elections in J&K. With a total of 800 lives lost in election-related violence—as disclosed by the prime minister to the Parliament—India went about touting that the mobilisation had helped the democratic process in J&K. Most of the violence was perpetrated by jehadi elements, who Pakistan repeatedly claimed were not under its control. These elements had stepped up their activities in the state after the ouster of the Taliban regime in Afghanistan. While the US was appreciative of Pakistan's position on the issue, it was necessary that India also understood the same.

The US Defence Secretary, Donald Rumsfeld, arrived in Delhi on June 20 for this purpose, four days after Armitage had left confident of the fact that de-escalatory moves had begun. The Rumsfeld mission had two objectives. The first was to impress upon the Indian leadership that Musharraf did not control all terrorists, especially jehadis, operating in J&K. It was, therefore, important that in the case of an attack like in Kaluchak India carefully understand the situation before implicating Musharraf or overreacting. His second objective in Delhi was to find out what peace moves India would be willing to take immediately and in the near future. India made it clear that it would wait to see results on the ground before its next peace move with Pakistan.

There had, however, been a decrease in infiltration after Musharraf's May 27 speech. Indian intelligence sources intercepted terrorist communication traffic and found out that Pakistan had instructed terrorists to lie low for four to six weeks. This was the period Pakistan had guessed it would take the US to arm-twist India into talks with Islamabad. Things went wrong for Pakistan when it learnt that India would not pull back its troops until the elections in J&K, nor would it talk with Pakistan until the latter dismantled terrorist camps in PoK.

Musharraf went into a belligerent mood and spilled the beans about the understanding he had reached with the US. Talking to *Newsweek* magazine, Musharraf said: "I have told President Bush nothing is happening across the Line of Control. This is the assurance I have given. I am not going to give you an assurance that for years nothing will happen." He further said that Armitage had not discussed the issue of dismantling training camps in PoK with him.

Instead he said, "I [Musharraf] have an assurance: I have been told by President Bush and deputy secretary Armitage that, yes, [India] needs to move forward on the initiation of a dialogue on Kashmir." To emphasise what was happening in J&K, Musharraf told the magazine, "I do not call it cross-border terrorism. There is a freedom struggle going on in Kashmir."[2]

Musharraf's tirade created an awkward situation for India. There was disappointment with the US which had indulged in doublespeak, saying something to India and cutting some other deals with Pakistan. It was also apparent that the US did not give any priority to terrorism against India. It was even suspected that the US had decided to silently endorse Musharraf's views on J&K, and was playing games with India. The CCS came to the conclusion that India should not expect the US to look after India's genuine concerns about Pakistan-sponsored terrorism. India would have to fight terrorism on its own, and the kowtowing to the US would have to end. The government's resolve to pursue an independent approach for tackling terrorism in J&K was reflected in the shifting of Foreign Minister Jaswant Singh, who was perceived as pro-US, to the finance ministry on July 1, 2002. This followed the elevation of L. K. Advani as the deputy Prime Minister, suggesting that India would finally take a tough stand against terrorism in J&K. The next day, Foreign Secretary Kanwal Sibal went public about US double standards regarding Pakistan, prompting Gen. Powell to pack his bags and return to the region—his third trip since 9/11. This time the US wanted to gauge if India was reviewing its nuclear policy and its relations with the US. Washington also wanted India to demobilise and start talks with Pakistan.

Arriving in Delhi on July 25, Gen. Powell found that not much had changed, except that India was coming out with more virulent rhetoric. For example, the deputy prime minister said that he dreamt of a united South Asia (*akhand Bharat*), a concept enunciated by his mentor, the late Deen Dayal Upadhyaya. This was just the kind of rhetoric Pakistan eagerly awaited. Gen. Musharraf complained that India, under the BJP rule, was not reconciled to an independent and sovereign Pakistan. Hence, there was the need now than ever before for both nations to demobilise and commence

---

[2] "Voices from a Hot Zone", *Newsweek*, July 1, 2002, p. 21.

talks, especially on the issue of Kashmir. After repeated US appeals to India for an early demobilisation, Operation Parakram was finally called off on October 16, 2002.

The Need for Talks

With Operation Parakram over, diplomacy should have taken precedence. The US and Pakistan wanted bilateral talks to commence under the Simla agreement. India's predicament was that little had been achieved by flexing military muscle for 10 long months. Pakistan had emerged more belligerent, and the US more supportive of its new-found ally. This was amply demonstrated by Gen. Musharraf, who congratulated his armed forces for having "earned the distinction of defeating the enemy without fighting a war".[3] The US, meanwhile, told India to go slow with its involvement in Afghanistan as it was not to the liking of Pakistan. On a visit to the US, India's national security advisor, Brajesh Mishra, discussed the issue with US officials.[4]

For India, talking with Pakistan at such a stage would have meant conducting negotiations from a position of both diplomatic and military weakness. Once talks began, the focus would necessarily be on the future of Kashmir. Pakistan had repeatedly said that for peace in the region, a solution to the Kashmir problem would have to be found. The US position was similar, with Gen. Colin Powell emphasising that Kashmir was important, if not the central issue for bilateral talks. Moreover, the UN Security Council resolution 1172, passed after the 1998 nuclear tests, unambiguously stated that Kashmir was the main cause of dispute between India and Pakistan.

India had agreed to discuss the Kashmir issue with Pakistan for the first time in 1994. However, the government of P. V. Narasimha Rao had also passed a unanimous resolution in Parliament at that time to get back PoK from Pakistan. In the same year, the Deputy Prime Minister, L. K. Advani, then the leader of the opposition, had told the media that once in power his government would get back PoK from Pakistan. On being asked if the BJP-led government

---

[3] "We Defeated the Enemy without a War", *The Hindu*, December 14, 2002.
[4] "The Matter is Behind Us", *The Hindu*, December 12, 2002.

would accept the LoC being made into a permanent border, Foreign Minister Jaswant Singh had asserted throughout his tenure
that "borders cannot be redrawn", implying that India would get
back PoK to unify the state of J&K. "The LoC", he had said, "is a CBM
[Confidence Building Measure]".

Between 1994—when both agreed to discuss the Kashmir
issue—and the 1999 Kargil war, the two sides went through a sterile modalities debate. The main issue of how to resolve the problem was overshadowed by the question of how to approach it.
Pakistan's position was that the core issue of Kashmir should be
discussed in isolation. According to India, the Kashmir issue was
only one of the many outstanding problems between the two
countries. Both sides finally agreed in 1997 to form eight "working
groups" to tackle all outstanding matters. The two main issues of
Kashmir and peace and security on the LoC were to be handled at
the foreign-secretary level. The remaining six issues relating to the
Siachen Glacier, the Tulbul barrage project, Sir Creek, economic and
commercial cooperation, terrorism, drug trafficking, and cultural
exchanges were to be discussed between the respective secretary-
level bureaucrats. This format of talks came to be known as the
"composite dialogue" interaction between India and Pakistan.

The election of Nawaz Sharif as the prime minister of Pakistan
with a clear majority in the National Assembly in February 1997
was greeted with a lot of euphoria. Optimists said Sharif, with cooperation from India, had an opportunity similar to what existed
between Rajiv Gandhi and Benazir Bhutto in 1989 to permanently
resolve the Kashmir problem. Such predictions glossed over certain ground realities: (a) In Pakistan the army, and not the political leadership, decided Kashmir policy; (b) 1989 was different from
1997, a time when the Pakistan Army perceived itself to be winning the proxy war in Kashmir; and (c) the leadership of Deve
Gowda and I. K. Gujral in India was pitiably weak. Things continued to drift at the political level until the Kargil war.

With the overthrow of the Sharif government in Pakistan, the
debate in India was whether it should talk with Gen. Musharraf.
Could the man who masterminded the Kargil operation against
India be trusted? For that matter, Could the Pakistan Army be
trusted? A senior Congress leader, Mani Shankar Aiyar, provided
an interesting viewpoint:

Do we [India] have an alternative? Ayub lasted eleven years.
Zia lasted eleven. "Democracy" [in Pakistan] lasted eleven. The
fact is the strongest political party in Pakistan is the army. Some-
times it runs the government itself. At others, it lends outside
support to the civilian authority. But any Pakistani politician
who backs the army is only storing up his own dismissal.[5]

Given the importance of the army in Pakistan's dispensation, an opportunity which could have produced results was lost in August 1992 when India's Defence Minister, Sharad Pawar, had extended an invitation to the Pakistan Army Chief, General Asif Nawaz Janjua, to visit India. It did not materialise because the Pakistan Army saw itself in a position of relative strength with regard to Kashmir. The next meaningful opportunity came with the advent of the Musharraf military regime in Pakistan. This thinking should have been the basis for the Agra summit between Vajpayee and Musharraf held on July 15–16, 2001.

Since the beginning of the insurgency in Kashmir in 1989, the Agra summit was the first time that Pakistan was coming to a summit meeting with two major weaknesses. First, in the post-Kargil scenario, the jehadis or the Taliban carried more clout in the Valley than the ISI-backed militants. This reality had forced Musharraf to praise jehad. Under the changed circumstances, where Pakistan had limited control over the jehadis, Musharraf could not have gone home with the sterile offer of a "composite dialogue" proposed by India. Nothing less than getting India to agree to the centrality of the Kashmir "dispute" or "issue" in normalising bilateral relations would have helped Musharraf cut a favourable deal with the jehadis. This explains why Pakistan was insisting the summit meeting be held without a prepared agenda, as India, which does not recognise Kashmir as a "dispute", may have retracted its summit invitation to President Musharraf had it known Pakistan's intention beforehand.

Second, on the surface, General Musharraf came to the summit meeting donning the four hats of president, chief executive, chairman of the Chiefs of Staff committee, and chief of the army staff, the last position being the most junior. In reality, Musharraf

---

[5] Aiyar, Mani Shankar (2000), *On the Abyss*, New Delhi: Harper Collins, p. 220.

drew his clout from being the army chief. In a Punjab-dominated Pakistan Army, it would have weighed heavily on Musharraf, a *mohajir*, to show results to his corps commanders. His psyche betrayed this yearning when, during his breakfast meeting with Indian media editors on July 16, he said that he would have had to come back to his ancestral home in Delhi if he could not show a positive movement in the Kashmir dispute.

For Musharraf, the Agra summit was a desperate attempt to curtail the growing clout of the Taliban in Kashmir. What Musharraf lost at Kargil to the Taliban, he wanted to gain at Agra. India, on the other hand, used the summit to please both the domestic audience by giving no quarters to Musharraf and the US by demonstrating willingness to talk with the architect of the Kargil war. In reality, both sides lost at the Agra summit because Pakistan was too sure of its agenda, and India appeared far too clueless.

Apparently, the only forward movement at the Agra summit was an agreement by both sides that the two main issues of the "composite dialogue" interaction—peace and security on the LoC and in J&K—should be upgraded and dealt with at the ministerial level. On the other hand, the weakness in future talks on J&K would be that India would have to interact with a civilian government in the "military-democracy" in Pakistan. The government of Pakistan would just be a facilitator and not the decision-making entity between India and the National Security Council of Pakistan headed by Musharraf. Simply put, Prime Minister Vajpayee would have to hold future summits with the dummy Prime Minister Jamali of Pakistan.

This would complicate talks, considering that the positions of India and Pakistan on Kashmir are dissimilar and hardened, with little common meeting ground. India wants to discuss three aspects of the Kashmir problem with Pakistan: the status of PoK, Pakistan's role in transborder infiltration across the LoC and its support to the militancy in J&K. India had demanded that Pakistan stop cross-border terrorism and dismantle the infrastructure in PoK that supports terrorism permanently. Pakistan, on the other hand, has its own set of three talking points regarding Kashmir. These are plebiscite or self-determination, reduction of Indian security forces—especially the army—in J&K and human rights violations by Indian security forces in the state. Pakistan has all along denied material support to the insurgents in Kashmir.

Such divergent views can be resolved only in two ways. Either the ground situation changes so drastically that Pakistan becomes either incapable of waging the proxy war in Kashmir, or no longer finds it cost-effective. This is possible if India goes to war with Pakistan and is able to decimate the bulk of its military machinery. This would get Pakistan to sincerely discuss the Kashmir issue in a proper perspective in the aftermath of the war. Alternatively, if India manages to bring about internal peace in Kashmir, Pakistan would have diminishing returns from its present proxy war. The latter is a more sensible and practical solution, but may not be achievable. Notwithstanding the J&K elections in September 2002, which brought in a coalition government committed to ending the insurgency, internal peace in the border state appears unrealisable. There are just too many differences between the state and the BJP-led central government. Moreover, with general elections due in 2004, the centre cannot be expected to run contrary to the BJP party thinking, which is against autonomy for Kashmir or talking with militants outside the guidelines of the Constitution of India.

The other way to resolve the issue is through mediation, which runs against India's mantra of bilateralism as enshrined in the 1972 Simla agreement. In practical terms, India has been slowly moving away from too much rigidity in bilateralism, as was evident during the 1999 Kargil war. In June 1999, General Anthony Zinni, Commander-in-Chief of the US Central command, met Prime Minister Nawaz Sharif and General Pervez Musharraf, which resulted in the Clinton–Sharif meeting in Washington on July 4, 1999, that de-escalated the war. The July 4 joint statement issued after the Clinton–Sharif meeting, amongst other things, sought "concrete steps to be taken for the restoration of the LoC". Subsequently, in March 2000, during his visit to India, President Clinton expanded on the theme in what came to be known as the US four "Rs" formula on Kashmir—the need to respect the LoC, show restraint, reject violence and restore the dialogue.

Humiliated by the forced withdrawal of troops from the Indian side of the LoC, Pakistan sought to play up another issue mentioned in the joint statement. "The president [Clinton] would take personal interest in resumption of bilateral dialogue" was interpreted as the US acceptance to be the mediator over Kashmir. This was hailed as a victory in the Pakistan media. The Indian media reflected that Delhi had not really discouraged the US to seek an early end to the Kargil war. However, the government did not commit any role for the US, formal or informal, in Indo-Pak relations.

Things, however, changed with Operation Parakram. Ever since the Kargil war, India had silently hoped that the US would understand its perspective of Operation Parakram, which was similar to the US-led Operation Enduring Freedom in Afghanistan in the aftermath of 9/11. From India's viewpoint, Pakistan was wrong in crossing the LoC, which led to the Kargil war. Further, Pakistan was again wrong in continuing to export terror into J&K, after the US-led world community had decided that terrorism, and countries exporting terrorism, need to be fought tooth and nail. By such righteous analogy, the US should have pressurised Pakistan to end terrorism in J&K, just as it asked the two countries to respect the LoC during the Kargil war. In this context, India welcomed the regular stream of visitors from the US and the UK during Operation Parakram. Prime Minister Vajpayee acknowledged the US role in the future would be that of a facilitator.[6] The US role in the region, therefore, became more institutionalised.

The US has been accepted as a facilitator by India primarily because of the nuclear weapon factor. On the Indian side, the nuclear deterrence played a role for the first time in curbing the escalation of the Kargil war. In one crucial closed-door meeting, Prime Minister Vajpayee expressed his apprehension about Pakistan using the nuclear weapon if India enlarged the conflict by crossing the LoC.[7] This underscored the need to stabilise the nuclear factor by implementing the Lahore declaration MoU, which was abandoned after the Kargil war.

From Tests to Lahore

The nuclear tests were a destabilising factor. The accompanying rhetoric by the Indian leaders made it worse. The day after India's first series of tests, Home Minister L. K. Advani told the media that Pakistan should realise the geo-strategic situation in the region had changed. India, he threatened, would deal firmly and strongly with Pakistan over Kashmir. This single statement which linked the

---

[6] "Voices from the Hot Zone", *Newsweek*, July 1, 2002, p. 20.
[7] This was told to the author by a high-ranking military officer.

threat of the use of nuclear weapons with Pakistan's proxy war in Kashmir worked to Islamabad's advantage. Pakistan thereafter repeatedly used nuclear weapons as instruments to influence political issues. A large section of influential people in Pakistan actively involved in Track-II or informal diplomacy painstakingly speak about the linkage between nuclear weapons and the resolution of the Kashmir problem.

Further, Pakistan found the justification in Advani's thoughtless statement to respond to India's tests with a series of tests of their own. The Pakistan premier, Nawaz Sharif, argued that: "Pakistan has been obliged to exercise the nuclear option because of the weaponisation of India's nuclear programme. This has led to the collapse of existing deterrence and has radically altered the strategic balance in our region."

Sharif offered to correct the destabilising factor caused by the tests in his first address to the nation after Pakistan's tests. The CBM offered to India was "urgent steps for mutual restraint and equitable measures for nuclear stabilisation". In addition, Pakistan reiterated its known position that it was prepared "to resume a Pakistan–India dialogue to address all outstanding issues, including the core issue of J&K, as well as peace and security". The latter issue of "peace and security on the LoC" was the Indian suggestion made to Pakistan by the 1994 non-papers. Sharif was willing to reconsider the Indian suggestion if India accepted a "non-aggression pact".

Pakistan essentially made three points after the tests. The first was a CBM offer to put into place a "nuclear stabilisation regime" along with the formation of a "nuclear risk reduction centre". The second was a pressing requirement to restart the bilateral dialogue on Kashmir and other issues. And lastly, Pakistan put on the block a regional test ban pact.

All three issues appealed to the US, which modified the Pakistan suggestion for a regional test ban pact to both countries signing the Comprehensive Test Ban Treaty. Washington added a fourth suggestion: a need for a ballistic missile regime. With India and Pakistan in possession of nuclear weapons, there was a pressing need for a "missile restraint regime". Realising the ground realities, the US adopted a new approach. Instead of seeking a "cap" or a "rollback" of Indian and Pakistani nuclear capabilities, it entered into a series of comprehensive security dialogues with both countries. A definitive outcome of these talks, spread over the fag end of the Clinton administration, was that nuclear weaponisation, at least in India, was slowed down. The US secretary of state made it clear that "We [the US] believe the South Asian nuclear tests of May 1998 were a historic mistake. And the UN Security Council Resolution 1172 makes it plain that the international community agrees with us."[8] The resolution of June 1998 urges India and Pakistan to give up their nuclear weapons capability and sign the Non-Proliferation Treaty as non-nuclear weapon states. The Clinton administration, at the time of leaving office in January 2001, made it abundantly clear that the non-proliferation issue was coming in the way of Indo-US relations realising their full potential. What it did not say was that unless India did not stop its nuclear weaponisation, relations could not be fruitful.

Regarding ballistic missiles, "the United States is no longer asking India and Pakistan not to test missiles or build more existing types of ballistic missiles or new ballistic missiles; all it now urges is no deployment of ballistic missiles", Assistant Secretary of State Karl Inderfurth told the Brownback sub-committee of the senate foreign relations committee on July 13, 1998. In reality, the US was pressuring India to go slow with testing of its ballistic missiles. The three US non-proliferation wishes with regard to India and Pakistan during the Clinton administration were: sign the CTBT, stop nuclear weaponisation and go slow with testing of ballistic missiles. Rhetorically, the US experts in the region said that India and Pakistan should avoid a nuclear and missile arms race.

After the nuclear tests, it was evident that India and Pakistan would need to evolve CBMs to tide over the destabilising factors—one created by the imminent nuclear weaponisation and the second pertaining to ballistic missiles, considering both sides had a comparable missile capability. This happened with the signing of the Lahore declaration on February 21, 1999, between Prime Minister Atal Bihari Vajpayee and Prime Minister Nawaz Sharif. The Lahore declaration had little to do with the problem of J&K or other issues between the two countries. Its operative part is the "Memorandum of Understanding" which broadly tackles four security-related issues:

---

[8] "Delhi must address N-issues", *The Times of India*, March 16, 2000.

- To give advance notice with respect to ballistic missile flight tests.
- To discuss respective nuclear doctrines and security concepts for confidence building in nuclear and conventional fields aimed at conflict avoidance.
- To set up a nuclear risk reduction centre to minimise risks of accidental or unauthorised use of nuclear weapons.
- To better the existing channels of communication.

Before the technical details as envisaged in the MoU could be worked out by the middle of 1999, Kargil happened. The war in Kargil was viewed with dismay by India as a breach of trust by Pakistan. The government was accused of naiveté when it was realised that a wily Sharif shook hands with Vajpayee after having given the nod to his army to plan the Kargil intrusions.

Pakistan's misadventure in Kargil provided the excuse for India to put on hold the Lahore declaration MoU. There was never much doubt that Vajpayee's bus ride to Lahore in February 1999, which resulted in the signing of the Lahore declaration, was not as spontaneous as was made out by both sides. The US pressure on both sides to concretise a bilateral nuclear and ballistic missile restraint regime was evident. Post-Kargil, India took the position that talks with Pakistan were possible only after it demonstrated sincerity by controlling infiltration into Kashmir.

In reality, the two issues of Kashmir and a need for nuclear and ballistic missile CBMs are unrelated. Irrespective of when, what or whether at all the two countries talk on Kashmir, there is an urgent need for both sides to start talks on nuclear and ballistic missile CBMs as mutually agreed in the Lahore declaration MoU. If not resolved at the earliest, these destabilising factors could have disastrous military consequences.

The US in the Role of Facilitator

The US desires a strategic relationship with India for two reasons: to ensure non-proliferation of nuclear weapons, and to seek greater transparency of India's defence matters. Respected Americans have suggested a middle path on proliferation while dealing with India and Pakistan. According to Dr. Henry Kissinger, "American policy should move from trying to pressure India and Pakistan to abandon their nuclear weapons programme to making them partners in a regime of nuclear restraint and in easing political tensions in South Asia." This could imply that India and Pakistan stop nuclear weaponisation, undertake not to spread nuclear and ballistic missile technology, and make efforts to ease tensions between each other. An American engagement in such a situation thus seems not only plausible but necessary.

On its part, India has already made a climb-down: from Prime Minister Vajpayee declaring India a nuclear weapon state in Parliament after the Shakti tests, and asserting that India had conferred this right on itself, to referring to India as a state with nuclear weapons within four years. This nuance in calling oneself a "state with nuclear weapons" instead of a "nuclear weapon state"—a terminology used for the five declared nuclear weapon powers—is not mere semantics. It indicates that India has agreed to a different status. In this context, it is interesting to note what Dr. Ashley J. Tellis, probably the most knowledgeable Indian–American, has to say:

> *India does not currently possess or seek to build a ready nuclear arsenal, contrary to views held by many within and outside the country. Essentially, India's nuclear deterrence consists of unassembled nuclear warheads, with their components stored separately under strict civilian control, and dedicated delivery systems kept either in storage or in readiness away from their operational areas—all of which can be brought together as rapidly as required to create a usable deterrent force during a supreme emergency.*[9]

Regarding the defence cooperation between India and the US, it is an unequal, on-again–off-again relationship. While it is fair that the US, as the sole superpower, cannot be expected to have an equal reciprocity of defence interests with India, the sad part is that India has been too willing to give more than it gets in return. This is galling; particularly after the 1998 nuclear tests when India has been in a position to stand up to the US taller than its stature would have otherwise permitted.

---

[9] Tellis, Ashley J. (2001), *India's Emerging Nuclear Posture*, New Delhi: Oxford University Press.

Apologists have made a case for a multifaceted defence relationship with the US implying that India is a rising power. According to them, a country which does not believe in free lunches, and has an annual defence budget of $396 billion as compared to India's $13 billion, will not seek a multi-dimensional interaction if its strategic interests were at odds with India. Prime Minister A. B. Vajpayee had set the tone of the defence relationship himself by describing the two democracies as "natural allies", a feel-good phrase which has subsequently been used by top US officials for India. At present, there are many more formal committees under the relationship than could be imagined during the Cold War.

Overseeing these interactions is the Defence Policy Group co-chaired by India's defence secretary and the US under secretary of defence for policy. Under this is the Joint Technical Group between the two defence research establishments, the Military Cooperation Group between the US Joint Staff and the Indian Chief of Integrated Defence Staff, and the Executive Steering Groups of the Indian Army, Air Force and Navy, which interact with their counterparts in the UN Pacific Command responsible for the region which includes India. There is also a Joint Working Group on peace-keeping, a Security Cooperation Group formed after the 9/11 events to discuss counter-terrorism-related issues, and a government-sponsored regular exchange between the defence research and analysis communities in both countries. In addition, there is an important strategic-level interaction, led by the Indian external affairs ministry, which deals with issues pertaining to weapons of mass destruction.

As a consequence of this, there has been bonhomie at military tactical levels between the two countries. Hardly a day passes without reports of combined training for humanitarian airlift, special operations training, small unit ground/air exercises, naval joint personnel exchange and familiarisation, and combined naval training exercises between US marines and corresponding Indian forces. Supplementing all this, there have been inspired reports— readily lapped up by a gullible media—that the US is seriously considering selling state-of-the-art weapons and technologies to India. All this, according to experts, means that the US has acknowledged India as a great (potential) power which it cannot do without for stability in Asia. India arrived on the US radar screen after the 1998 nuclear tests, and the bilateral defence relationship has since strengthened by leaps and bounds.

The problem with the above thesis is that it is too good to be true. Indian analysts have simply not paused to think what is pushing, or at other times stalling, this defence cooperation. The moot question from India's viewpoint is whether it is getting what it desires most—defence and dual-use technologies—from the defence cooperation. After the 1998 tests, the US had imposed across-the-board economic and technological sanctions, putting into operation its Enhanced Proliferation Control Initiative (EPCI). Two hundred Indian organisations or entities were put on the prohibited list. After 9/11, the Bush administration removed all sanctions against India and Pakistan, although certain restrictions have remained in place under the US non-proliferation act and related congressional stipulations. Only 24 entities remain on the restrictive list at present. Importantly, these entities include India's nuclear facilities that are not under IAEA (International Atomic Energy Agency) safeguards—the Defence Research and Development Organisation, Bharat Electronics, and India's Rare Earth Organisation. Although importing sophisticated technologies is no longer subject to the EPCI, US export licences are still necessary, which, needless to say, would depend on the US thinking about India at that time. However, it is certain the US would give India nothing that would help in research pertaining to nuclear weapons, ballistic missiles and supercomputers. It would be erroneous for India to conclude that a strategic interaction with the US could result in tangible technology gains. This is because acquisition, control and denial of technology has emerged as the principal tool of future warfare; there is little possibility of the US sharing even medium-level technology with India in certain defined areas.

The US has redefined rules for new members of the Missile Technology Control Regime (MTCR). New MTCR members are required not to export any dual-use technologies, and have also been denied a sharing of technology with original MTCR members. Further, after 9/11, the US has made its end-user restrictions for weapons and technology given to friendly western nations and Israel more stringent. What the US has given and offered India is low-level and old technology. For example, Pakistan already has the ANTPQ-37 gun-locating radars that the US sold recently to India. There were reports corroborated by senior government officials that the US instructed Israel not to give any high-tech equipment to India which could disturb the conventional balance with Pakistan. India has been negotiating for at least three Phalcon Airborne Warning and Control Systems (AWACS) to be used with Ilyushin-76 aircraft procured from Russia, and components of the Arrow-2, an anti-tactical ballistic missile system to be used with the indigenous Akash surface-to-surface missile. Even worse, the US maintains pressure on Russia to ensure that it does not sell high-level technology to India, something which China clandestinely gifts to Pakistan.

India, on the other hand, signed a General Security of Military Information Agreement (GSOMIA) with the US in August 2002. Under the wraps of the GSOMIA, the US, in essence, has two objectives. First and foremost, the US does not want to be surprised a second time after the shock of India's May 1998 nuclear tests, when it was caught unawares. Moreover, the world (read, the US) believes that a conventional war between India and Pakistan could easily escalate into a nuclear exchange. Hence, there is a need for a better understanding of India's security policymaking and military matters through high-level institutionalised interactions.

Simply put, the US now understands the need to constantly nudge India for more transparency in defence matters. Defence transparency, after all, means different things for different nations. For developed nations led by the US that have an out-of-area operational role, transparency in defence matters implies deterrence. The more they show their superior weaponry, and talk about their novel strategies and issues of operational art, the more it would deter nations which are likely to create mischief. On the other hand, for developing nations like India and Pakistan, whose armed forces are meant for the nation's defence, deterrence comes from hiding their weapon modifications, military strategies and defence planning. This leaves the others guessing about their capabilities and intentions.

In the short term, the US wants to understand the Indian defence establishment in its totality. This would help it to prepare for pre-emptive and preventive measures should India's ambitions soar. On the other hand, cumulative knowledge about India's military prowess acquired over time would assist the US in deciding whether India could be a bulwark against China in the Indian Ocean region.

The other objective of the US through the GSOMIA is to keep India's nuclear ambitions in check. The US has repeatedly said through its high-ranking officials that its core objective of a strategic dialogue is to persuade India to cap its nuclear capabilities at the present level. The US has not, and will not, accept India as a nuclear weapon state. This was the essence of the Jaswant Singh–Strobe Talbot rounds of talks held in the aftermath of the nuclear tests. And this remains the credo of the Bush administration. India, unfortunately, has failed in its nuclear weapons diplomacy. Its nuclear weaponisation has been checkmated even as it has permitted greater access to the US into its defence establishment.

Confidence-Building Measures

Most of the CBMs worked out by the strategic community are rarely accepted by the leadership of India and Pakistan because they are unrealistic and irrelevant. For example, there have been suggestions to have an "Open Skies" treaty between India and Pakistan within 250 kilometres of the border. The fact that there are offensive land formations cantoned within this area on both sides is overlooked. Another CBM hotly sought to be sold is the need for hot-line communications between the two air forces and navies as it exists between the two armies—the two director generals of military operations—for multiple redundancy linkages. Such a CBM is of little use when the Pakistan Army alone decides issues of war and peace. Hot lines were instituted between the two air forces after the 1971 war, but were later discontinued. Another CBM has been an ironic one; it appealed for an arms cut, and was made after retirement by the late Gen. K. Sundarji, who drew up the most ambitious armament plans as the army chief. Not surprisingly, the senior military brass did not endorse such thinking. According to Gen. Sundarji, "because a nuclear deterrence is in place, it should not be difficult for India and Pakistan to agree on mutual conventional force reductions". However, he added, "I realise we would meet resistance to force reductions from the military establishments on both sides of the border."[10] The trouble with Sundarji's argument is that not many in the military see the linkage between nuclear and conventional arms, and a reduction of forces is dependent upon improved relations between the policy

---

[10] "The World Power Structure in Transition", General K. Sundarji, *USI Journal*, January–March 1993.

makers in India and Pakistan. The two militaries are merely following the instructions of the establishment—the army in Pakistan,
and the political-bureaucratic combine in India.

A CBM which Pakistan keeps offering, both formally and infor-
mally with sincere regularity, is a no-war pact: Zia-ul-Haq suggested
it in 1981; Sharif proposed it in June 1998 after the nuclear tests,
calling it a non-aggression pact; Musharraf offered it in September
2000 while addressing the UN Millennium Summit in New York, and
again in January 2002 when India and Pakistan were on the brink of
war. The reason why India cannot accept it is that it undermines
the 1972 Simla agreement which commits both sides "to resolve
all issues bilaterally and peacefully". As long as the Simla agreement exists, there is little use of a no-war or a non-aggression pact.

During Operation Parakram, a particular CBM was tossed
around by the US with regularity. It related to joint patrolling by
India and Pakistan to ascertain infiltration across the LoC. Ironically, this CBM exposed the ad hoc and disjointed thinking of the
Indian government. Even as Prime Minister Vajpayee suggested
this CBM at the Conference on Initiative and Confidence Building
in Asia at Alma Aty in June 2002, Defence Minister George Fernandes,
who was not aware of what the premier had said, vehemently
rejected the proposal. The Indian Army's position in rejecting the
proposal was a practical one. Once patrolling started in a terrain
not altogether conducive to such effects, Pakistan could legiti-
mately deny responsibility for any infiltration that continued
thereafter. Such a difficult situation could lead to more outside
pressure on India for monitoring of the LoC by external observers,
which would benefit Pakistan. India did not share Islamabad's
keenness to position UN monitors on the LoC, as it was opposed
to third-party mediation on J&K. The prime minister, unfortunately, was more interested in scoring brownie points. When Pakistan
understood the import of what India had said, it asked the world
community to pressurise India to formally send the proposal.
Nothing was heard from India thereafter.

A CBM which has not received due importance is one which
outlines the need to establish a nuclear weapons and ballistic
missiles regime between India and Pakistan. Pakistan test fired a
series of nuclear-capable ballistic missiles during Operation
Parakram. Considering that it has sufficiently accurate guidance
systems and solid propellant for its ballistic missiles, both acquired

from China, it remains uncertain whether the Pakistan Army
would use them with conventional or nuclear warheads. Similarly,
there is a mismatch between the declaratory nuclear policies of
India and Pakistan. Delhi advocates a no-first-use nuclear policy,
which Islamabad rejects. For these reasons, it is critical that the
two sides start talks on these issues. Such talks should be undertaken formally by civil and military officials, and not by unofficial
or Track-II channels. Even though an Indo-Pak dialogue on Kashmir
and other issues can wait, an understanding on nuclear and missile issues cannot.

Summary

- The single reason which stopped the Indian political leadership from starting the war was the fear that Pakistan might use
  its nuclear weapons.
- The US role as a facilitator between India and Pakistan was
  formalised.
- The US made it known that Pakistan was its close ally in the
  war on terror, and that India's military action against Pakistan
  would displease the US enormously.
- Despite the US acknowledgement that Pakistan was indeed responsible for infiltration, Washington brushed aside India's repeated
  calls to label Pakistan as a state sponsoring terrorism.
- Pakistan did not betray anxiety about Operation Parakram, with
  Gen. Musharraf remaining defiant throughout the 10-month
  long mobilisation.
- The coercive diplomacy by India failed to check cross-border
  infiltration across the LoC.
- None of the other Indian demands, like the list of 20 wanted
  criminals, were met because of this so-called coercive diplomacy.
- With 800 dead in terrorist violence related to elections in J&K,
  India declared that mobilisation had helped keep Pakistan's
  nefarious designs in check.
- There is a need for India to starts talks with Pakistan over the
  nuclear and ballistic missiles regime, and the formation of a
  nuclear risk reduction centre. The guidelines are available in
  the memorandum of understanding of the 1999 Lahore declaration between India and Pakistan.

5

Nuclear Threat: Perceptions and Realities

Even as India's Operation Parakram was underway, Pakistan test fired a series of ballistic missiles in May and October 2002. On the first occasion, it fired its long-range Ghauri-I or Hatf-V, Ghaznavi or Hatf-III, and Abdali or Hatf-II missiles. On the second, it fired the Shaheen-I or Hatf-IV missile twice. The significance of the timing was that an Indian attack into PoK appeared imminent in June, which was subsequently confirmed by Prime Minister A. B. Vajpayee. Further, people close to the government kept hinting about taking Operation Parakram to its logical conclusion—a war inside PoK—during October and November.

India pooh-poohed the tests on both occasions. New Delhi had earlier scoffed at media reports in the United States in September 2000, quoting their intelligence sources, which alleged Pakistan's superiority over India in ballistic missiles. The government spokesperson dismissed Pakistan's ballistic missile firing as something that did not impress "us". India's defence minister, George Fernandes, said that there was no need for Pakistan to test its ballistic missiles considering they were not indigenous, but acquired missiles. The tests, he declared, would have no effect on India's strategic thinking, its policy on Kashmir or the ongoing Operation Parakram.

While Fernandes' statement remains debatable, there has been a method in Pakistan's behaviour. For example, despite warnings and allurements from the United States, Pakistan followed India's May 1998 nuclear tests with its own series to "restore the strategic balance". Similarly, until India's Agni-II test firing on February 17, 2001, all ballistic missile test firings were immediately countered, laced with taller claims by Pakistan. Once Pakistan managed to more than match India's ballistic missiles—besides having its military in the saddle—there was no need for it to reply to India's test firings until the launch of Operation Parakram.

This time around, Pakistan was sending a straightforward message, both to the international community and India, that it had the political will and military wherewithal to exercise the nuclear option, should it become necessary. It is important to expostulate on both issues—political will and military capabilities—to appreciate Pakistan's nuclear threat. It is irrelevant whether Pakistan would indeed exercise its nuclear option in a war with India. The issue is how India's political and military leadership conceive the nuclear threat, as this is what constitutes a deterrent for Pakistan. To appreciate the significance of Pakistan's tests, it becomes necessary to do a reality check of what constitutes nuclear deterrent, which includes national perception and resolve, doctrinal approach, size of nuclear arsenal, delivery systems, nuclear command and control systems, and the threshold factor.

National Perception and Resolve

It is traditional wisdom that a nation with a credible nuclear deterrent would automatically have a focused thinking and a national resolve demonstrable through its political and military will to exercise the nuclear option in conformity with a declared doctrine, should a situation so demand. Moreover, as greater transparency implies a credible deterrence, efforts would be made, however modest, to publicly put into place key features of nuclear command and control. The cases of Pakistan and India are quite different, and hence need elaboration.

Pakistan's nuclear weapon and ballistic missile programmes, unlike India's, are Indo-centric. This has given Pakistan a singular determination to remain much more resolved on the issue than India. The result has been that India, with a sound technology base, started its nuclear and ballistic missile programme much before Pakistan, only to arrive at a contestable situation about whose programme leads the other at present. The good thing for Pakistan has been its obsessive commitment not to lag behind India, which helped put its two advantages to good use. The first was that Pakistan's nuclear weapons and ballistic missiles programmes have been unflinchingly under the Pakistan Army since

Gen. Zia-ul-Haq's time. Any ambiguity on the issue was subsequently removed by Gen. Pervez Musharraf. Unlike in the case of India, Pakistan ensured that it did not succumb to outside (read, the United States) pressure to either stop or go slow on its programmes, whatever the reasons. For example, during most of the eighties, when Pakistan was fighting the US proxy war in Afghanistan, Washington repeatedly tried to persuade Islamabad to give up its nuclear weapons programme in return for conventional weapons largess. Washington could only politely nudge Islamabad on this crucial issue because as early as 1981, when Pakistan got a hefty economic and military assistance worth $3.2 billion for fighting the American war in Afghanistan, Islamabad made it clear to Washington that "it would neither compromise on her nuclear programme nor accept any external advice on internal matters".[1]

According to a former Pakistan army chief, Gen. Mirza Aslam Beg, "the US deliberately overlooked evidence from its own official, Richard Barlow (posted in the American embassy in Islamabad), that Pakistan had nuclear capability in 1987. It was only when the Soviet Union withdrew from Afghanistan that they accepted Barlow's report as correct".[2] Similarly, in 1994, when Nawaz Sharif was the prime minister, the US offered Pakistan an attractive conventional arms package including F-16 aircraft in exchange for a "cap" on its nuclear weapons programme. Instead of the prime minister, it was the Pakistan Army Chief, General Abdul Waheed, who replied to the US by saying, "F-16 or no F-16, Pakistan will not compromise on its national security [read, nuclear weapons capability]".[3]

To finally settle the issue about who would control Pakistan's nuclear and strategic assets, President Pervez Musharraf formalised the role of the military in the government on August 21, 2002.[4] The National Security Council, chaired by Musharraf himself—he would be a triple hatter: the President of the Islamic Republic, the

---

[1] Lt. Gen. Arif, K. M. (1995), *Working with Zia: Pakistan's Power Politics 1977–1988*, Karachi: Oxford University Press, p. 341.

[2] *The Guardian*, London, March 7, 1996.

[3] *The Asian Age*, June 9, 1994.

[4] "I say, if you want to keep the military out, you have to get them in, and I mean every word of it", General Pervez Musharraf, quoted in "Pak Military is now in Government", *The Times of India*, August 23, 2002.

chairman of the NSC and the army chief for the next five years—comprises the three service chiefs, the chairman of the Chiefs of Staff Committee, the prime minister, the four chief ministers, the leader of the opposition and chairpersons of both houses of Parliament. The NSC has been structured as a supercabinet and a watchdog over the cabinet headed by a democratically elected prime minister. Considering the president has the power to dismiss an elected prime minister, it would be fair to conclude that the government will concern itself only with the internal running of the country.

This arrangement would put to rest the hopes of an elected prime minister in Pakistan meddling with the nation's nuclear assets and thinking. For example, former Prime Minister Benazir Bhutto had said that nuclear weapons were assembled without her knowledge during the height of the 1990 tensions with India over Kashmir.[5] The then army chief, however, asserted that she was always in the picture.[6] Subsequent to President Musharraf's diktat, the unfortunate issue for the outside world, and especially for India, is that an elected civilian leadership has been formally discarded from the strategic assets policy loop. This has removed the desired checks and balances on the nation's nuclear weapons programme. The good thing is that the world now knows who to do business with.

Pakistan's other advantage has been its "strategic partnership" with China. Translated into reality, it has meant two things. First, notwithstanding the close watch by the United States intelligence agencies on Beijing's murky proliferation record, China has ensured that Pakistan remains well geared to meet the Indian nuclear weapon and ballistic missile challenge. Further, by assisting Pakistan to maintain a conventional arms near-parity with India, China, by design, has helped minimise the risk of an early use of nuclear weapons in a war by Pakistan. Both issues are of great import and require a detailed expostulation to understand the dynamics underlining Operation Parakram.

Within weeks of conducting the nuclear tests, India putatively slowed the next logical step, nuclear weaponisation, however modest it might be. Immediately after the nuclear tests, Prime Minister Vajpayee, in his missive to President Clinton, emphasised

---

[5] NBC News, December 1, 1992.
[6] "Pakistan's Nuclear Doctrine", *Defence Journal* (Pakistan), No. 11/12, 1993.

"national security" as the sole reason for the explosions. On July 17, 1998, the then Foreign Minister, Jaswant Singh, diffused the focus of the tests and gave the ethereal reason of "strategic autonomy" for the nuclear big bang. Thereafter, for India it was all about hugging the US leadership through photo opportunities, a presidential visit to India, and by welcoming senior US officials and other European dignitaries to Delhi—India had "arrived", we were told.

The US, however, had no such illusions. After the initial anger which led to the UN Security Council Resolution 1172 of June 6, 1998, demanding that both India and Pakistan "refrain from weaponisation and from deploying nuclear weapons", the US changed tack. The world's leading power engaged India in a series of talks—the Jaswant Singh–Strobe Talbot talks—to both understand India's security perspective and to empathise with it. However, the US bottom line remained, and still remains, that India abide by UN Resolution 1172. Senior officials of the Bush administration, including Secretary of State Gen. Colin Powell and John S. Wolf, the assistant secretary of state for non-proliferation, have publicly said that the nuclear genie should not go any further out of the bottle than it already has. The US thinking has been that if India could be leashed on the nuclear issue, Pakistan would automatically exercise nuclear restraint.

Regarding indigenous ballistic missiles, India has been routinely pushed around by powerful nations who give the utmost care to their national security. For example, Prime Minister P. V. Narasimha Rao postponed a planned test flight of the Prithvi missile on the eve of his visit to Washington in May 1994 because he did not want wrong signals to mar his trip. Similarly, Prime Minister I. K. Gujral ordered Prithvi missiles to be moved back from forward storage areas in Jalandhar in June 1997 after the US protested against their proximity to Pakistan. The Indian prime minister failed to explain the military rationale behind the move to the US leadership. The missiles were not deployed, but had been moved for storage into their designated locations according to routine military self-operating procedures. By the intervention of the prime minister in such a matter, the command and control of a simple battlefield support weapon system was raised to the political level.

The story of Agni has been the same. Between the testing of a Prithvi and an Agni, the US has favoured putting the brakes on the latter programme from its very inception. Washington has made no secret of the fact that it wants India to go slow on Agni, which is an Intermediate Range Ballistic Missile (IRBM). According to former US secretary of state, Madeleine Albright, the basis for engaging India after its nuclear tests would be when "there is no further nuclear testing, and deployment and testing of missiles".[7] The Bush administration has confirmed a similar resolve in the matter. This explains the roller-coaster development of Agni—a total of a mere six test flights (one of which was a failure) since 1984. Three test flights each have been conducted preceding and following the 1998 nuclear tests until Operation Parakram. The Agni was initially conceived as an IRBM, but was soon designated as a "technology demonstrator" to escape international opprobrium. It was once again called an IRBM after the nuclear tests. Even as the status of Agni remained undecided, it was evident that the armed forces would be severely handicapped if they could not rely on this weapon system in the near future.

Doctrinal Approach

Too much fuss has been made about the differing nuclear doctrinal approaches of India and Pakistan. The former has adopted a nuclear no-first-use policy as against Pakistan's first-use one. Analysts on both sides of the divide have interpreted the two approaches to mean various things: Pakistan would use its nuclear weapons early in a war; Pakistan's nuclear doctrinal approach seeks to neutralise India's conventional military superiority; Pakistan's nuclear capability bestows on it the option and the freedom to continue the proxy war in Jammu and Kashmir without much fear of an Indian retaliation.

Discerning people know well that such opinions are academic rather than real. Few military professionals believe that Pakistan will use nuclear weapons first in a war with India; just as the latter, notwithstanding the doctrine, may pre-empt if a nuclear assault from Pakistan looks imminent. Pre-emption, after all, is inbuilt in the doctrine of nuclear deterrence, which India espouses.

---

[7] "Clinton Calls for United Plan to Avert Arms Race in Subcontinent", *The Times of India*, June 5, 1998.

On the Indian side, this doctrine has placed the enormous burden of building a credible deterrent for second-strike capability. The National Security Advisory Board (NSAB) prepared a draft nuclear doctrine and explained that the concept of a credible minimum deterrence would be based on a triad of nuclear forces comprising aircraft, mobile land-based missiles and sea-based assets. The doctrine was unpalatable to the United States, which saw in it a burgeoning arms race in the sub-continent. Even before a debate could be initiated on the draft doctrine—a document which was released by National Security Advisor Brajesh Mishra himself— the then Foreign Minister, Jaswant Singh, publicly rubbished the document. Instead, he left the question of India's nuclear forces sufficiently vague by saying that "the minimum nuclear deterrence was a dynamic concept firmly rooted in the strategic environment, technology imperatives and national security needs, and the actual size, components, deployment and employment of nuclear forces will be decided taking into account all these factors".

Implicit in Jaswant Singh's move was the indication that the government did not wish to sour relations with the US, and that the military would not be integrated into the nuclear weapons policy loop too soon. The government has since continued with an approach where only the political leadership, and select scientists from the Atomic Energy Commission, Bhabha Atomic Research Centre and the Defence Research and Development Organisation, have full knowledge of the Indian nuclear weapon capability. This mindset has resulted in the political leadership believing that nuclear weapons are mere political weapons to provide deterrence rather than for actual use. For this reason, India's political leadership has found it difficult to live with Pakistan's nuclear first-use policy, which suggests a use of nuclear weapons.

Size of Nuclear Arsenal

Four and a half years after the nuclear tests, the basic question is no longer why India conducted the Shakti tests, but whether it has undertaken follow-up actions necessary for national security. Knowledgeable people have given ample justification for the need for India to end the ambiguity in its nuclear weapons policy. For example, J. N. Dixit, a former foreign secretary, has given two reasons for

India's nuclear tests.[8] The first is that "there are a number of countries with a nuclear weapons presence in this entire region, one of
which Pakistan has threatened to use nuclear weapons missiles
capabilities against India more than once. Pakistan's relations with
other nuclear weapons powers such as China and the US cannot
be ignored by India". The second reason for the Shakti tests was
that "conducting the tests was necessary for India to ascertain for
itself what its capabilities were, to make the Indian public generally aware of these capabilities, and to impart a sense of confidence". In short, "the tests have infused a sense of confidence and
decisiveness in India's foreign and defence policies".

Leave alone the public at large, the biggest dilemma confront-
ing the military leadership has been that they are not well informed
about the country's nuclear weapons capabilities. The scientific
leadership has shared with the military only part, and not the
whole, of what constitutes nuclear deterrence. This obviously has
the nod from the political leadership, which has deliberately kept
the military on the fringes of the nuclear policy loop. Perhaps the
reason for doing so is that India's nuclear weapons capabilities
are not what have been proclaimed to be. In any case, there have
been hyped claims followed by meek clarifications which have
left people wondering about the truth. For example, even before
the dust kicked by the nuclear explosions had settled in the wide
expanse of the Pokhran desert, Dr. Kalam declared in a gung-ho
manner, "India's nuclear weaponisation is complete. We [India]
have the size, range, performance and the system management to
weaponise whatever is needed." Dr. Kalam's colleague, Dr. R.
Chidambaram, the chief nuclear scientist for the Shakti tests, was
more circumspect. According to the latter, India could make thermonuclear weapons of 200 kt yield. Dr. Chidambaram later
revised his position while addressing a select group of artillery
officers,[9] saying that the country could make thermonuclear
weapons of 300 kt yield.

Notwithstanding the constantly shifting positions regarding
nuclear weapons capabilities, India shocked the world when it

---

[8] Dixit, J. N. (2002), *India-Pakistan in War and Peace*, New Delhi: Books
Today, p. 333.
[9] During a conference at the School of Artillery, Devlali, November 7 and
8, 2001.

conducted a series of nuclear tests, and more so thereafter, when it declared what had been achieved by the tests. The three tests conducted on May 11, 1998, had yields of 0.2 kt, 15 kt, and 45 kt. The two tests on May 13, 1998, had yields of 0.3 kt and 0.5 kt. According to Drs. Chidambaram and Kalam, the tests achieved the following. First, they provided critical data for validation of capabilities in the design of nuclear weapons of different yields for different applications and different delivery systems. This implied that India could make nuclear weapons of a whole range of fission, thermonuclear and low-yield varieties termed Tactical Nuclear Weapons (TNWs). Except for the fission weapons, the other claims have been hotly contested by international scientists and especially Indians like Dr. P. K. Iyengar, a former director of the Atomic Energy Commission. Analysts who have been working on India's nuclear weapons capability believe that the fusion test was a failure.[10]

Second, the tests validated concepts for the long-term shelf life of device components and optimisation of the yield-to-weight ratio. Simply put, it meant that India could make optimised nuclear warheads of a wide variety for various operational needs with a long shelf life for mating with different delivery systems, notably ballistic missiles. And importantly, from the technical standpoint, India's computer simulation capabilities were claimed to have increased so much that it would now be possible to conduct sub-critical experiments of zero yield, should it become necessary.

What comes out unambiguously about the above claims and counterclaims is that after the Shakti tests, India does possess a reliable fission device capability which can be converted into high-assurance nuclear weapons. The yield of such weapons has been put at 15 to 20 kt. According to Western assessments, towards the end of 1999 India possessed between 240 to 395 kg of fissile plutonium which could be converted into 45 to 95 nuclear weapons.[11] Ironically, the Indian military launched into Operation Parakram knowing just so much about its own nuclear weapons capabilities. A senior general involved with the planning of Operation Parakram confirmed, in private, that the government had assured them of the existence of such a nuclear weapons capability within the country. Should Pakistan decide to exercise its nuclear weapons

---

[10] *Seminar*, September 2002, p. 74.
[11] "Nuclear Rivals", *The Economist* (newspaper), May 25, 2002, p. 27.

option, Indian scientists, in accordance with the country's second-strike nuclear policy, would be in a position to assemble nuclear weapons in a reasonable time frame for an assured retaliatory strike. The government further assured the military leadership that there would be adequate nuclear warning, and friendly nations had promised help in this regard.

However, this was what the military knew even before the Shakti tests. For instance, Prime Minister P. V. Narasimha Rao had instructed Dr. Kalam in April 1995 to set up a special cell at the DRDO to speed up efforts to build weapons—including storing the nuclear core in several strategic sights across the country and not just at Bhabha Atomic Research Centre in Trombay, and working out a mechanism of mating the core with its assembly in the shortest possible time when the need arose.[12] In operational terms, therefore, the Shakti tests did not amount to much. The military leadership knew as little and as vaguely about its own nuclear weapons as it did during the 1990 tension—supposedly the first crisis after Pakistan confirmed its covert nuclear weapons capability—between India and Pakistan.

Many reports in the media during Operation Parakram highlighted the anxiety of the Indian Army leadership regarding Pakistan's possible possession of TNWs. A recently retired general, Lt. Gen. B. D. Shekatkar, confirmed to a magazine[13] that Pakistan had TNW capability. Apparently, these have been given to Pakistan by China after India and Pakistan declared themselves as overt nuclear weapon states. (China is the only country besides the United States and Russia which has TNWs in its armoury. It is common knowledge that over 95 per cent of nukes with China are of a non-strategic variety, mated with its medium and short-range ballistic missiles.) A top serving general, on condition of anonymity, said that Pakistan may possess low yield nukes—between one to five kt. According to the same source, there was no information about Pakistan having sub-kt yield weapons, as China itself was unlikely to possess such sophisticated weapons; and if it did, it would be hesitant to pass it to Pakistan.

---

[12] Chengappa, Raj (2000), *Weapons of Peace*, New Delhi: Harper Collins Publishers India, p. 391.
[13] *Outlook*, June 10, 2002, p. 44.

TNWs are nuclear weapons with low yields of sub-kt to 10 kt suited for military targets. For example, a five kt yield TNW would bring about total destruction in a little over a one-mile radius. The sub-kt weapons with yields from 0.05 to 0.5 kt are also referred to as mini-nukes. Because TNWs are meant to inflict damage on a battlefield up to operational levels, in military parlance these are also called Theatre Nuclear Weapons. Belonging to the non-strategic category of nukes, TNWs are miniaturised weapons that can be delivered by short-range ballistic missiles, cruise missiles, air-to-surface and air-to-air missiles, artillery shells, and as atomic demolition munitions. As a rule of thumb, TNWs of lower yields are more complex, difficult and expensive to manufacture. Proponents of TNWs justify them on the following grounds:[14]

- They deter the use of TNWs by the enemy.
- They provide flexible response over the whole range of possible military threats.
- They offer nuclear military options below the strategic level.
- They help to defeat large-scale conventional attacks.

Built into the war scenario, it has been argued by defence analysts that if an Indian conventional assault manages to go deep inside Pakistan, the latter is likely to use TNWs to halt the Indian blitzkrieg. Another doomsday scenario depicted shows Pakistan using TNWs early in a war to pre-empt the Indian armoured columns from making headway inside Pakistani territory. Yet another scenario, the most dreaded one, shows TNWs in the hands of Islamised generals who could hold the entire region to ransom.

There are two presumptions in these scenarios: First, because Pakistan's conventional forces are inferior to India's, the former would neutralise its military weakness by employing nuclear weapons. Second, Pakistan would hesitate less to use its TNWs, meant for military targets, than strategic nukes meant for city busting that would cause enormous collateral damage. According to analysts, India's retaliatory massive nuclear strike would be assured if Pakistan undertook city busting. However, should Pakistan use its TNWs in self defence on its own soil, India may have second

---

[14] Kanwal, Gurmeet (2001), *Nuclear Defence*, New Delhi: Knowledge World, p. 94.

thoughts on its nuclear second strike. Herein lies the importance of the Pakistan Army's possession of TNWs.

Considering that the Indian political leadership has ruled out a possession of TNWs, which runs contrary to the stated no-first-use nuclear policy, analysts argue that India is at a grave disadvantage vis-à-vis Pakistan. The latter abides by a first-use or a nuclear-flexible response policy. In focused terms, the propounded single reason why India finds it difficult to go to war with Pakistan is that the latter has TNWs, which, unlike strategic nukes, are seen as usable weapons. The suggested Pakistani nuclear response appears plausible to analysts because Pakistan shares its nuclear first-use policy with the western powers. For example, during the Cold War, the Eastern Europe theatre was strewn with TNWs because the United States wanted to upset the Warsaw Pact conventional weapons superiority by an early use of TNWs.

Fortunately, the Indian military does not think like these analysts influenced by the West. First and foremost, there is nothing called a TNW in regional military thinking. Considering Pakistan's elongated geography and the fact that many of its high-value targets are close to the border, with a large population living in close proximity to the border on both sides, the defining line between strategic and tactical nuclear weapons is extremely blurred. Moreover, a TNW implies a decentralised command and control of nukes for timely action, something which the Pakistan General Headquarters would never do. This automatically precludes the possibility of nukes getting into the hands of Islamised generals.

Instead of TNWs, a more appropriate phrase in this context would be a "tactical use of nuclear weapons", suggesting both a tight command and control over nukes, and their likely use in a battlefield. The possibility, however, of Pakistan using nukes early in a war is virtually nil, considering that it matches India in conventional arms strength for a short-duration war. In military terminology, Pakistan enjoys parity with India at the operational level of war. The key issue for Pakistan is that the war should not exceed more than two weeks or so, as the chinks in its armour would start showing then. Pakistan, for this reason, has discarded a no-first-use nuclear policy. This does not mean it intends to use nukes early in a war, but Pakistan has ensured that in a war, the domestic and international pressure on India to end war at the earliest would be intense and swift. Considering that Pakistan is bleeding India white in a low-cost proxy war, this is exactly what Islamabad desires by its possession of nuclear weapons.

From Pakistan's perspective, the technological gains from its nuclear explosions on May 28 and 30, 1998, were of equal import as strategic considerations. As Prime Minister Nawaz Sharif declared, the explosions were conducted to restore the strategic balance with India. Moreover, according to analysts, "the test conducted on May 30 reportedly has a low, one to six kt yield. This test was of a better design and its aim was to test a warhead which could be fitted on a ballistic missile".[15]

It is an open secret that China passed on its fourth fission weapon's atmospheric test design of its Dong Feng-2A missile armed with nuclear warheads using Uranium 235 as fissile material to Pakistan. After Pakistan got a tested missile warhead design from China, its next problem was to reduce the weight of the original Chinese warhead. As the smallest nuclear devices are plutonium weapons, based on the critical mass of Plutonium 239, there arose the need to procure plutonium for missile warheads.

This was done in two stages: First, Pakistan opened the alternate route of plutonium by the mid-eighties. In addition to the plutonium production reactor at Khusab, a 300 MW plutonium extraction plant was set up at Chasma with Chinese help. Second, the break-up of the Soviet Union led to the disintegration of control, command and safeguard arrangements governing its nuclear material. Pakistan shopped extensively with Russia for plutonium, technology, and even for experts in nuclear engineering and weapon systems.[16] The clandestinely procured limited plutonium was employed by Pakistan to design composite cores containing a mix of both fissile materials—plutonium and enriched uranium—thereby reducing the overall weight of a nuclear missile warhead. The yield of the warhead was probably enhanced by employing tritium. There are confirmed reports that Pakistan received a tritium extraction plant from a company in Germany.[17]

---

[15] The Kargil Review Committee (2000), The Kargil Review Committee Report, New Delhi: Sage Publications, p. 196.

[16] Dixit, J. N. (1998), *Anatomy of a Flawed Inheritance*, New Delhi: Konarak, p. 187.

[17] Albright, D. and T. Zamora (1989), "India and Pakistan's Nuclear Weapons: All the Pieces in Place", Bulletin of Atomic Scientists, June, p. 21.

Pakistan's efforts for a better and reliable warhead for ballistic missiles finally attained fruition with its nuclear tests. Moreover, according to the Central Intelligence Agency in its annual 1999 report to Congress, a summary of which was published in the *Washington Times*, Chinese proliferation activities in Pakistan increased manifold since the 1998 nuclear tests, in violation of its 1996 pledge to stop assistance to Islamabad's nuclear and missile programmes. There was also a reference to the unsafe guarded plutonium production plant set up at Khusab in 1998 with Chinese help.

Delivery Systems

India announced its intention to make indigenous missiles in 1983 with the launch of an Integrated Guided Missiles Development Programme (IGMDP). The IGMDP was to develop a 2,500 km Agni IRBM, a 150 km Prithvi battlefield support missile, two quick-reaction surface-to-air Akash and Trishul missiles, and an anti-tank Nag missile. Subsequently, modifications were made in the programme for political and operational reasons. For example, Prithvi was decided to be made in three versions with a 1,000 kg payload: a 150 km battlefield missile, and a 250 km and 350 km medium-range missile. The 350 km missile called Dhanush was to be the naval version, while the 250 km one would go to the air force. Further, Akash was proposed to be modified for an anti-missile role. The Agni series has two versions: the Agni-II and the recently test fired Agni-I. Development work is said to be in progress on Agni-III, which will have a range of 3,500 km and is expected to be test fired towards the end of 2003. At present, except for the battlefield-support Prithvi missile and Agni-II,[18] all others missiles are at various development stages.

The battlefield-support Prithvi, with a 150 km range and carrying a payload of one ton, was inducted into the Army in 1994 as the 333 Missile Group under the newly raised 40 artillery division. Unfortunately, this Prithvi version has at least four technical and

---

[18] Government of India (2002), "Limited production of 2000 km range surface to surface missile Agni-II commenced and induction being planned", *Milestones of Success*, New Delhi: Ministry of Information and Broadcasting, GOI, October 15, p. 13.

maintenance limitations: First, at a time when most missiles the world over use solid propellants, Prithvi has a liquid propellant. The latter has a larger specific impulse and can deliver greater pay-loads to longer distances. However, liquid propellants, being highly corrosive, are difficult to handle in the field and during tactical movements. The trade-off is a solid fuel system's operational sim-plicity and faster reaction time for the liquid fuel system's supe-rior performance. This missile limitation could have been offset by regular training, which India, under US pressure, has never con-ducted for its army. Second, Prithvi lacks a proven terminal guid-ance system for accuracy. The suggested Prithvi consistency is a Circular Error Probability (CEP) of 150 m at its maximum range, implying that 82 per cent rounds will fall within a radius of 150 m if it is fired at a 150 km target. The best missile of the Prithvi class in the world is the Russian Tochkas, which has a 15 m CEP at 100 km.

Third, the Prithvi has a low terminal velocity, and hence its high-explosive monolith warheads will not be able to penetrate hardened fortifications on the border. The missile's other planned warheads like cluster sub-munitions and high-explosive earth shocks, which could be utilised against soft targets, are not ready. The reason for Prithvi's low terminal velocity is that unlike Pakistan's Ghaznavi, the body of Prithvi does not separate from the warhead, which results in low aerodynamic forces during its launch and the re-entry phase into the denser part of the atmosphere. Fourth, the distribution of a single weapon system to three services—the army, air force and navy—is an unnecessary strain on scarce resources and also causes maintenance problems. Nowhere in the world are surface-to-surface ballistic missiles in the armoury of any other service except the army.

The army is not unhappy with Prithvi's CEP, which is a closely guarded secret in the first place. Claims made in this regard vary from a CEP of 150 m to 25 m at maximum range. Noted scientist Dr. A. P. J. Abdul Kalam[19] suggested a 50 m CEP for the missile, while the Prithvi project director, Dr. V. K. Saraswat,[20] mentioned a 25 m CEP. Considering that the CEP is the measure of consistency, the army has reservations about the missile's accuracy. There is thus

---

[19] Kalam, A. P. J. Abdul (1999), *Wings of Fire*, New Delhi: University Press, p. 145.
[20] "Boosting the Arsenal", *India Today*, February 29, 1996.

a fear that the Prithvi, used with conventional warheads, may wreck unacceptable collateral damage due to the high population density on both sides of the Indo-Pak border.

The Army's opinion, therefore, is divided over the employment of Prithvi. A powerful section of the military feels that the missile should be used only with nuclear warheads. The argument is that because the missile travel time between India and Pakistan is less than five minutes, a conventional missile is likely to be mistaken for a nuclear one. Other reasons which collaborate this thinking are the limitations imposed on the use of Prithvi. The fire of the present Prithvi unit will be controlled by the army headquarters, keeping in mind the overall situation, likely enemy reaction, likely reaction of the international community, and the discussed technical and operational limitations of the weapon system. If the government has made up its mind that Prithvi will be used only with a nuclear warhead, there is little need to have it in large numbers.

Ground realities, however, tell a different story. The government has cleared the raising of at least two more Prithvi missile groups, which indicates a more widespread use for the missile. Senior army personnel feel that Prithvi should be used in a conventional mode for interdiction purposes on targets like bridges and ammunition dumps to both supplement the Air Force and relieve it for strategic tasks. An alternative employment of Prithvi could be for harassment purposes which would have a damming psychological effect on the enemy.[21] This would indeed be a novel employment, considering that firepower is traditionally expected to bring destruction and attrition alone. A section of officers opine that in the absence of a formal missile understanding or a missile stabilisation regime with Pakistan, there is a need for the government to declare that Prithvi would not be used with nuclear warheads for deterrent purposes. This opinion gains credence as the DRDO has started work on replacing the liquid propellant of Prithvi with solid fuel, which, once accomplished, would require less preparation time, have a much longer shelf life and be quicker to respond.

The Agni IRBM missile is yet to enter service. On May 31, 2001, the then defence minister, Jaswant Singh, had announced to a meeting of the Defence Consultative Committee that a limited

---

[21] A proponent of this thinking is the recently retired vice-chief of army staff, Lt. Gen. V. K. Oberai.

serial production of Agni-II had begun, and the IRBM would enter service in 2002. According to a government report released by Deputy Prime Minister L. K. Advani on October 13, 2002, the Agni-II still awaits induction.[22] The army, which will receive the IRBM, has got clearance from the government to raise an Agni Missile Group—work on which has already begun.

The Agni-II is reportedly mobile through both rail and road, has a two-stage solid propellant rocket motor with a strap-down Inertial Navigation System, and has achieved a range of 2,000 km with a one-ton payload. After two successful test flights, the government decided to induct Agni-II into the army as "the weapon is a land-based deterrent and only the Army has the logistics strength to handle the missile".[23] India also test fired a shorter-range version of the Agni series, called Agni-I, on January 25, 2002. This single-stage missile powered by solid propellant fuel has a range of 700 km with a payload of one ton. Defence Minister George Fernandes informed the Parliament that Agni-I would have one more test before getting into production and induction modes.[24] When in service, Agni-I will fill the operational gap between the Prithvi-II missile, with a range of 250 km, and Agni-II.

During Operation Parakram, only Prithvi was in service for India. Considering the debate on the employment of Prithvi, and the tight control imposed on its firepower by the government, India's preferred nuclear weapons delivery system would have been aircraft—MiG-27, Mirage-2000H and Jaguar. The recently inducted limited numbers of SU 30MKI aircraft, of course, were not available at that time for the nuclear role.

Pakistan, in comparison, has a wide variety of proven missiles. In early 1989, the Army Chief, Gen. Aslam Beg, surprised the world by announcing a sudden breakthrough in making ballistic missiles. Pakistan's interim prime minister, Moeenuddin Qureshi admitted in 1992 that between 1989 and 1992, China gave certain missiles to Pakistan which did not transgress the Missile Technology Control Regime. These were Abdali or Hatf-II missiles with a range of 80 km carrying a 1000 kg payload. Between 1991 and 1994, China

---

[22] GOI (1998), cited in note 18 above.

[23] Gupta, Shishir, "Air Battles", *India Today*, August 20, 2001.

[24] "Agni-I will be Inducted Soon", *The Times of India*, July 25, 2002.

gave at least 84 M-11 missiles to Pakistan, which came to the notice of US intelligence services. To take the US heat off China, Pakistan let these missiles remain in crates near Sargoda and, with China's approval, established contacts with North Korea in 1993 to buy its ballistic missiles. Pakistan bought 12 North Korean two-stage, liquid-propellant No Dong-I missiles and renamed them Hatf-V or Ghauri-I. Similarly, certain numbers of longer-range No Dong-II missiles were purchased and called Hatf-VI or Ghauri-II.

By late 1997, Pakistan had acquired the manufacturing capability of M-11, a mobile, solid-propellant missile capable of carrying a 500 to 700 kg warhead to a range of 290 km, and renamed it Hatf-III. A missile production unit was set up at Fateh Jung under the aegis of the National Development Complex with Chinese help. In addition to Ghaznavi, this production unit made the smaller-range Abdali missiles as well. Also commissioned in 1997 was a solid-fuel plant to manufacture all key solid-fuel ingredients.

Beginning 1998, Pakistan embarked on a twin approach regarding ballistic missiles. The Khan Research Laboratories under Dr. A. Q. Khan was responsible for improving the liquid-propellant Ghauri series, or No Dong missiles. The National Development Complex under Dr. Samar Mubarakmand was asked to work on the solid-propellant Shaheen series with Chinese help. Shaheen-I, re-named Hatf-IV, with a range of 700 km and a 1000 kg payload, was fired by Pakistan on April 15, 1999. The need for the twin channel arose because the US was keeping a close watch on Chinese proliferation, and the Pakistan government was encouraging an intense competition between its two competing scientific establishments, Khan Research Laboratories and National Development Complex. In sum, Ghaznavi and Abdali have been in production in Pakistan since 1998. The longer-range Ghauri and Shaheen series are available in limited numbers and have been improved upon with China's help.

Two other areas of Chinese assistance in missile and nuclear weapons to Pakistan deserve attention. Unlike Prithvi, Ghaznavi and Abdali use a solid propellant and have proven guidance and control systems acquired from China. Similarly, unlike Agni, which uses a strap-down Inertial Navigation System, Pakistan's long-range missiles have improved INS procured from China. The best of the strap-down INS are known to provide an acceptable accuracy only up to 1,500 km, beyond which an improved INS is needed. China is known to have mastered the INS technology for its DF-5 ICBM sometime in the late eighties. The second issue relates to Pakistan's nuclear weapons. Unlike India, which has never tested a nuclear warhead for missiles after it closed its option by signing the 1993 Partial Test Ban Treaty, Pakistan has a proven, dynamically tested nuclear missile warhead design, which has been further refined by its 1998 nuclear tests. Therefore, unlike India, Pakistan's preferred nuclear delivery system will be its unstoppable long-range ballistic missiles, the Ghauri and Shaheen series, in addition to the aircraft.

Regarding the employment of ballistic missiles with conventional warheads, it would, amongst other factors, depend upon numbers available with both sides. It sounds ironic that India, which first started the indigenisation of its Prithvi, may not have more numbers than Pakistan's comparable missile. India's Prithvi production has been controlled because the user was unhappy with the limitations. Further, between 1991 and 1996, when Pakistan was struggling to clandestinely acquire the manufacturing capability of M-11, the Indian government succumbed to US pressure on Pakistan's persuasion to go slow with Prithvi testing.

Pakistan, under the circumstances, is likely to use its ballistic missiles both in the pre-emptive mode in conjunction with its air force, and also reactively as the intentions of India's strike forces become clear. The first option will help Pakistan to offset the inferiority of its air force vis-à-vis the Indian Air Force. Under joint battlefield air interdiction programmes, Pakistan will use its missiles against headquarters, artillery and tank concentrations, and logistics nodes. This would help the Pakistan Army tremendously, as the air effort is usually not available for two important interdiction tasks because of the limited air force resources of both countries: handling enemy artillery and tackling a series of land objectives, and shifting of enemy reserves in a contiguous corps zone. Considering that the expected battles would be fluid, flexible and with a shallow penetration, a sizeable use of ballistic missiles would keep enemy commanders on tenterhooks.

The basic difference between the use of ballistic missiles by both sides will be governed by their respective mindsets. Pakistan will use its ballistic missiles aggressively and liberally to make up for its shortcomings in air power and land-based firepower. India, on the other hand, will remain conscious of the fact that Pakistan does not subscribe to the nuclear no-first-use doctrine, and that the two countries should have entered into a missile stabilisation regime in order to set out mutually acceptable ground rules.

Nuclear Command and Control

Pakistan has always given importance to nuclear command and control apparatus, which in essence is about an effective and fool-proof management and delivery of nuclear assets. Immediately after the nuclear tests, Pakistan's former army chief, Gen. Mirza Aslam Beg, claimed that the nation had formed a formal National Nuclear Command Authority under the prime minister. The latter, however, had delegated full authority to carry out a nuclear strike to the army chief. Considering that Prime Minister Nawaz Sharif had garnered sufficient constitutional clout during his last days in office, Gen. Beg's announcement sounded plausible.

One of the first tasks of the National Security Council in Pakistan, which was formed after Gen. Musharraf usurped power on October 12, 1999, was to create a command and control structure for nuclear weapons. The London-based *Jane's Defence Weekly*[25] reported that Pakistan had announced the formation of a National Command Authority (NCA) headed by the head of government on February 2, 2000. The NCA would be responsible for policy formulation and would exercise employment and development control over all strategic nuclear forces and strategic organisations.

The NCA has two committees—the Employment Control Committee (ECC) and the Development Control Committee (DCC). As the apex body for nuclear decision-making, the ECC is headed by Gen. Musharraf. This committee has the foreign minister as its deputy chairman, and includes the defence and interior ministers, the Chairman of the Joint Chiefs of Staff committee (CJCSC), the three chiefs of staff, director general of the Strategic Plans Division and representatives from strategic organisations. The DCC, meant for developing nuclear weapons, and delivery and auxiliary command, control and intelligence systems, is also headed by Gen.

[25] Farooq, Umar (2000), "Pakistan Tests New Missiles and Revises Command Structures", *Jane's Defence Weekly*, February 16, p. 26.

Musharraf, with the CJCSC as its deputy chairman. A Strategic Plans Division, headed by a lieutenant general, was established at the joint services headquarters to provide secretariat support for the NCA and its two committees. A Strategic Force Command (SFC), which heads the nuclear forces, is reportedly commanded by Lt. Gen. S. M. Amjad. Pakistan reportedly has a National Command Post (NCP) at Faisalabad and an alternative site at the air force base in Chaklala. Its biggest advantage is that its military, which will use nuclear weapons in case the need arises, knows and controls all nuclear weapons capabilities. It is an open secret that though the head of government heads the NCA, his role is notional rather than real. The real authority regarding all aspects of strategic assets undoubtedly rests with President Musharraf.

In India, nuclear command and control is as nebulous as any other aspect of the nation's strategic assets. A few months after the nuclear tests, a journalist close to the government[26] disclosed that the Chiefs of Staff Committee had approved a comprehensive paper prepared by the defence planning staff and had forwarded it to the government for approval. The salient points of this paper are worth mentioning:

- The government should set up a National Strategic Nuclear Command (NSNC)—a tri-service organisation including experts from related fields like atomic energy, defence research and development, telecommunications, and information technology.
- An NCA headed by the prime minister needs to be formed. The NCA should comprise the prime minister, the ministers for defence, external affairs, home and finance, the national security advisor, the Chiefs of Staff Committee, and the general commanding officer of the NSNC.
- An NCP should be set up.
- The tasking of tactical nuclear weapons should be done by the operational commands of the three services in consultation with the NSNC.

---

[26] Singh, Manvendra (1998), "Who Should Control Nuclear Button? Armed Forces Have a Proposal", *The Indian Express*, September 1, 1998. Manvendra Singh is Finance Minister Jaswant Singh's son.

While the authenticity of the above paper was never ascertained, the draft nuclear doctrine prepared by the NSAB with government backing emphasised the importance of a credible nuclear command and control infrastructure, especially for a second-strike capability. This, however, was found too ambitious by the US and the government decided to place it in deep freeze. However, when asked, the government has been quick to declare that India does have a nuclear command and control infrastructure according to its own needs. What remains baffling is how it intends to have an assured second-strike capability when the basic institutions and infrastructure needed for nuclear weapons are not in place.

Let us take the institutions first. The biggest lacuna has probably been the non-creation of the post of Chief of Defence Staff (CDS). The recommendation of the Group of Ministers, which was released by Home Minister L. K. Advani in February 2001, mentions: "The Chiefs of Staff Committee has not been effective in fulfilling its mandate. It needs to be strengthened by a CDS and a Vice-CDS." Besides various other functions, the CDS would exercise administrative control over nuclear and strategic forces through the office of a Strategic Forces Command, and thus would provide single-point military advice to the government. To be designated as the "Principal Military Advisor" to the defence minister, the CDS, as the bridge between the civilian political leadership and the military, would assist in all areas of nuclear strategy, force structure and, importantly, operations. Regarding nuclear strategy and force structure, the CDS would provide valuable military advice to the civilian leadership, which comprises generalists and technocrats from the scientific community. Nuclear operations, which would include targeting, deployment, the state of alert and readiness, and what mix of weapons and delivery systems to use—after the use of nuclear weapons has been authorised by the political executive—are all military decisions best left to military professionals.[27]

Instead of the CDS staff, the government did a U-turn and created a post called Chief of Integrated Defence Staff, which was not even mentioned in the Group of Ministers report. Speaking to

---

[27] Kanwal, Gurmeet, (2001), *Nuclear Defence*, New Delhi: Knowledge World, p. 146.

the media in September 2002, on the completion of a year since inception, the Chief of the Integrated Defence Staff (CIDS), Lt. Gen. Pankaj Joshi, expressed his inability to answer questions regarding the creation of a Chief of Defence Staff (CDS). However, he said that a Strategic Force Command (SFC), with all nuclear delivery assets under its administrative control, would be raised soon. The general further clarified that the three tasks of the CIDS, namely, management of defence with the government, administration of defence with the defence ministry, and management of war-fighting within the armed forces, were progressing satisfactorily. The general was simply flying kites, and hoping that none in the media would pip him to the post. While he succeeded that day, the armed forces as a whole lost because of the infighting and succumbing to political pressure.

Just as no organisation can function without a head, India's nuclear weapons status is both meaningless and dangerous without a CDS. Such a head alone can fulfil the three suggested tasks because he, unlike a CIDS, will not report to the three service chiefs, but would be senior to them. This status of CDS is silently unacceptable to the service chiefs as they see him usurping their powers regarding defence management and management of war-fighting over a period of time. This weakness of the services has been exploited by the political leadership to defer the creation of a CDS.

Even though the government agreed to the creation of a CDS, it later developed cold feet. Once the CDS came into being, the government, sooner rather than later, would be obliged to share the nation's nuclear weapons capabilities with him. The government is hesitant to do so because the capabilities may not exactly be what have been suggested. Until a CDS is formed, an SFC is optimally unrealisable. A CDS alone should have administrative control over the SFC, which could have two organisational options. Either all nuclear delivery assets could come under the SFC, which is an expensive and unaffordable proposition, or it could provide the secretariat to the CDS on nuclear operational aspects, while nuclear assets remain with the respective services.

There is also a need for a credible National Command Authority (NCA). Simply saying that the final authority to use nuclear weapons rests with the prime minister is not enough. The prime minister heads the Cabinet Committee on Security (CCS), which is the highest decision-making body. However, the CCS needs regular professional advice on all matters of national security and, most importantly, on nuclear aspects. This can be achieved by a National Security Council (NSC) that has the same composition as the CCS plus the National Security Advisor and the Deputy Chairman of the Planning Commission. The present NSC has three grave shortcomings which render it ineffective. First, the NSC does not have an independent secretariat, as the erstwhile Joint Intelligence Committee has been reconstituted as the NSC secretariat. Second, while the post of NSA should be a full-time job, the present incumbent, Brajesh Mishra, doubles as the principle secretary to the prime minister. And third, the weakest link of the NSC is its third tier, the National Security Advisory Board (NSAB), which is a conglomeration of outside experts with little access to official thinking and documents.

The shortcomings of the NSC need to be removed, a CDS as an independent channel of military advice to the defence minister needs to be created, and the devolution of command of the NSA needs to be put down in writing. Even if this is being done to maintain secrecy, the Parliament should be informed that such precedence in writing does indeed exist.

In addition to the NCA, which codifies the civil-military relations for nuclear weapon purposes, there is a need to create a secure infrastructure for the NCA in the shape of a National Command Post (NCP). This becomes more urgent considering that India has adopted a nuclear no-first-use policy. The importance of an NCP, where the entire nuclear command authority would be moved during the warning period prior to the outbreak of hostilities, can hardly be overemphasised. The NCP should be spacious enough to accommodate the entire CCS, the NSA, the cabinet secretary, and the CDS/Chiefs of Staff Committee, with the accompanying operational and intelligence directorates. Considering that in the event of a nuclear strike the present North and South block buildings would constitute ground zero, the NCP should be located at a safe distance, preferably outside Delhi. Till an NCP is constituted, there is a need for an interim NCP, which, according to reports, has been established "somewhere in the vicinity of the prime minister's office in Delhi".[28] If true, this is indeed dangerous as

---

[28] "India's Nuclear Doctrine Unclear", *Jane's Defence Weekly*, October 18, 2000.

even an underground location at the suggested ground zero location may not be capable of withstanding a 20 kt blast from a ground burst. There are, however, conflicting indications on the NCP. Some senior army officers say that it exists and is capable of withstanding up to 20 kt-yield nukes. Others opine that nothing of this sort exists, as plans have yet not moved beyond the consultation stage.

A leading US analyst, Dr. Ashley J. Tellis, is of the opinion that a static NCP is not a good idea. Making a hardened NCP, say, 60 m below the surface, and ensuring that communications from such a structure are not vulnerable to interdiction would be a Herculean task. There is also the problem of maintaining secrecy of the location from Pakistan. Dr. Tellis feels that there would be technical, operational and financial hurdles for India if it decides to make static command posts which can withstand a 15 to 29 kt nuclear blast or the US B61-11 earth-penetrating nuclear warhead. He suggests three alternate options. The first and the most burdensome solution consists of configuring some kind of airborne command post. This could be done with assistance from Russia and Israel.

The second option is to upgrade all "communication suites, resident databases, and mission-planning equipment in existing Indian operations rooms to serve as nuclear command posts in an emergency. While these centres are no doubt soft targets that can readily be interdicted, upgrading all of them would diminish the problem of command vulnerability simply by increasing redundancy."[29] The benefit of this option would be that command posts in far-flung operations rooms at various command levels could be used as alternate nuclear command posts, a move which would help maintain operational secrecy vis-à-vis Pakistan. The third option would be to develop a mobile, land-based command post. The advantage of this would be that mobile command posts would be equipped with all manner of long-distance, beyond-the-line-of-sight wireless communication equipment on board. In addition, their movements would be relatively difficult to track in real time and, built in sufficient numbers, they could allow for redundancy. It becomes obvious that whatever choices for NCP the government adopts, there must be enough inbuilt operational secrecy

---

[29] Tellis, J. Ashley (2001), *India's Emerging Nuclear Posture*, New Delhi: Oxford University Press, p. 590.

and secure communications, especially when links would have to be established with far-flung centres that have warheads and delivery systems. Although cost would always be an inhibiting factor, what needs to be clarified is that a credible nuclear deterrent is as much about nuclear warheads and tested delivery systems as it is about a reliable command and control infrastructure.

Threshold Factor

India's political leadership came face-to-face with Pakistan's nuclear threat during Operation Parakram. Prime Minister Vajpayee said at the United Nations on September 18, 2002, that Pakistan was using nuclear blackmail to support terrorism. Ironically, within hours of its May 1998 nuclear tests, India had done exactly that: Home Minister Advani declared that Pakistan would have to review its support to terrorists in Kashmir. The question to be asked is what happened since May 1998 for the Indian political leadership to feel the heat of Pakistan's nuclear blackmail.

Similarly, four and a half years after the nuclear tests by India and Pakistan, the then Indian presidential candidate, Dr A. P. J. Abdul Kalam—who had steered the controversial Defence Research and Development Organisation for seven long years from 1992 to 1999 and was a key architect of the Shakti tests—told the media on June 19, 2002 that "nuclear weapons had helped avert war". He was referring to Operation Parakram, and few questioned Dr. Kalam's pronouncement. Considering that India, and not Pakistan, was supposedly poised to launch a military campaign inside PoK, how was a turning back because of the nuclear weapons factor to India's advantage? A better interpretation of Dr. Kalam's announcement would be that nuclear weapons poured cold water on India's offensive military plans.

Fortunately, the Indian military leadership does not share Dr. Kalam's conviction because it knows that in the context of India and Pakistan, a conventional war and a nuclear exchange are two separate entities. Irrespective of differing nuclear declaratory doctrines, both sides would resort to nuclear weapons under extreme compulsion. This is apparent as both sides spend scarce finances to not only maintain large conventional forces, but also ensure that asymmetry in conventional levels does not happen. The key for both sides in avoiding a nuclear war is to maintain competitive conventional forces, which, surprisingly, have similar operational stances and war doctrines. Fortunately, neither side views nuclear weapons as a replacement for conventional military strength.

India's weakness vis-à-vis Pakistan, however, stems from the fact that unlike Pakistan, its military has minimal knowledge about its own nuclear weapons capabilities. On the other hand, the political leadership, which knows these capabilities, does not understand the military's conventional capabilities and rarely consults them on nuclear matters. This wide gap has resulted in different thinking on the nuclear threshold factor by the two. The military understands that a conventional war with reasonable political aims and achievable military objectives is possible with Pakistan below the nuclear threshold level; the political leadership thinks otherwise.

Surprisingly, the political leadership's fear of nuclear weapons rubbed off on the military brass during the 1999 Kargil war. This was an occasion when the political and military leaders were meeting on a daily basis and having regular consultations about the conduct of war with Pakistan. According to the then Army Vice-Chief, Lt. Gen. Vijai Oberai,[30] the Army Chief, Gen. V. P. Malik sent a confidential letter to his army commanders stating, "nuclear weapons are political weapons and will not be used in war-fighting". Two aspects about nukes were troubling the army chief. There was a need to assure his command that the military leadership did not believe Pakistan would use nuclear weapons in a war. However, the political leadership's repeated apprehensions on the matter could not be dismissed out of hand. In addition to this dilemma, the army chief was probably not sure of the scientific community's capabilities to deliver on time, should the need arise.

It is one thing to have a weaponised and ready or unweaponised and dormant deterrence; it is quite another to have a credible nuclear deterrence. Dr. Ashley Tellis has praised India's unique nuclear weapons posture, calling it "strategically active and operationally dormant". Explained in general terms, it means that all elements of nuclear weaponisation have been accomplished, but have not been assembled as a whole. The nuclear cores are in the custody of the Bhabha Atomic Research Centre, the non-nuclear

---

[30] In an interview with the co-author of this book.

components are with the Defence Research and Development Organisation, and the delivery systems are with the defence services. What Dr. Tellis does not mention is that such a position was attained even before the 1998 nuclear tests. What is needed now is a credible nuclear deterrent. The answer lies in having greater transparency. Such transparency will provide more assurance to both the military and political leadership, and help the country negotiate better with Pakistan on nuclear risk reduction and confidence building regarding ballistic missiles.

Summary

- The nuclear weapons factor worked to Pakistan's favour during Operation Parakram. India's political leadership was worried that Pakistan had a lower nuclear threshold.
- India had only the Prithvi missile as compared to a range of proven ballistic missiles in Pakistan's possession.
- Pakistan's preferred nuclear delivery system would have been its unstoppable ballistic missiles, in addition to aircraft. India would have relied on its aircraft alone for a nuclear mission.
- Pakistan was expected to use its ballistic missiles aggressively, with both conventional and nuclear warheads.
- India's biggest drawback vis-à-vis Pakistan is that its military is not fully in the nuclear weapons policymaking loop.
- India needs both a CDS and a credible nuclear command and control system.

6

Conventional Prowess: Truths and Untruths

Professionals acknowledge that India's edge in conventional military capabilities over Pakistan is slender. According to the Kargil Review Committee Report, "On the Indian side, it had been made abundantly clear that the Indian Army has not for sometime enjoyed a punitive edge over the Pakistan Army to adopt an effective proactive strategy."[1] A more definitive assertion comes from the army doctrine written under the aegis of the Army Training Command (ARTAC): "On our Western borders [with Pakistan], a conventional conflict would probably be fought under conditions of near parity, both in qualitative and quantitative terms."[2]

After the spending spree of the eighties under Prime Minister Rajiv Gandhi and Army Chief Gen. K. Sundarji, the annual defence budget was given short shrift by Gandhi's successors. According to a former Army Chief, Gen. S. Roychowdhury, "It was more than obvious that when the Narasimha Rao government embarked on its economic liberalisation back in the nineties, it also quietly pushed issues like defence and national security very low down on its list of priorities."[3] He adds, "Our [army's] detailed assessments

[1] The Kargil Review Committee (2000), *The Kargil Review Committee Report*, New Delhi: Sage Publications, p. 77.
[2] Headquarters, Army Training Command (1998), *Fundamentals, Doctrine and Concepts: Indian Army*, Shimla: Headquarters, Army Training Command, p. 57.
[3] Roychowdhury, Shankar (2002), *Officially at Peace*, New Delhi: Viking, p. 156.

of national security, repeatedly presented to Narasimha Rao and his successive prime ministers, as well as to Mulayam Singh Yadav during his tenure as defence minister, could well have been scripts for Bollywood fantasies for all the attention that was paid to them." The general further says that, "Our apparent tolerance towards Pakistan's provocations and blatant terrorist attacks was actually due to the run-down in our military capabilities for decisive puni-tive action, caused by the government's economic preoccupation with the demands and compulsions of a free market economy. Effective counter-offensive capabilities were the precise area where the Indian Army's potential had been greatly eroded."[4]

Even as poor defence spending eroded the military's conven-tional capabilities, three developments in the nineties compounded the troubles of the defence forces: Pakistan started a proxy war in J&K, ballistic missiles between India and Pakistan arrived on the scene, and both countries conducted nuclear tests and declared themselves as nuclear weapon states. Hence, instead of being ready to fight a high-intensity war with Pakistan, India was forced to prepare for the entire spectrum of war scenarios: a low-intensity war, which could lead to a high-intensity conventional war, and a possible nuclear exchange.

Moreover, as a consequence of reduced defence budgets, India was compelled to look inwards for procurements. Indigenisation became the buzzword. The Defence Research and Development Organisation (DRDO), with an uninspiring track record, suddenly assumed an added importance. Instead of giving the DRDO a shake-up and seeking technical reviews of some of its high-profile projects, the government went about pampering them in the hope that they would deliver. The defence services were forced to dilute general staff qualitative requirements for indigenous weapon sys-tems, strike deals for imports by accepting sub-standard comparable indigenous items, and waylay urgent modernisations. The DRDO's stature, on the other hand, rose sharply. Irrespective of operational requirements, the DRDO became the final authority in deciding which weapon systems would be imported or made in the country.

Common sense demanded that India seriously review its national security perspective to meet new threats and accompanying

---

[4] *Ibid.*, p. 158.

challenges, and look afresh at the gamut of procurements, including indigenisation. However, what happened was just the opposite. Prime Minister A. B. Vajpayee said after the 1998 nuclear tests that a Strategic Defence Review (SDR) would be conducted to obtain a holistic view of India's military threats and security challenges. This was undertaken by the National Security Advisory Board—a motley gathering of retired bureaucrats, military officers and experts with little access to official thinking and documents—which completed its task in March 1999. The SDR, however, was never made public. Under criticism, the government declared that the SDR needed an upgrade by the NSAB and, once completed, it would be called the National Security Review.

The 1999 Kargil war, meanwhile, jolted the existing ad hoc regime on national security to an extent. Under severe domestic criticism, the government constituted the Kargil Review Committee in July 1999 with a limited mandate to look into the episode. Following the committee's recommendation, the government formed four task forces—border management, defence management, intelligence, and internal security—which led to the Group of Ministers (GOM) recommendations made public in February 2001. Even though the implementation of the GOM recommendations has been slow and piecemeal, the government did not miss the opportunity to announce, on the completion of its three years in office in October 2002, that national security has been its primary achievement. The truth is that in the absence of a holistic security review, and a comprehensive policy which takes into account the changed and new threats and challenges, the defence forces have been weakened.

Instead of wholeheartedly addressing the need to strengthen the nuclear and conventional capabilities of the armed forces, the debate in India has been on how warfare has changed in a nuclear environment. This would have been fine provided analysts knew what exactly India's nuclear capabilities are. Pakistan, meanwhile, has diligently focused on two tracks. On the one hand, it has made known through its diplomats and analysts, both civilian and military, that its putative nuclear first-use policy should not be undermined. An impression has been created that Pakistan could use its nuclear weapons in a variety of ways: in a pre-emptive mode, early in a war, when the going gets tough, or when ultimately pushed to the wall by India's conventional forces. This has instilled uncertainty amongst Indian planners, and especially the political leadership which believes that Pakistan's rash military leadership cannot be trusted with nuclear weapons.

Pakistan's military leadership, meanwhile, understands the need to have a separate nuclear and conventional deterrent against India. In common terms, it means four things. First, Pakistan must maintain a credible strategic parity with India in nuclear weapons and delivery systems. Second, Pakistan should maintain an operational level parity vis-à-vis India in conventional forces. Third, the escalation of a conventional war to a nuclear one can be prevented once Pakistan has accomplished the first two requirements. And fourth, such deterrence gives Pakistan adequate space and manoeuvrability to continue with its low-cost proxy war in J&K.

Operational-Level Parity

The operational level is the intermediate level of war between strategic and tactical levels, and helps translate strategic aims into a workable military method of war-fighting in a theatre. It is provided with the requisite military assets for this purpose by the strategic level. The tactical level, therefore, refers to a single battle, while the operational level implies a war which is a series of battles. The operational level can be successful because of good firepower, coordination, training and surprise, in spite of lesser overall numbers of manpower and equipment. Translated into military terminology, these levels refer to an "offensive" and an "attack". The former is undertaken by the strategic and operational levels of war, and the latter by tactical-level formations. While an "attack" is advocated to be launched with a numerical superiority of 3:1, successful "offensives" have been launched with parity.

In India, this level of war was reassessed by the Army Training Command in 1998:

> In limited or general war, the regional Command is the operational level since it is responsible for the design and control of operations, allocating specific and limited tactical missions to the corps under its control. The corps is the highest level tactical formation which has no fixed establishment, but which holds reserves of supporting arms, particularly of artillery,

*engineers and aviation, which may be allotted to divisions
temporarily for specific operations. The corps commander's
ability to concentrate these arms for particular tasks and to
commit a reserve of a division or more gives him the means to
influence the battle in a decisive fashion.*[5]

In Pakistan, the General Headquarters (GHQ) directly controls the
field forces through the 9 Corps headquarters. This is an unwieldy
arrangement, as vast field forces are controlled by a monolith GHQ.
In operational terms, this has been an abiding source of interfer-
ence in combat operations at tactical levels by the GHQ. During
exercise Zerb-e-Momin in 1989, intermediate headquarters Army
Reserves North and Army Reserves South were tested to control certain number of corps: HQ ARN controlled 1, 30 and 4 Corps, and
HQ ARS headed 2, 31 and 5 Corps. While this operational concept
found favour with the GHQ, it was thought imprudent to permanently create the post of a regional operational boss akin to India's
general-officer-commanding-in-chief or regional operational
commander. The official explanation that the creation of ARN and
ARS headquarters was impossible in the light of financial constraints is a spurious one. The real reason is that the army chief
prefers the 9 Corps commanders to be under him, rather than the
two powerful regional commanders. However, Pakistan has sought
to meet this operational requirement by regular training.

In addition, both armies have adopted a peculiar operational-level
stance. Serious scholars who study the two armies are astonished
to find a tremendous amount of combat power locked into pure
forward defences. The reason for this is that both the militaries
have no option when faced with a similar unspoken political term
of reference: No loss of territory is acceptable in the politically
vital areas of Punjab and the state of J&K. Both armies therefore
display an identical operational-level stance. Corps-level formations in both armies have a nomenclature which is unique in name
and role in the world.

The first are called the Holding Corps. These are defensive in
nature, with very limited offensive capabilities. Except for absorbing an enemy offensive, this force is not employed to its full during

---

[5] Headquarters, Army Training Command (1998), cited in note 2 above,
p. 54.

an all-out war. The holding formations are capable only of launching limited local attacks to straighten out bulges and enclaves on the Line of Control. These also help the strike formations by stepping up and manning obstacles breached by them, so that strike formations do not fritter away their strength. However, these forces cannot be used for the initial build-up of assault troops.

In addition, both armies have strike or offensive corps. These are heavy formations built around an armoured division and are supported by infantry divisions, reinforced general support artillery, engineers in brigade strength (as corps troops), a transport column, etc. These forces are fully mobile on tracks or wheels, and can establish a bridgehead across a manned obstacle and break out against an opposition at least into the operational depth. These troops can also be used to restore an adverse situation by mounting a general counter-attack. This task would not be undertaken unless the enemy achieves full strategic surprise, which is unlikely. In addition to the strike formations, both countries have a few infantry formations as army or theatre reserves, capable of both defending a corridor left behind by the fast moving armoured and mechanised formations, and providing logistics to these strike formations.

The extreme forward defensive operational stance adopted by both countries is based on built-up, heavily fortified linear obstacles called Ditch-Cum-Bandh—irrigation canals converted for defence with the home bank raised, or nodal point defences in deserts where a chain of water and communication centres are held in strength with concrete bunkers and pill boxes and linked with a defensive minefield. Called DCB by India and the canal defences line by Pakistan, it has a continuous minefield along the far side to a depth of 1,000 m to 2,000 m. Twin obstacles of this nature have come up in sensitive defended sectors, and in some areas yet another minefield may be found hugging the home side.

Additional strengthening comes from a combination of the following factors: the border outposts on both sides are reinforced to provide early warning; all appreciated approaches expected to provide a black-top road (tracks for corps logistics) on the home side for a likely break-out have delaying/advanced positions turned into strong points; beyond the minefield(s), a surveillance screen of small teams carrying automatic weapons and anti-tank rocket launchers has been established; machine gun nests are interspersed within the minefields; and concrete bunkers embedded irregularly on the far side, and more evenly on the near side, are impervious to direct hits by medium/heavy artillery shells or even conventional 450 kg bombs. Further, the bunkers are camouflaged and blend well with the DCB or irrigation canal defence and are extremely difficult to spot.

These elaborate defences have been built over decades. The philosophy of such a linear deployment was suggested by the US to Field Marshal Ayub Khan. It was argued that a good way to offset the perceived numerical superiority of India was for Pakistan to focus on the quality of equipment and to "hold ground by firepower". These linear defences are meant to ensure that the enemy is not given a free run, provided a 12- to 24-hour warning is given to holding formations, which is not difficult. The enemy's main effort would be easily identifiable, as the time taken to breach and then establish a strong bridgehead will give the opposing operational commander time to gather his wits and sift information to identify the main attack from secondary ones or other deceptive measures. Thereafter, resources could be released to form mobile strike force(s) for pre-emption or a reactive counter-offensive.

Unlike the Maginot line, which was outflanked, or the Saddam line in Kuwait, which collapsed on contact with the allied forces in the 1991 Gulf war, the linear defence line between India and Pakistan is formidable. A hardened concrete construction, it cannot be outflanked because it is a continuous stretch of over 2,000 kilometres from Chammb in J&K to the middle of Rajasthan. These obstacles are of the terrain model, around which integrated combined arms deployments are effected, both against ground and air threats of considerable magnitude.

A vertical envelopment of this defence line is not possible for either country as it would require assets of the scale of the US 101 Airborne Division, which was emplaced in depth in the 1991 Gulf war. In the subcontinent, no more lift capability than that of a reinforced infantry battalion helicopter is available. Moreover, creating a deep ground link in enemy territory will be all the more difficult. The net result of this operational stance is that India does not have any qualitative or quantitative advantage over Pakistan.

The main objection to this stance is that no one knows how to utilise the massive forces available with the holding corps after one side's main effort goes through successfully. For example, if

Pakistan pre-empts and manages to break out its main effort through India's defence line, the huge amounts of manpower and equipment locked in with India's holding formations along the Line of Control will be rendered useless. Against this backdrop of operational-level parity and the peculiar operational stance in the form of fortified linear defences, the primary reason for avoiding a full-scale war seems clear enough.

Yet another advantage of the Pakistan Army is that unlike India, they work admirably at the strategic level. They formulate national security policies and decide budgetary allocations for defence. Nuclear policy, weaponisation options, and command and control of nuclear assets are the sole responsibility of the GHQ. Further, the Pakistan Army's ease of manoeuvre at the strategic level allows it to maintain the tempo in a fluctuating conflict-crisis situation. Indo-Pak relations, after all, are a continuum on the scales of war. And more importantly, the decision to go to war in Pakistan rests with the armed forces, despite the occasional facade of democracy. This provides an advantage to the GHQ in terms of timing, place(s), methods and even objectives for war vis-à-vis India.

Since Pakistan has strategic-level advantages in command and control, it also enjoys wider choices and options in planning and execution at the operational level of war. In addition, Pakistan operates on interior lines of communication and can mobilise its holding formations to move into battle locations in a maximum of 96 hours. Its mobile strike reserves can be simultaneously concentrated. While the Indian Army, which operates on exterior lines of communication, can mobilise its holding formations in the same time frame, the concentration of army strategic reserves and its accompanying logistics build-up will take between seven to 10 days. This provides a tremendous advantage to Pakistan in the initial stages of war, and hence its doctrine of "offensive defence". The major military problem for Pakistan is not a lack of strategic depth, but the fact that too many of its politically sensitive targets are close to the border with India.

Pakistan, with an edge over India at this level of warfare, is proactive, while India is reactive. A clear advantage in strategic command, control and coordination enjoyed by the Pakistan armed forces is a powerful force multiplier, overlooked by scholars when evaluating military balances. It is another matter that Pakistan's operational level of war is surprisingly weaker, and has in the past led to disastrous consequences: Pakistan's military policy and plans rarely survive the contact of forces in battle.

New Thinking

The arrival of nuclear weapons, ballistic missiles, and, most importantly, better Reconnaissance, Surveillance and Target Acquisition (RSTA) has led to a fresh thinking within the Indian Army. It has been argued that the present operational stance of holding every inch of sensitive territory was necessary because the means to gain an early warning about the enemy's offensive plans were inadequate. With the coming of Unmanned Aerial Vehicles (UAV)/Remote Piloted Vehicles (RPV), better ground and air sensors, long-range fire delivery means, and Precision Guided Munitions (PGMs), the depth battle should assume importance over contact battle. On the one hand, this implies that instead of the enemy mass, the centre of gravity, defined as the enemy's vulnerability, should shift towards its RSTA, communications, logistics bases, and command and control centres. This calls for a coordination hitherto unavailable between the land-based and airborne firepower.

On the other hand, the concept and role of the holding corps should be reviewed to dispense with the present method of linear deployment of troops. The army has already renamed its Holding Corps to Pivot Corps. This is to both banish a defensive connotation implicit in the word "holding", and also emphasise a change in thinking that is aggressive and proactive. A denial of territory by observation and fire rather than by physical presence will enable the Pivot Corps commander to keep the combat potential of almost his entire infantry and mechanised forces intact as reserves for exploiting opportunities to launch offensive action.

The vast manpower and equipment with the pivot formations should, therefore, be utilised by having only light screening forces along the border. The linear obstacles which have been built over a period of time should, however, be regularly maintained so that their defence potential continues to be exploited gainfully. Heavy concentrations of mobile forces should be emplaced at certain locations, enabling them to advance on at least two axes of attack (and logistics) to bolster their respective main efforts. The single problem with this thinking is that it runs contrary to the political terms of reference of holding sensitive ground in both countries. Implementing such a strategy would thus require the political nod.

Implicit in the new thinking is again the need for strengthening land-based and airborne firepower. Fire raids deep inside enemy territory would help achieve an element of surprise and make interdiction more meaningful in conjunction with the air force. An "anvil of fire" should thus replace the traditional anvil formed by a pivot of manoeuvre, freeing strike forces to punch hard. The raising of an artillery division indicates that artillery will be employed on a theatre basis to optimise its availability. The operational philosophy is likely to be changed to "attack by fire, manoeuvre and occupy" from the present, "manoeuvre, fire and occupy".

The other doctrinal issue that land commanders are debating on is the concept of Deep Strike. According to the army doctrine: "The Indian Army believes in fighting the war in enemy territory. If forced into a war, the aim of our offensive(s) would be to apply a sledgehammer blow to the enemy. The Indian Army's concept of waging war is to ensure a decisive victory and to ensure that conflict termination places us at an advantageous position."[6] This suggests manoeuvre, which instinctively leads army commanders to debate between attrition and manoeuvre.

Before aspects of this debate are discussed, it becomes relevant to assess how ballistic missiles with conventional warheads may affect the depth and contact battlefield. Understandably, the army could become less dependent on immediate close air support (called battlefield air strike by the Indian Air Force) for the forward line of troops, both in offensive and defensive operations. The deep battle could be fought with ballistic missiles being the main source of disruptive firepower, which will include economic targeting— power stations, gas and oil installations, oil tank parks, etc.

This would lead to a major problem for military planners on both sides: how does one mask the forward concentration of strategic mobile reserves and a build-up of the respective logistics support bases, called corps maintenance areas? With the coming of better RSTA means, and considering that the human intelligence on both sides is excellent, these attractive targets for ballistic missiles will be difficult to hide. Ways will have to be found to dispense these vulnerable concentrations. Apart from wide dispersal,

---

[6] *Ibid.*, p. 11.

the logistics bases will have to be masked and will probably merge with those of the defending corps. At present, to minimise a loss of strategic surprise, most of the mechanised forces of both armies are located close to the border. For example, Pakistan's 1 Corps, a massive offensive formation located in Kharian and Mangla, does not need rail carriage. For this elite formation, disruption by Indian missiles will obviously have to come at road communication bottlenecks.

Ballistic missiles will help in the destruction and disruption of enemy strike reserves without physical occupation of heartland territory. The doctrinal shift because of land-based firepower—including ballistic missiles, rockets and long-range precision artillery—will emphasise on the destruction of forces and supporting infrastructure rather than pose an overwhelming threat to territorial integrity. Unfortunately, in the usage of ballistic missiles with conventional warheads, Pakistan scores over India as it has sufficient numbers, solid-propellant fuel, and assured accuracy. Given the advent of television and the 1999 Kargil war, which brought the gory battlefield into peoples' homes, it will be necessary for military planners to ensure minimum collateral damage.

Pakistan's employment of its ballistic missiles is expected to follow the Chinese Peoples' Liberation Army (PLA) thinking, which now places importance on its Conventional Missile Forces (CMFs), considered more usable than nuclear ones. In consonance with the PLA's concept of high-tech warfare, it has sought greater terminal accuracy of its ballistic missiles and has integrated them into theatre united campaign programmes. The CMFs would be employed in conjunction with the air force to allow the latter to retain sorties for achieving air supremacy. In a significant development, the PLA has converted DF-21 and DF-25 IRBMs, initially intended for nuclear use, into conventional ones.

The Pakistan Army, which controls its ballistic missiles, has reportedly procured better guidance systems from the PLA, and is likely to use them early in a war. The Indian Army, on the other hand, would be forced to react to Pakistan's usage of ballistic missiles. At present, the fire of India's sole Prithvi ballistic missile is controlled by the army headquarters, which is supposed to first take clearance from the political leadership for retaliation purposes. However, in the absence of an understanding on the usage of ballistic missiles, both sides would be under enormous pressure to prevent each other from misreading the type of warhead used.

Against the backdrop of an evolving anvil of fire and RSTA, and considering that India improves its ballistic missiles and employs them with caution, the relevance of deep strikes through manoeuvres becomes tempting. It would also be necessary for the Indian Army to dovetail Pakistan's offensive-defence doctrine while making its own operational plans. As an offence is best replied to with pre-emptive offence, Indian Army commanders would have to assess Pakistan's nuclear threshold level sector by sector. As suggested in the army doctrine, the Indian Army would need to plan to seize a long narrow strip of Pakistani territory in theatres with lower nuclear threshold levels, and seek to manoeuvre with the strike forces in areas with higher nuclear threshold levels.

Alarmists, however, point out that it would be too dangerous a game to assess Pakistan's nuclear threshold levels, and that it would be best for the Indian Army to indulge in the option of deep-fire attacks with minimal manoeuvre and seizure of territory. It can be argued that both sides would attempt to force the opponent by a shallow penetration to expose its main offensive forces to battle. In fact, options exist for preventing a coherent deployment of Pakistan's Army Reserve North. In the deserts, allowing Pakistan's Army Reserve South to get into waterless desolate tracts before being encircled and destroyed would keep matters below the subcontinent threshold. While the commanders would know best, unnecessary caution because of the nuclear weapons factor could be self-defeating. The Indian Army must call Pakistan's nuclear bluff with military sensibility.

The Air-Land Battle: A Problem Area

The army's new thinking necessitates an aggressive and proactive posture, which demands air-land battle capabilities. Unfortunately, an abiding operational concern in both countries is that the much-needed concept of an air-land battle is more theoretical than real. Pakistan, however, has an advantage over India as its army is more powerful than the other two services, and is hence in a position to dictate terms. The need for an air-land battle can hardly be overemphasised, considering that India has a territorial dispute with Pakistan, in which a war will essentially be a land battle with an overwhelming and sustained support from the air force. The premium on time placed by nuclear weapons on India and Pakistan calls for "jointness" in the conduct of operations as an essential prerequisite. According to a former army chief, Gen. S. Roychowdhury, "The Indian army must acquire true Land-Air warfare capability. This can definitely not be a single service effort and will require a good deal of intensive overtime work with the Indian air force to synergise the collective intellects and capabilities of the two services in joint conceptualisation, training, and most importantly, induction of weapons and battle support systems."[7]

Gen. Roychowdhury has made the whole issue of "jointness" sound easy and plausible. The ground realities tell a different tale because of the huge doctrinal gap between the army and the air force. The army, in stages, wants a Chief of Defence Staff, and bi-service and tri-service operational commands leading eventually to integrated commands—the ultimate aim of a Unified Command being a joint doctrine, joint intelligence and joint plans. According to the army, "the present system of first formulating respective service plans and then attempting their interface needs to be reversed".[8] The army feels that "Counter Air Operations for gaining favourable air situation over the battle area need to be considered as part of the air-land battle, and need to be closely dovetailed with it." It adds, "The best judge to decide and demand air effort is, however, the man controlling and fighting the land battle."

The air force does not agree with the army's thinking, much less with its requirement of a Unified Command and a CDS. It opposes any move towards limited air assets being parcelled out. Instead, it feels that the focus should be on "unified thinking". "Only by doing so can we move towards true joint planning, which could then be translated into an effective and integrated war-winning solution."[9] Being a strategic force, the air force gives primacy to offensive and strategic tasks that involve the control of the air: "the control of the air is vital for the success of not only air operations, but also for the success of virtually all types of surface and sub-surface operations".[10] Close Air Support (CAS) operations, considered most important by the army, are viewed as just the

---

[7] Roychowdhury, Shankar (2001), "Limited Conflict", *Indian Defence Review*, June, p. 86.

[8] *Ibid.*, p. 132.

[9] *Doctrine of the Indian Air Force*, Restricted, 1995, p. 106.

[10] *Ibid.*, p. 71.

opposite by the air force, which refers to them as Battlefield Air Strikes (BAS).

The air force prefers Battlefield Air Interdiction to BAS, the difference between the two being in the proximity of targets to friendly forces and the control arrangements therefore needed. In short, once the balloon goes up, the air force would prefer to focus on its strategic and offensive tasks for at least five to eight days to gain a favourable air situation or a localised air superiority, if not an air supremacy. For the army, CAS operations—both planned and immediate missions—and support by attack helicopters, which should be treated as part of CAS operations, would help maintain the momentum of land battle. It becomes axiomatic that the divergent operational thinking of the army and the air force can only be unified by having a Chief of Defence Staff, which appears unlikely.

Modernisation and Operational Logistics

Modernisation, which has generated a constant debate in the armed forces, is about a concurrent induction of new technology and a reorganisation of present military structure. Because of the paucity and uncertainty of funds, the modernisation debate within the three defence services revolves around whether the approach should be capability-driven, resource-driven or threat-driven. To derive maximum benefits from modernisation, the services indulge in triplication of work by making plans from different perspectives. In spite of this, it is not uncommon for the five-year perspective plans of the services to lapse without any allocation of funds. Even worse, the capital outlay in the annual defence budgets is generally grossly underutilised because of bureaucratic slovenliness. Various defence scandals exposed after the Kargil war have provided yet another excuse for bureaucratic inaction.

As a result of all this, India's combat edge vis-à-vis Pakistan has eroded over the years. A report in a leading newspaper in October 2002 quoted the Parliamentary Standing Committee on Defence as saying that India's conventional superiority over Pakistan's military in April 2002 was barely 1:1.2. This had come down from the 1:1.7 superiority that India enjoyed over Pakistan during the 1971 war (remember, even when Pakistan lost its eastern wing to India for various reasons, it stood matched on India's western front).

What is little known is that during the Kargil war, India's combat edge over Pakistan stood at a mere 1:1.1. This figure was given by the then Army Chief, Gen. V. P. Malik himself, while addressing a select group of serving and retired defence personnel at the United Services Institution in Delhi immediately after the war. He also said, "The army's modernisation programmes are in a state of terminal illness. Our conventional combat edge over Pakistan has been eroding with every passing year. Unless additional funds are earmarked, future planning is not possible and the erosion in combat edge will soon become uncorrectable."

One of the reasons why Gen. Musharraf started the Kargil war was the common knowledge that India's conventional capabilities had weakened. India's defence services were starved of funds throughout the 1990s. Defence allocations hovered around 2.4 per cent of the GDP, when it should have been at least 3 per cent. During the tenure of Gen. B. C. Joshi in 1984, there were deficiencies in equipment alone to the tune of Rs 18,000 crore even on an 80 per cent authorisation. Little wonder then that after Operation Parakram was over, the Army Chief, Gen. S Padmanabhan, told the media that he had sought an annual defence allocation of 3 per cent of the GDP.

The reduced annual defence budgets have meant four things. First, there has been pressure on the army to reduce its strength, as nearly 60 per cent of the army's annual allocation is spent on pay and allowances. It is little appreciated that unlike the capital-intensive air force and the navy, where a trade-off between technology and manpower is possible, the Army's Case is different. With overstretched commitments to prepare for a conventional war with Pakistan and China, and the continuing counter-insurgency operations, it is not possible to reduce the army's manpower, estimated at 1.2 million. The former Army Chief, Gen. Malik, sought to do so in 1998 by reducing the army strength by 50,000 in a non-field-force review, and attempted to utilise the money saved on pay and allowances for modernisation. After the Kargil war a year later, the army was forced to increase its manpower commitment by raising a new corps in J&K. The present army strength stands at 1.2 million, not including the Rashtriya Rifles, which has grown to a strength of 75,000.

Second, the DRDO has benefited from reduced defence budgets, disproportionate to its technical capabilities. In the nineties, with the focus on indigenisation, the DRDO should itself have sought a technical review of most of its high-ticket items like the Arjun tank, Light Combat Aircraft, Advanced Light Helicopter, Pinaka Multiple Launch Rocket System, Advanced Technical Vessel or nuclear-powered submarine, Trishul and Akash surface-to-air missiles, and Nag anti-tank guided missile projects. A decade later, at the turn of the century, none of the above projects have delivered satisfactorily. In some, the battlefield requirements have overtaken the original general staff requirements; in others, the import component has risen alarmingly, resulting in cost escalations and maintenance problems because of the assemblage of components from various countries; and in the rest, inordinate delays have forced the services to seek an import of comparable weapon systems.

Third, a lack of a financial commitment for perspective and annual defence plans has led to ad-hocism in defence purchases. The focus has been on matching Pakistan's acquisitions rather than building our own capabilities and doctrines after a holistic review of military threats. For example, India signed a contract for 320 T-90 tanks with Russia in February 2001 after Pakistan acquired the same number of T-80UD tanks from Ukraine between 1997 and 2000. Consequently, there has been a mismatch between the service doctrines and the needed weapon systems.

Fourth, reduced defence budgets have affected operational logistics adversely. Instead of providing product support and seeking incremental upgrades on existing weapon systems, scarce finances are being spent on tangible items, such as new weapon platforms. It is not uncommon to find that substandard lubricants, oils, and spare parts have been purchased, which both shorten the life of weapon systems and place its crew at risk. The perennial attitudes of both civil and military bureaucrats who are hesitant to lock capital in spares and such intangible items have added to the war-wastage reserves not being maintained optimally. Another culprit has been the inadequate and substandard storage capacity of high-wastage items and ammunition in depots. Notwithstanding claims by ordnance services of fully computerised inventories, after the Kargil war it was found that the exact availability of logistics stores and even ammunition was not known. Considering that there would be an immediate international clampdown on the sales and aid of equipment, stores, and ammunition, India would need to keep the inventory management nightmare in mind before deciding on the duration of a war.

There are reasons to suspect that storage figures are not calculated based on operational research database, and are intuitive and even empirical derivations. Little wonder that India faces the prospect of being surprised by the actual expenditure rates. In any case, the air force and the navy are always short of finances. A way out of this dilemma for India is to deliberately control the intensity of engagements. To do this, it will have to wrest complete initiative from Pakistan after the first week or so of war as a means to control its battlefield operational logistics requirements.

Operational logistics has been a lesser problem for Pakistan when compared to India. Its flow of strategic military sustenance from China has been regular unlike the case of India, which is still to recover fully from the break-up of the Soviet Union. India signed a military-technical cooperation agreement with Russia in 1994, and hopes that by 2010 most of the critical spares and assemblies needed for maintaining equipment of Russian origin with the Indian defence services would be indigenised.

Slippages in the Indian Air Force

All is not well with the Indian Air Force (IAF), though the bean-counting of assets suggests otherwise. Compared with the Pakistan Air Force (PAF), the IAF is sitting pretty at 39 combat squadrons against the PAF's 20. However, unlike the PAF, the IAF has a very high accident rate. While bird hits account for about 30 per cent of IAF accidents, the major culprit is inadequate training. Umpteen high-powered committees on aircraft accidents have pinpointed the reasons for high rate of accidents. According to the September 1997 report of the Abdul Kalam (now the president of India) committee on fighter aircraft accidents, human error caused by unsatisfactory training and aircraft maintenance are responsible for maximum mishaps. The committee's major recommendation was that there should be an early induction of Advanced Jet Trainers (AJT), in addition to other sweeping improvements in training standards, including increased use of simulators. Simulators are a good low-cost option for various aspects of pilot training like ground attack, navigation and even air combat. However, since simulation cannot replace real airborne training, AJTs are a must.

In his first stint as Defence Minister, George Fernandes had confirmed to the Defence Consultative Committee that the AJT would be finalised by December 2000. The deadline has expired even as new competitors have recently emerged for the British Aerospace Hawk aircraft, which was nearly decided upon. The government has put the procurement of AJTs, sought for the past 18 years, on the back-burner, and the IAF is hesitant to spend scarce resources on simulators. A former chief of the air force confirmed, in private, that the scanty budget allocations were having an adverse operational impact on the IAF. One such impact was on flight safety, as flying hours were being reduced and maintenance was also suffering. One would recall a drastic reduction in flying hours between 1991 and 1996 because of the collapse of the Soviet Union which resulted in an acute shortage of spares and product support for aircraft of Soviet origin. The MiG-29 pilots are required to routinely fly 250 hours a year, and Mirage pilots average over 200 hours. The IAF, however, has clarified in the Annual Report 2000–2001 of the ministry of defence that accident statistics have actually come down. This has been possible after various operational safety management workshops were conducted to reduce, if not completely eliminate, human errors by aircrew and servicing personnel.

In the larger sense, the two major questions emerging from aircraft accidents are how good the IAF pilot training and aircraft health are compared to the Pakistan Air Force (PAF). Compared with their Indian counterparts, the PAF pilots are young and well-trained. A PAF squadron commander takes charge at the age of about 34 years, six years earlier than the IAF. Even worse, with the two-year retirement extension given by the present government to servicemen, group captains in the IAF are being forced to command transport squadrons and helicopter units. Further, unlike in India, military service in Pakistan is a prestigious career, where young men come from well-to-do families. Understandably, the housing facilities at forward air bases in Pakistan are better than those in India. The impact of all this on the morale is too obvious to need elaboration.

Pilot training in the PAF is extremely rigorous, orderly and effective. According to Pushpinder Singh[11] who has done

---

[11] Singh, Pushpinder (2000), "Scenario 2015: The Pakistan Air Force", paper presented at the IDSA seminar on Air power in India's Security, October 9–10.

commendable research on the PAF, of the 20 combat squadrons with the PAF, only 12 are full-fledged combat units. The remaining eight squadrons are all concerned with operational and conversion training; but this commitment varies according to the demand for pilots, and most of them have operational roles to fulfil. Five of these squadrons are commonly referred to as Operational Conversion Units (OCU), and a good proportion of their effort is directed towards providing a steady stream of qualified aircrew. Each of the five major types of aircraft in the PAF inventory is supported by an OCU squadron.

The other advantage with PAF pilots is that they have flown all major advanced aircraft in friendly Islamic Gulf countries. Since the seventies, PAF pilots have been working with the air forces of Saudi Arabia, Abu Dhabi, UAE, and even Turkey. PAF pilots working with the Royal Saudi Air Force flew F-15 aircraft combat missions during the 1991 Operation Desert Storm against Iraq, and are thus familiar with high-tech warfare. The PAF, therefore, has more high-tech orientation than their IAF counterparts. In addition to all these advantages, their numbers are large when compared to the IAF.

For example, the IAF graduates about 150 of its own pilots annually, of which nearly 100 go into fighters. The remaining join the large, 500-strong aircraft transport and helicopter aircraft crew. In contrast, the PAF also trains about 150 pilots annually, all of which go into the fighters. In Pakistan, the helicopter pilots are trained by the army, and it has a small number of transport aircraft. Therefore, a situation exists where the PAF, with less than half the combat aircraft of the IAF—400 aircraft verses 750 aircraft—annually graduates about as many combat pilots. The implication is that compared to the IAF, the PAF not only has younger pilots, but also maintains a much higher pilot-aircraft ratio. In common terms, this means that in a war, even with smaller combat numbers, the PAF would be able to sustain a much higher sortie rate than the IAF.

In addition, the IAF will have to factor in about 50 to 100 additional sophisticated aircraft joining the PAF "on loan" from friendly Islamic nations which employ PAF pilots. For example, the PAF could get UAE-owned and PAF-flown Mirage-2000-5s, or utilise the Saudi E-3A Sentry AWACS to monitor Indian aircraft and direct PAF air defences, or procure the F-16 now being built for the UAE by Turkey.

Even in the area of maintenance, which is also responsible for high accident rates, the PAF is more comfortably placed than the IAF. Since the eighties, the IAF has introduced 25 different types of aircraft, including variants, while the PAF has inducted five basic types. Maintaining the IAF fleet, which originates from different countries, is a nightmare.

The IAF modernisation plans have also not kept pace with its doctrine, which was first written in 1995. According to the doctrine, the IAF has four fundamental goals.[12] However, even a brief look at these goals makes it evident that the IAF is nowhere near achieving these goals.

- Offensive operations priority has been upgraded along-side the focus on air defence. The concept of air defence has been revised and replaced by strategic or deterrent air defence. Deterrent air defence differs from the earlier concept as it implies that after absorbing the enemy's initial air effort, the IAF will be able to maintain a higher relative strength as the conflict progresses.
- Acceptance of economy versus escalating costs, and the tendency towards worldwide structured disarmament—in essence, the acceptance of a reduction in force level. Air Chief Marshal S. K. Kaul, who was responsible for the IAF doctrine and induction of Russian SU-30 aircraft, had envisaged "a total of up to 34 combat squadrons by the year 2005 of which one-third should be multi-role in performance".[13] On the one hand, the IAF is nowhere near having such numbers of multi-role aircraft. On the other hand, the senior IAF brass appear to have changed their mind and are thinking of a fleet of 60 combat squadrons.
- A greater emphasis on the acquisition of force multipliers such as AWACS, mid-air refuelling, and electronic warfare, in order to maximise the impact of the existing force, and to make up for any probable reductions in that force at a later date. Even as the first of the six contracted mid-air refuelling aircraft arrived from Uzbekistan in February

---

[12] Sawhney, Pravin (1997), "India's First Airpower Doctrine Takes Shape", *International Defense Review*, June.
[13] *Ibid.*, p. 33.

2003, it is all too evident that there are major slippages in the acquisition of the above force multipliers.

• Work towards improvements in command, control, communications and intelligence structure, and a revamped, modernised air defence network.

Notwithstanding the ambitious planning, the IAF appears to be riddled with procurement problems. The Light Combat Aircraft (LCA) which was to replace the ageing MiG-21 fleet is nowhere in sight. Insiders are of the opinion that even if the LCA joined the IAF by 2008, its technology would have been completely overtaken by new operational requirements. The MiG-bis upgrades are extremely slow, and the Jaguar and MiG-27 need an urgent upgrade. According to the Annual Report 2001-2002 of the ministry of defence, "the original IAF version of Jaguar Navigation and Weapon Aiming Sub System needs an avionics upgrade". The same report says that "the MiG-27 aircraft too needs an avionics upgrade to improve its operational effectiveness by day and night". However, due to financial constraints and other priorities in the IAF, this has not happened till now. According to top IAF sources, as many as 100 MiG-27s may be unserviceable.

Pushpinder Singh, an aviation expert, says that though the PAF has only a relatively limited number of combat aircraft at its disposal, it is better oriented towards multi-mission capability. According to calculations, even though the IAF has maintained its 1971 edge of 3:1 in terms of interdiction tonnage, the PAF has quantum-jumped its long-range strike tonnage to approach near parity with the IAF.

Army, Mobility and Firepower

Pakistan, in the last decade, has kept sufficient focus on mobility in a tactical battlefield. In the nineties, Pakistan's armoured strength had suffered slippages, resulting in reports that armoured regiments were being reorganised in blocks of 35 tanks instead of the usual 45 tanks. Such a depletion of tanks in a regiment does not have a tactical basis. By end-1999, the tank position had improved substantially, and the regiments had gone back to a war-establishment of 45 tanks with a priority to divisional armour regiments, corps reconnaissance regiments, strike corps and independent armoured brigades. Between 1997 and the beginning of 2000, Pakistan acquired

as many as 320 T-80UD tanks from Ukraine. At present, the bulk
of Pakistan's armour consists of Chinese T-85 (125 mm smooth-
bore), T-80, upgraded T-59 and T-69 tanks. Pakistan has two strike
corps each centred on an armoured division. Its 5 Corps based in
Karachi has reportedly what amounts to an armoured division
without a formal headquarters, although one could be created if
required.[14]

The introduction of newer and upgraded tank fleet had led
western analysts to conclude that Pakistan had a qualitative edge
over India's armour by the year 2000. This created concern in India,
and quick-fix solutions were sought, with three main options being
assessed. The DRDO was bent on giving the indigenous Arjun tank
to the army. Even after nearly 25 years of development, the tank
has enough flaws to be unacceptable to the service. With a 58-ton
weight, it is difficult to transport the tank by rail as it protrudes
beyond the permissive limits on either side of the tank transport-
ers used. It has poor operational mobility, the engine suffers from
overheating problems in desert conditions, its fire control system
has reached the development limit, and with imported assemblies
from different sources, the tank is a maintenance nightmare. Instead
of scrapping the project, it was decided that the army would accept
three regiments worth of Arjun tanks by the year 2010. One such
regiment has been raised and equipped.

Meanwhile, the search for the main battle tank shifted to an
improved version of the existing T-72M1—being assembled at Avadi
since 1988—or a new tank of Russian origin. Considering that the
existing fleet of T-72M1 tanks needed an upgrade, one solution was
to procure the cheaper Russian T-72S tank with a powerful 840
horsepower engine. The T-72S could accommodate up to three
tons of additional armour on the turret for protection of the tank
and, in addition to a total of 52 ammunition rounds, it could carry
four Russian SS B 119M missiles with a range of four kilometres.
The tank had been extensively trial tested in the country and the
army was satisfied with it. The Russians had offered the requisite
technology transfer, and it could be assimilated with minimum
fuss and manufactured on the existing production line of the T-72
tank in Avadi.

---

[14] Cloughley, Brian (1999), *A History of the Pakistan Army*, Karachi: Oxford
University Press, p. 344.

The army, instead, settled for the Russian 125 mm calibre T-90 tank. The deal to procure 124 tanks off the shelf and progressively assemble another 186 in India was signed in February 2002. About 40 tanks have arrived and all the 310 tanks are expected to be in service only by 2005. The purchase of T-90, meanwhile, has led to the slowdown of operation Bison—the upgrade programme for nearly 1,500 T-72 tanks. The T-72 needs a night fighting device, a good fire control system, more protection and a new power pack. It needs a fire control system, with a laser range finder which should be slaved to thermal imagers for night vision. Thermal imagers are supercooled cryogenic supersensitive detectors with an ability to detect military objects against an ambience where everything above an absolute zero temperature radiates heat. While thermal imagers can solve the problem of recognition during day and night, identification of objects comes with training. The latter is only possible if priority is given to the tank upgrade programme. Overall, therefore, the state of the armour leaves much to be desired.

The guiding philosophy of field artillery has been to standardise the calibre of weapons in service and to seek ammunition compatibility with guns of the same calibre but from different countries of origin. There is also a need for long-range artillery and accompanying surveillance means. Five operational considerations have influenced this thinking:

- The changes in potential targets in Pakistan as linear defences and supporting field works along the border with India are heavily reinforced with concrete fortifications. A successful engagement of hardened defences is possible only with heavier-calibre shells with higher terminal velocities.
- The expansion of mechanised forces within the armies of India and Pakistan has underscored the need for larger-calibre artillery systems and higher rates of fire.
- There has been a determination to reduce the logistics complexities of operating guns of 14 different calibres through a programme of rationalisation.
- The development of better roads and tracks in India's mountains means that many mountain guns can be dispensed easily.
- With the availability of better RSTA systems, the depth of a traditional battlefield has increased manifold.

Against this backdrop, the state of land-based firepower has been no better. One of the lessons of the Kargil war was the need to have long-range artillery. It has been argued that if India had the Russian 70 km-range 12-barrel Smerch multi-barrel rocket launchers in its inventory, it could have threatened Skardu in the northern areas and put tremendous pressure on the Pakistan Army. Meant to cover the gap between the maximum range of 155 mm-calibre artillery guns and the minimum range of the Prithvi missile (provided it could be used with conventional warheads), the Smerch was cleared by army headquarters for induction into service in the eighth plan (1992-1997). One regiment each was to come in the eighth, ninth and 10th plans. Considering that the development story of the indigenous 39 km-range, 212 mm, 12-barrel Pinaka MBRL was the same as that of the Arjun tank, the army had favoured a combination of three Smerch and one Pinaka in a rocket regiment. However, given the government delay in procuring Smerch, by 1998 the army revised the rocket regiment organisation to have three Pinaka and one Smerch system. The government is understood to have been in the final stages of negotiations on Smerch towards the end of 2002, even as the Pinaka, with accuracy problems, was ready for induction. The story of seeking Russian help to upgrade the Soviet-designed 122 mm BM-21 GRAD area weapon system with a range of 20 km is no better. The artillery has a total of five GRAD regiments, which it wants to retain in service till the end of the 12th plan. The enhancement of the GRAD range from 20 to 35 km was sought in the early nineties. Russia offered to do so, but government clearance is still awaited.

The artillery had purchased 480 guns of 130 mm calibre worth 24 regiments at throwaway prices between 1993 and 1994 after the break-up of the Soviet Union. Hundred guns came from the Czech Republic, while 380 came from Russia. The proposal was to upgrade these guns to a 45-calibre barrel and also conduct feasibility studies to further upgrade them to 52 calibre. Similarly, it was also proposed to have a total of six regiments of Self-Propelled (SP) 45-calibre guns. Ultimately, the artillery sought around 400 SP 155 mm systems. Amongst other options, the indigenisation route suggested was to mount an SP turret on the Arjun tank chassis. The South African LIW T6 155 mm/52 calibre turret system was successfully mounted on an Arjun chassis (Bhim project) and trial tested in 1999. However, nothing further has been heard of the matter.

The net result of all this is that the artillery division raised in 1988 lacks the needed punch. To be orbated with the strike corps, the only artillery division in the army includes two gun brigades, one composite brigade comprising Surveillance and Target Acquisition means, a Prithvi missile group, and a rocket regiment.

Pakistan, on the other hand, is consolidating its available artillery in its strike corps to form a second artillery division. Its artillery division has under its command the corps independent artillery brigade, corps artillery brigade, armoured division artillery brigade, and at least one or two air defence gun-missile regiments of Chinese origin formed into a composite air defence brigade. (The basic fire unit is one PL-9 missile launcher and two twin-barrel air defence guns served by one fire control radar.)

Moreover, the Pakistan Army has a unique reconnaissance and support battalion with each infantry division. Each has three composite companies as part of the three brigades, armed with anti-tank firepower (106 mm RLs [Rocket Launchers] and ATGM [Anti-Tank Guided Missile]) and medium/heavy small-arms fire. Having no equivalent in the Indian Army, these battalions are mobile, and are expected to be employed with strike corps reconnaissance regiments and various division armoured regiments.

Pakistan also has firing data computers available at the battery level; its meteorological data is accurate and it has a lead in SP artillery. This results in accuracy and mobility of firepower, which offsets the numerical advantage in artillery pieces with India. In terms of accuracy and mobility, the Pakistan artillery has somewhat of a lead over India.

Overall, at the tactical level, both sides are strong in defence. With the current levels of availability of night observation devices with both armies, the defending forces have an edge over manoeuvre forces. While night movement by large mechanised forces is feasible, combat is not. The infantry and artillery can manage combat at night, but it will not be possible for the mechanised forces. In any case, opening an active infrared at night will be disastrous. Passive observation devices like thermal imager fitments are still not freely available in tanks and ICVs (Infantry Combat Vehicles). However, the extensive deployment of image intensifiers by India gives its defensive and holding formations an edge over Pakistan. There are indications that both countries have given high priority to equip reconnaissance and surveillance forces with night-vision devices as a step towards all forces acquiring the capability to fight at night.

Summary

- The Indian and Pakistan armies are nearly matched at the operational level of war.
- The Pakistan Air Force has quantum-jumped its long-range strike tonnage to approach near parity with the Indian Air Force.
- Pakistan is expected to use its ballistic missiles with conventional warheads in both the depth and contact battles to supplement its air force. Unlike India's Prithvi, Pakistan's ballistic missiles use solid propellants and have better guidance systems acquired from China.
- For the envisaged short and intense full-scale war, true air-land capabilities are a must. In the obtained circumstance, the synergistic effort of closely coordinated joint operations will not be available.
- The army's new thinking necessitates an aggressive and proactive posture. It requires a restructuring of security instruments to provide versatile and balanced forces, greater induction of technology, greater flexibility in force levels and organisations, and greater inter-services coordination, which are not available at present.
- The land-based and air firepower and mobility of India leave much to be desired.

7

After Operation Parakram

Ten months, 130 soldiers' lives lost in laying mines on the border, an expenditure of over Rs 8,300 crore, heavy wear and tear of military equipment, lowering of the troops' morale, and displacement of villagers from the border areas—after all this and more, Operation Parakram failed to meet its singular objective of stopping cross-border terrorism across the LoC. Yet, Prime Minister Vajpayee insisted that the operation met its goal as it enabled the execution of the Jammu and Kashmir assembly elections, notwithstanding the additional 800 lives which were lost in the electoral process. This was certainly a very high price to pay for any election, no matter how crucial it might have been. In any case, the government's insistence that the army mobilisation was meant for state election has few takers. When Operation Parakram was launched, the state elections were 11 month away.

Perhaps the failure of Operation Parakram lay in its genesis. It was not a deliberately thought-out action, but a knee-jerk reaction to the terrorist attack on the Indian Parliament on December 13, 2001. The government simply got carried away as there was pressure to do something equally spectacular to show the domestic audience that India meant business. The US had to be told that the no-nonsense letter sent by Prime Minister Vajpayee (emphasising that India's patience was not unlimited) to President Bush after the October 1, 2001, terrorist strike on the J&K assembly was no idle threat. Most importantly, it was hoped that President Musharraf would cower under India's military threat.

The mobilisation was extraordinary in many ways. To begin with, the government did not issue any directive to the armed forces either in writing or verbally outlining what was sought by Operation Parakram. Nearly eight months into the operation, the government made a feeble attempt to put together a few objectives—mostly afterthoughts like the need for free and fair assembly elections in J&K—which were sent to the Chiefs of Staff committee in a draft form for comments.[1] However, before these could be formally issued, the operation was called off.

In military terms, Operation Parakram was initially undertaken to support the army's campaign across the LoC in J&K. The army's Northern command (responsible for the J&K theatre), which has been battling infiltration since 1990, was well-versed with the changing profile of terrorists, the infiltration routes, and the Pakistan's ISI and Army's role in running terrorist training camps—which included providing them with launching pads, and covering artillery and small arms fire to facilitate their crossing into the border state. The Northern command had long argued the need to cross into PoK and capture such Pakistani positions which helped terrorists slip into J&K. Similarly, the army headquarters was of the view that a tactical alteration of the LoC to ensure that infiltration stopped or declined considerably should be acceptable to the government and even the world. India, after all, was not doing a Kargil on Pakistan, but was simply ensuring that Pakistani army positions close to the LoC be placed at a tactically disadvantageous position to discourage infiltration. Should Pakistan agree to stop all help to militants in J&K, a status quo could be considered. Given such a military thinking, the army knew its military aims and hoped that the war would remain confined to J&K. Operation Parakram was, therefore, a bottom's-up operation conceived by the Northern command and was accepted by an angry and shocked political leadership numbed by the assault on Parliament.

However, by the time India sounded the second clarion call (the first time was in January) after the terrorist attack on army families in Kaluchak on May 14, 2002, the army's plans had grown ambitious. The military leadership decided to engage Pakistan in a full-scale conventional war to destroy its strike formations. The logic behind the bold military aim was that once the centre of gravity of Musharraf's military—his offensive formations—was destroyed,

---

[1] Interview with a senior army officer.

he would be compelled to curtail cross-border terrorism, and might agree to sincere bilateral negotiations. The army argued that Musharraf would not use nuclear weapons until Pakistan's vital interests were hit. While the destruction of its army's offensive prowess would certainly be a major setback, it would not be reason enough for Pakistan to start a nuclear war. Understanding the gravity of the situation and its own limitations against pressing Pakistan too hard, and appreciating India's viewpoint, President Bush said that India had the right to defend itself. The US, thus, issued advisory warning to its citizens to leave India and Pakistan, even as it started making plans to shift its forces (it occupied five air bases in Pakistan then) deployed against the Taliban and Al Qaeda out of Pakistan.

Once the US made it known that it was unwilling to apply too much pressure on India to restrain itself, and on Pakistan to stop cross-border terrorism permanently, India's political leadership developed cold feet. On the one hand, India felt let down by the US stand—it was hoped that the US would support India wholeheartedly against Pakistan, as it did during the 1999 Kargil war. On the other hand, Pakistan's nuclear deterrent had worked successfully on India's leadership. Therefore, unlike the January standoff, this time the Indian leadership was much too willing to lap up Pakistan's fake assurances, given through the roundabout US route, that it would cease infiltration across the LoC. Meanwhile, an emboldened Musharraf struck a deal with the US that in return for a temporary cessation of infiltration, the US would persuade India to start talks with Pakistan over Kashmir.

As it became clear to India that neither Pakistan nor the US was suitably impressed by the mobilisation, it was time to call off the operation and think of gains which could be attributed to it. One such gain was elucidated by Foreign Minister Yashwant Sinha on January 14, 2003: "The visible result [of India's mobilisation] was that the President of Pakistan himself said on more than one occasion that he was committed to fight against terrorism. He would not support any terrorist activity in Kashmir—we got the assurance."[2] Given that Musharraf's definition of terrorism is dissimilar to India's, and that the US is not averse to Pakistan's game plan, India's bold declaration rings hollow.

---

[2] "Talking with Yashwant Sinha", *The Indian Express*, January 14, 2003.

Irregular War

In retrospect, Prime Minister Vajpayee correctly commented that not going to war with Pakistan in January was a mistake, given that the Indian Army's aims for war at that time were quite modest, and hence attainable. Unlike Pakistan, India has adequate trained forces in J&K for operations inside PoK. Gen. Musharraf would have been in a bind, as it would have been suicidal for him to use nuclear weapons subsequent to a few tactical losses of territory in PoK. If he had moved forces from the Afghanistan front to India, they would have needed time for familiarisation, which was not possible. Cornered, Pakistan had few options then, one of which was spelled out by Gen. Musharraf when he addressed his troops on December 30, 2002. "Pakistan had planned an unconventional war if Indian troops had crossed the LoC", he said. Unlike what many analysts thought, by unconventional war, as Musharraf explained later, he did not mean a nuclear one. What he meant was that Pakistan would have used both regular and jehadi or irregular troops against India. A war would have provided an easy passage for militants across the LoC. Once inside, these jehadis would have made the task of the Rashtriya Rifles and other counter-insurgency security forces of securing the army's internal lines of logistics and communications difficult. This, in turn, might have ensured the unavailability of the RR as the second line of defence on the LoC to check infiltration.

Pakistan's war strategy of using irregulars in J&K is not new—it was at the heart of the 1999 Kargil war. This was the first operation where the Pakistan Army and jehadis operated in close coordination. Unfortunately, when Pakistan signed the declaration between President Clinton and Premier Nawaz Sharif under pressure from the US in Washington on July 4, 2001, and decided to withdraw its forces from across the LoC, the jehadis interpreted it as Pakistan's military defeat. Supported and motivated by the Taliban and Al Qaeda, these jehadis held their own until the forceful removal of the Taliban regime in Afghanistan.

After the events of 9/11, and emboldened by the growing strategic closeness between the US and Pakistan, Musharraf has been working hard to win over jehadi groups like the Lashkar-e-Taiyyaba and Jaish-e-Mohammad. Notwithstanding strong links with the Al Qaeda and Taliban, these jehadis are finding it increasingly difficult to operate in J&K without Pakistan's help. Musharraf wants jehadi cadres located in J&K, comprising various nationalities, to work closely with the pro-Pakistan indigenous Hizbul Mujahideen militants. The release of the chiefs (Masood Azhar and Hafiz Saeed) of these outfits—jailed after President Musharraf banned these terrorist organisations in his famous speech on January 12, 2001—within a year explained that Pakistan was succeeding in its endeavour. The LeT has been renamed as Jamaat-ud-Dawa and the JeM will now be called Tehrik-i-Khuddam to beat the US blacklist.

During his visit to J&K in January 2003, Deputy Prime Minister L. K. Advani correctly assessed the emerging pessimistic security situation in the turbulent state. While confirming that infiltration continued unabated across the LoC, he pointed out that maximum infiltrators are of foreign origin. Defence Minister George Fernandes, who accompanied the senior minister, said that about 3,000 Pakistan-sponsored terrorists are on Indian soil and as many numbers are waiting to cross into India. He also confirmed that Al Qaeda operators are harboured in Bangladesh. Interestingly, the US defence secretary, Donald Rumsfeld, had said on a visit to India in June 2002 that Al Qaeda terrorists were waiting for an opportunity to cross the LoC in J&K, a statement which was subsequently denied by the US. This was then done not to oppose India's position that all terrorists crossing into J&K were controlled by Pakistan. While understanding the new realities, India would do well to prepare for a showdown with Pakistan over J&K on its own steam.

Therefore, on assuming command on January 1, 2003, Army Chief Gen. N. C. Vij visited J&K for obvious operational reasons. The Northern command in J&K, after all, could initiate action that might snowball into a full-scale conventional war. Therefore, short-notice military responses to possibly spectacular terrorist attacks were discussed. The army is now apparently well-geared to conduct raids and limited actions across the LoC. Local commanders in J&K have been authorised to order a limited action without clearance from above. The army chief was given assessments on continuing infiltration, countermeasures being taken, deficiency of equipment and ammunition, and performance of various sensors placed along the LoC. The requirements of the Rashtriya Rifles (RR), which is fighting counter-insurgency operations (CI ops), and the morale of the troops received special attention. The morale factor assumed importance as the political indecisiveness during Operation Parakram did not go down too well with the troops.

Given the fact that the RR is the pivot of India's CI ops in J&K, the status, funding and future of this force should be a matter of some import. The less than optimal performance of the Unified Headquarters, tasked for CI ops under the state chief minister, owes much to the centre's reluctance to catch the bull by the horn. Once the status of the RR, with a present strength of 75,000 soldiers, is decided—its mandate expires on March 31, 2003—the command and control problems amongst security forces fighting terrorism would be alleviated. Therefore, the issues that need to be spelt out clearly are whether the RR comes under the defence or the home ministry, whether it is a permanent force, and whether it is part of the regular army or a paramilitary force. If these matters are not resolved soon, the RR may not be available as the second line of defence on the LoC in the event of a war. The task of protecting the internal lines of logistics and communication from jehadi attacks would overwhelm the counter-insurgency forces no end.

Another important issue is that of the morale of the troops. While it is important to boost the morale of our own troops, it is equally essential not to underestimate the professionalism of the Pakistan Army. Instead of helping to clear cobwebs, analysts close to the government have been circulating stories about the Pakistan Army. Consider the following: "The first myth is the assertion that the Pakistan military has no role to play in Afghanistan in the immediate aftermath of 9/11. The second myth is the assertion that the Pakistan military is a disciplined cohesive unit which takes its orders from the top and that there is no room for any kind of religious zealotry or rogue autonomy."[3] These observations are based upon a story which appeared in Pakistani papers, widely circulated in the Indian media. The story[4] is about a decorated soldier of the Pakistan Army who left for Afghanistan after the events of 9/11 to fight alongside the Taliban. There he found hundreds of Pakistanis from militant organisations like JeM, LeT and Harkat-ul-Mujahideen, and even officers from the Pakistan Army

---

[3] Bhaskar, Uday C., "Lifting the Smoke Screen", *The Times of India*, January 3, 2003.

[4] Gul, Imtiaz, "Abdul Nasr the Pak soldier, Abdul Nasr the Talib", *The Friday Times*, Lahore, December 31, 2002.

and the ISI who had assembled in support of the Taliban regime. This particular soldier contracted malaria and was sent back to Pakistan. The important thing about this story—which was deliberately omitted by the Indian analysts—is that he tried to get back into the Pakistan Army, but was rejected.

Since the eighties, the Pakistan Army under Gen. Zia-ul-Haq was indoctrinated to fight the Red Army in Afghanistan in the name of religious affinity with the mujahideen. After the ouster of the Red Army from Afghanistan, the closeness between the mujahids and the Pakistan Army and ISI grew, and the Islamisation of the Pakistan Army continued fervently. At the heart of Zia's Islamisation of the Pakistan Army was the quest for strategic space in Afghanistan. Interestingly, the Pakistan Air Force and Navy, which had little contact with the mujahids, remained insulated from Gen. Zia's Islamisation drive. The Pakistan Air Force and Navy focused upon professionalism alone. Professionalism in the Pakistan Army, however, had an added requirement—that officers should preferably have had a working tenure or so with the mujahids.

This policy continued until the 1999 Kargil war, after which the jehadis listened more to the Taliban regime in Kandahar than the military and intelligence dispensation in Pakistan. Islamabad's tactics for seeking strategic space in Afghanistan had misfired. Even as Musharraf was resolved to reverse Zia's policy of Islamisation of the Pakistan Army after he signed to fight international terrorism, it would take a long time for the well-cemented links between the khaki establishment and the mujahids to snap. There are indications that Pakistan Army officers and soldiers who decided to fight with the Taliban are now being dismissed from service. The inescapable conclusion is the opposite of what some Indian analysts have said; the Pakistan Army is moving away from Zia's Quranic concept of war towards professionalism in both regular and irregular war.

The Indian military leadership understands this shift, and has decided to plug the chinks in its own armour with regard to a regular war. The focus is now on quality more than quantity. Even as a few high-profile weapon platforms like Smerch multi-barrel rocket launchers, ANTPQ-37 weapon-locating-radars and high-altitude unmanned aerial vehicles are desired, specialised ammunition and weapons' upgrades must assume importance. For example, there is a need for more Krasnopol (155 mm laser-guided artillery ammunition) and aerial precision-guided munitions. The newly inducted T-90 tanks are without night-fighting devices, thus incapable of operating at night. Much of the T-72 tank fleet is also plagued with problems. Not only does it lack night-fighting capabilities, fire control systems and good communications, there is also a shortage of specialised ammunition—the list goes on and on. The good thing is that France and Israel have offered help in these areas. Unfortunately, the Defence and Research and Development Organisation continues to promise indigenisation in the same areas. The government must take the decisions now; otherwise, as in the 1999 Kargil war where Rs 2,175 crore was spent on equipment that arrived much after the war was over, the frittering of forex would become unavoidable.

Though Operation Parakram failed to meet any political objectives, it did turn out to be a fruitful exercise in operational terms. The operational gains of this mobilisation are listed below.

- Today the army is confident of employing its dual-tasked forces, which were moved from the Chinese front in the east to J&K in the west against Pakistan. These include up to three divisions and a corps headquarters. Given that the government has decided to call the demobilisation of the army a strategic relocation, these additional forces in the J&K sector will not move to their peacetime locations in a hurry.
- The army was able to devise bold operational plans and train troops accordingly. It was unusual for the army to have moved its three strike corps to the Thar desert for the June war. On assuming command of the army, Gen. N. C. Vij, who was the vice-chief of army staff during Operation Parakram, said: "In times of war, the role of the army is to occupy [territory] and others [air force, etc.] come in support of it."[5] The general was probably hinting that for the June war, the army and the air force had achieved a high level of coordination through the refining of war plans and training. The attained inter- and intra-services cooperation was indeed a major operational gain.

---

[5] "We will not Lower Guard on LoC", *The Hindustan Times*, January 1, 2003.

- The army achieved a high level of coordination with the railways and civil administration for strategic movement of forces across the country. This would help a future mobilisation, if needed, to be much smoother and faster.
- The army was able to find shortcomings in its mobilisation drills and evolve new self-operating procedures.
- The importance of the special forces and commando units with infantry battalions on the LoC was highlighted. Army Chief Gen. Vij hinted that the special forces had done a good job, and would hence get special attention, implying better equipment and communication. These indicate that the army plans to raise a few more special forces for J&K.

Even as another Operation Parakram has a robust future, India would need to be clear on two fundamental issues: One, the political leadership should have enough resolve to withstand enormous US-led world pressure to end a likely war before its sought objectives have been met. And two, the military gains of Operation Parakram cannot be frittered away—the next war with Pakistan should logically be a full-scale conventional war.

India's Nuclear Capability

Operational gains notwithstanding, Operation Parakram seems to have jolted the Indian political leadership out of its slumber. Probably the single most important realisation which emerged from the June stand-off with Pakistan is that there is a need to honestly re-examine India's nuclear weapons credibility. While the political leadership did not entirely disbelieve the military's argument that Pakistan would not use nuclear weapons too soon in a war, and that its nuclear threshold was high enough to fight a full-scale conventional war which could even lead to a near destruction of its offensive forces, the real worry was about our own nuclear weapons capabilities. The question that kept the Indian political leadership on tenterhooks was whether Pakistan was deterred by India's nuclear arsenal. The answer, of course, was an unambiguous negative. India's political leadership had misgivings about its own nuclear declaratory and employment policies; about the fact that the military did not have full knowledge about the nation's nuclear weapons capabilities and that the nuclear delivery systems left much to be desired. These issues assumed an added urgency after India realised that the US and the world would not come to its rescue in the fight against Pakistan-sponsored and -supported terrorism in J&K. Moreover, the Indian armed forces had trained themselves for a successful full-fledged conventional war, which could not be ruled out in the future.

Against this backdrop, the government announced its nuclear policy on January 4, 2003. The nuclear declaratory policy was less ambitious than the draft nuclear doctrine prepared by the National Security Advisory Board (NSAB) in July 2000, which was rejected by the then Foreign Minister, Jaswant Singh. The NSAB's nuclear doctrine spoke about the need for a triad of delivery systems: aircraft, land-based mobile ballistic missiles, and sea-based assets— something which openly suggested a nuclear arms race and was unacceptable to the US. While rubbishing the draft nuclear doctrine, released by National Security Advisor Brajesh Mishra himself, Jaswant Singh spelt out a non-ambitious and rather ambiguous nuclear doctrine in a lengthy interview to a newspaper.[6] The post-

---

[6] "India's Nuclear Doctrine", *The Hindu*, November 28, 1999:

- India shall maintain a minimum nuclear deterrent and shall undertake necessary measures to ensure its credibility.
- India has declared a moratorium on undertaking any further underground nuclear test explosions, but R&D activities including computer simulation and subcritical tests will be conducted as necessary.
- Development work on an extended-range Agni missile is under way and a successful flight test was carried out this year. Additional flight testing would be undertaken in a manner that is non-provocative, transparent, and consistent with established international norms and practices.
- India has declared a no-first-use doctrine. This has implicit in it the principle that India shall not use nuclear weapons against non-nuclear weapon states.
- In order that our minimum deterrent be credible, we shall adopt and maintain a deployment posture that ensures survivability of assets. Such a posture, obviously, provides for greater safety and security.
- India will not engage in an arms race. We shall not, therefore, pursue and open-ended programme.
- A civilian command and control system, with necessary safeguards, shall cater for possible contingencies.

Parakram nuclear doctrine was closer to the Jaswant Singh doctrine than the NSAB nuclear doctrine.

India's nuclear doctrine highlighted eight imperatives about the nation's declaratory policy:

- A credible minimum deterrent will be built and maintained.
- A posture of "no first use" will be adopted—nuclear weapons will only be used in retaliation against a nuclear attack on Indian territory or on Indian forces anywhere.
- Nuclear retaliation to a first strike will be massive and designed to inflict unacceptable damage.
- Nuclear retaliatory attacks can only be authorised by the civilian political leadership through the Nuclear Command Authority.
- Nuclear weapons will not be used against non-nuclear weapon states.
- However, in the event of a major attack against India, or Indian forces anywhere, by biological and chemical weapons, India will retain the option of retaliating with nuclear weapons.
- There will be a continuation of strict controls on the export of nuclear and missile-related materials and technology, participation in the Fissile Material Cut-off Treaty negotiations, and observance of the moratorium on nuclear tests.
- There will be a continued commitment to the goal of a nuclear weapon-free world through global, verifiable and non-discriminatory nuclear disarmament.

India's nuclear doctrine highlighted a new issue: the right to retaliate with nuclear weapons even against a biological and chemical attack on India or Indian forces anywhere in the world. While enough debate was generated in the media on the need for such incorporation, the real story came from elsewhere. Three days after

---

- India's commitment to global nuclear disarmament remains undiluted. We will continue to work with other like-minded countries and take initiatives for moving towards a nuclear-weapons-free world. We also seek to negotiate CBMs, both in the conventional and nuclear fields, with the aim of reducing lack of trust in the region.

the government made the nuclear doctrine public, the NSAB, in what appeared to be a deliberate leak to the media, suggested two important matters as part of its annual review of India's security policy. A call was made to review India's no-first-use nuclear doctrine, and it was advised that India should not close the option to conduct further nuclear tests, should they be scientifically necessary. The suggestion to review the no-first-use doctrine was not entirely new. From time to time, analysts had suggested India should dispense with the asymmetry in its doctrine vis-à-vis Pakistan. Considering that Pakistan adamantly stuck to its first-use nuclear doctrine, India was automatically placed in a more difficult and demanding position. There was a need for India to safeguard its nuclear assets and leadership from a putative first strike from Pakistan—which would have good intelligence information on India—before embarking on a suitable retaliation. Be that as it may, the crux of this debate has been more academic than real. In reality, under supreme exigency conditions, all nations retain the option to change their declaratory policies. India cannot be an exception to the rule.

The surprise, however, was the NSAB suggestion that India should not close the option to conduct nuclear tests, if necessary. This recommendation gets a boost from the fact that Pakistan has a proven nuclear missile warhead design from China. This was refined and improved for better weight-to-yield ratio by Pakistan after it opened up a plutonium fissile procurement route in addition to its enriched uranium one with China's help. In comparison, India had closed the option of testing nuclear warheads for ballistic missiles after it signed the 1963 Partial Test Ban Treaty prohibiting overground testing needed for missile warheads. India has the onerous challenge of both matching the nuclear warhead credibility of Pakistan's ballistic missile, and developing higher-yield nuclear warheads for longer-range ballistic and cruise missiles against China. In essence, further nuclear tests may be inescapable if India wants to have credible nuclear warheads to instil a high assurance level within its military forces and deter enemies. The lack of this could probably be one of the reasons for the government's hesitance to share the nation's full range of nuclear capabilities with the defence services.

This shortcoming is discernable in India's nuclear doctrine. Nearly five years after the nuclear tests, India provided a glimpse of the operationalisation of its nuclear doctrine. The government announced[7] that the Nuclear Command Authority would comprise a political council and an executive council. The political council would be headed by the prime minister, while the national security advisor (NSA) would lead the executive council. Chaired by the prime minister, the political council would be the sole body to authorise the use of nuclear weapons. Meanwhile, the executive council would provide inputs for decision-making to the political council and execute orders given by it. In addition, the government approved the appointment of a commander-in-chief, Strategic Forces Command (C-in-C, SFC) who would manage and administer all strategic forces.

The government should have taken these steps earlier to generate confidence in the mind of the public and to deter Pakistan. The composition of the political council is likely to be similar to the CCS, including the ministers of home, defence, finance, external affairs and the NSA. The executive council under the NSA would have the three services chiefs, chiefs of the Defence Research and Development Organisation, Bhabha Atomic Research Centre, the intelligence agencies, the Defence Intelligence Agency, the chairman of the Joint Intelligence Committee, and the cabinet secretary to say the least. Meanwhile, the C-in-C, SFC, working under the present system of the Chiefs of Staff Committee (COSC), would at some stage become the custodian of the strategic forces.

Attempting to clarify the brief government statement regarding the SFC, the chairman of the Chiefs of Staff Committee, Admiral Madhvendra Singh,[8] made three relevant points to the media. First, the training in nuclear weapons and servicing of delivery systems would be the responsibility of the individual services. Second, the utilisation and use of nuclear weapons would be the prerogative of the newly formed SFC. And third, while the ballistic missiles will be transferred to the SFC initially, the Indian Air Force would soon decide on the transfer of its nuclear capable fighters to the SFC.

This means that the government has made up its mind to employ the Agni and Prithvi missiles exclusively with nuclear and conventional warheads respectively. Once the Agni missile group has been

---

[7] Government of India Press Release (2003), "The Cabinet Committee on Security Reviews Operationalisation of India's Nuclear Doctrine", January 4, New Delhi: GOI.
[8] "New Command to Decide on Nuke Use", *The Asian Age*, January 17, 2003.

raised by the artillery, the group with its accompanying parapher-
nalia would come under the operational control of the C-in-C,
SFC, while being administered, trained and serviced by the artillery. The physical management of the Agni missile group by the
SFC, though agreed to in principle, is years away and depends
upon the impending tests of Agni-I and Agni-II, the *inter se* relationship between the three service chiefs within the COSC, and
the available finances to create an elaborate infrastructure within
the SFC. The case of nuclear-capable aircraft being physically given
to the SFC is different.

Unlike the Agni missile group, which will be dedicated for use
with nuclear warheads, the Indian Air Force cannot afford the
luxury of having aircraft dedicated to nuclear delivery. The meagre air assets will necessarily have to be kept on a dual role—the
air force will keep the option of using its earmarked and modified
aircraft meant for nuclear use to deliver conventional payload as
well. For this reason, the air force has not yet decided about trans-
ferring its aircraft to the SFC. While this is completely justified
from its perspective, it cannot be pleasing to the army, which
would also like to retain the Agni missile group under its command. The C-in-C, SFC, will set up its secretariat and hope to get
some inputs from the executive council, routed through the COSC,
about India's nuclear weapons capabilities for nuclear planning
purposes. Like the existing Chief of Integrated Defence Staff
(CIDS), who has completed a frustrating year under the COSC in
October 2002, the SFC cannot be expected to do much better.

Rendering India's position even more precarious is the fact that
Pakistan already has a variety of operational systems—Ghauri,
Ghaznavi, Abdali, and Shaheen. Amidst much fanfare, the Ghauri
and Shaheen ballistic missiles were inducted into the Pakistan
Army by Gen. Musharraf on January 3, 2003, and February 28, 2003
respectively. India, on the other hand, has a single operational
Prithvi missile, while the induction of the Agni is at least a year
away. With India having decided to use Prithvi with conventional
warheads, the only nuke delivery platform at present is aircraft.
And here lies the problem: Unlike India, Pakistan would give priority to its ballistic missiles as a delivery system for nukes, with
aircraft as the stand-by platform. Considering that ballistic missiles are unstoppable and immune to air defence systems, the
success of Islamabad's nuclear strike, should it so decide, is assured.
India's nuke delivery with its aircraft—SU 30, Mirage-2000 and

Jaguar—would remain uncertain, problematic and dangerous. Simply put, India does not have a single completely assured delivery platform for nuclear weapons.

In this context of nuclear vulnerability, India has sought a high-profile defence package from Russia. During a visit to Moscow in January 2003, Defence Minister George Fernandes confirmed that "Gorshkov is part of the package agreed to in the inter-governmental agreement, and all three deals would be signed together".[9] The package comprises the 44.5-thousand-tonne Admiral Gorshkov aircraft carrier, two Akula-class nuclear-propelled submarines and four TU-22M3 maritime reconnaissance aircraft, which are actually long-range, nuclear-capable bombers. The minister expressed hope that the deal would be signed by May 2003. In addition, India has sought Israel's anti-missile Arrow system technology to reconvert the indigenous surface-to-air Akash missile from an anti-aircraft to an anti-missile system. The urgency in seeking the weapon systems from Russia is indicative of the fact that India wants a credible and assured nuclear delivery system—something it probably does not have. It is reasonable to assume that India does not have a high assurance level of nuclear warheads for its ballistic missiles, which itself has not been developed fully. Considering that none of the aircraft with the Indian Air Force would be reliable enough to beat Pakistan's air defences completely, the leasing of TU-22 bombers makes operational sense.

The Importance of being Gen. Pervez Musharraf

Conducting a successful foreign and defence policy is more about strategic clarity than anything else. Strategic clarity does not imply a complex thinking process or the need to be a genius. All it requires is an ability to grasp changing ground realities, and an understanding that states are guided by their own national interests more than any other factor. Powerful nations become so because they have the capability to accurately appreciate ground realities or strategic imperatives faster than others, in addition to being

---

[9] "Russia gives Nuclear Edge to Indian Defence", *The Sunday Times*, January 19, 2003.

able to influence events befittingly to benefit their national interests. This, in essence, is what strategic clarity is all about.

Unfortunately, India has equated strategic clarity with moral clarity. There is hardly any country, including the US, which does not publicly accept that Pakistan continues to indulge in cross-border terrorism across the LoC into J&K. All know that Pakistan created the Taliban in Afghanistan and helped Osama Bin Laden befriend the Taliban supreme leader, Mullah Omar. While empathising with India's viewpoint, the world does not reject Pakistan's viewpoint either. The world does not disbelieve Pakistan when it says that it stands against terrorism of all sorts, including the Taliban and Al Qaeda. Pakistan itself has been a victim of terrorism. However, according to Pakistan, what goes on across the LoC is not terrorism, but a freedom struggle being waged by indigenous militants who should not be stopped from freely moving across the divided J&K—Indian occupied Kashmir and *Azad* Kashmir. Considering that Pakistan has pledged moral and political support to this indigenous struggle, Islamabad cannot be expected to indefinitely curtail the movement of militants within an area which should rightly belong to them, or so the argument goes.

The problem with Pakistan's righteous position, however, is that it does not explain its material and military infrastructure support to militants—after all, there are no arms manufacturing factories in J&K. Hundreds of sophisticated arms caches captured by Indian security forces from militants in J&K have all come from Pakistan. Moreover, a majority of foreign militants or jehadis in J&K are Pakistani nationals, out of which some are retired Pakistani soldiers. India has provided indelible evidence of Pakistan's direct and multifaceted involvement in J&K through its army and ISI to the world community. Yet, the world does not endorse India's position that "the epicentre of terrorism in our region is Pakistan and the adjoining areas of Afghanistan".[10]

This should spur India to ask itself what is probably a moot question: How important is Gen. Musharraf to the US? The US, after all, has accepted Pakistan's unique form of democracy, where an elected prime minister can be dismissed by his own army chief.

---

[10] Sibal, Kanwal (2003), "Challenges Ahead—India's Views on Regional Development", *The Indian Express*, January 3.

This concession cannot be the outcome of the single reason that Musharraf has pledged to fight against terrorism. India should dispassionately assess the relevance of President Musharraf and the region comprising Afghanistan, the Central Asian Republics and Iran for the US. Considering that there will be unabated US pressure on India to talk with Pakistan, it is pointless to deny its existence or to aimlessly wait for Musharraf to stop infiltration across the LoC.

India has accused Pakistan of being the epicentre of terrorism, as it is exporting terrorism into J&K and has been an active supplier of nuclear weapons technology to North Korea. The US does not deny either of the charges against Pakistan, but has a different perspective on them. It is worth mentioning that before 9/11, US intelligence agencies had identified three threats facing the nation: Bin Laden; the increasing availability of weapons of mass destruction—chemical, biological and nuclear—including weapons proliferation concerns; and the rise of Chinese power, military and otherwise.[11] After 9/11, the US focus has been on Bin Laden and his Al Qaeda brand of terrorism, and the non-proliferation of weapons of mass destruction (WMD). A doomsday scenario for the US is the prospect of nukes falling into the hands of Al Qaeda. Considering that Pakistan is the only Islamic nation which has nuclear weapons, the West's largest concern is that Islamabad should not have a regime either incapable of keeping its nukes under tight control or having sympathies with the jehadis.

Even as Musharraf supports the US, he is playing on its fears for reasons of his own. First, not only does the war against terrorism enable him to reverse the process of Talibanisation of the Pakistan society, it also helps him regain the strategic space in Afghanistan which it lost to the Taliban. Second, Musharraf has also managed to wrest a silent assurance from the US that it would not push him too hard on terrorism in J&K, thereby ensuring that his position within the Pakistan Army remains powerful. Barring a few tactical alterations, this has been the understanding between the US and Pakistan on J&K.

Pakistan is not the only country to cut a deal on terrorism with the US. Russia and China, the two traditional sceptics of US policy, have both come around to share the US viewpoint on terrorism

---

[11] Woodward, Bob (2002), *Bush at War*, New York: Simon & Schuster, p. 35.

and proliferation, two issues which are at the core of President Bush's war on terror. Facing indigenous terrorist insurgencies, these powers initially made a pact with Washington that if it promised not to interfere in their internal matters, they would support the United States' war—Operation Enduring Freedom—in Afghanistan. Russia has been fighting militancy in its break-away Chechnya republic, while China has been battling with Muslim Uighurs in its Xinjiang province. Both powers mutually support anti-terrorism actions launched by each other in their own countries. After their national agenda was accepted by the US, both countries have acknowledged that the scourge of terrorism and proliferation needs to be addressed seriously.

Until 9/11, it was probably unthinkable for Russia to accept the unilateral scrapping of the 1972 ABM treaty by the US with barely a murmur. The idea of NATO enlargement in countries bordering Russia no longer raises the hackles of Russian military brass, and the presence of US troops in the former Soviet Central Asian Republics no longer means a declaration of war. Russia and China understand geopolitics and the consequent writing on the wall that the epicentre of international terrorism is closer to them than the US. It is for this reason that the Shanghai Cooperation Organisation (SCO)—comprising Russia, China, the four former Soviet republics and the recently joined Uzbekistan—formed to resolve border differences between the member states has re-focused itself towards collectively fighting terrorism.

India, on the other hand, jumped on the US bandwagon within hours of 9/11 and offered everything without asking for anything, in the naïve belief that terror was a universal menace and therefore should not be compartmentalised. One year later, the epicentre of terrorism for the world is still Afghanistan and not Pakistan as India understands it. The terrorists are the Al Qaeda and its various offshoots who swear by the corrupted version of jehad, and not the Pakistan-supported, so-called Kashmiri freedom fighters. The implicit suggestion is that there are bad terrorists whom Pakistan is fighting against as an indispensable partner in the US-led war on terror, and there are good terrorists, whom the world will not fight as that may dislodge President Musharraf.

In Pakistan's military democracy, President Musharraf derives his power by being the chief of army staff. The least Musharraf must do to stay in power is to retain the unflinching loyalty of his army brass. For this reason, once he signed up on the side of the US-led war, Musharraf got rid of his two close colleagues—ISI Chief Gen. Mahmood Ahmad and Deputy Chief of Army Staff Gen. Muzzafar Usmani. The two were responsible for the coup against Nawaz Sharif in October 1999 which brought Gen. Musharraf to power, and had masterminded the involvement of the Taliban in the 1999 Kargil war with India. They had to go because they were Taliban and Al Qaeda sympathisers. Even as Musharraf cleanses the army and the ISI of jehadi loyalists, he has to ensure that the so-called freedom struggle in J&K remains on the boil. It is certainly a difficult job, but not an impossible one for Musharraf considering he is aware that the US would not dump him for fear of nuclear weapons falling in the hands of the jehadis. And his army brass is equally pleased with Musharraf so long as undiluted terrorism continues in J&K.

Sensing that the US-led war against terror would be a long one, Russia, India's strategic ally and a major world power, sought its own strategic foothold in the war. In August 2002, Russia established a Consultative Group on strategic stability and a Joint Working Group (JWG) on counter-terrorism with Pakistan to engage the latter on the issues of developments in Afghanistan and the adjoining region, and international terrorism. This indicates that Russia has also grasped the importance of Musharraf for stability in the region and exchange of views on the fight against the Al Qaeda brand of international terrorism. There is little gainsaying that the two would discuss bad terrorists only. It would be interesting to note how Russia balances its two JWGs—one with Pakistan discussing bad terrorists, and the other with India focusing on so-called good terrorists. The lesson for India here is that like the major powers Russia and China, India would have to fight its own terrorists before it fights international terrorists in the US-led war.

On the question of nukes being loose in Pakistan, which may fall in the hands of terrorists and their sympathisers, India is unwittingly buttressing Pakistan's case. It is Musharraf's argument that given his fight against the jehadis, it is of paramount importance that he stays in power to safeguard Pakistan's strategic assets. The US is petrified at the prospect of a moderate Musharraf getting replaced by a fundamentalist general in Pakistan. This explains why the US let Musharraf turn democracy on its head in Pakistan. In October 2002, Pakistan conducted the most farcical election in its history where national political leaders were barred from contesting, and the newly elected prime minister, Mir Zafarullah Khan Jamali, took oath to continue the policies of President Musharraf—who, through a rigged national referendum, gave himself a five-year extension—rather than defend the Constitution. Ironically, the Constitution itself was emasculated to suit the supreme leader rather than serve the people.

The prospects of Musharraf getting overthrown is so alarming for the US that it has decided to downplay Pakistan's blatant proliferation of nuclear weapons technology to North Korea. The US officials could not have been too surprised when North Korean officials admitted, in the course of high-level bilateral talks in October 2002, that they were pursuing a Uranium enrichment programme in violation of international agreements—the NPT and the 1994 Agreed Framework with US which Pyongyang had signed to shut down its plutonium-based nuclear programme. The US intelligence agencies had surely kept the administration informed about the Pakistan–North Korea clandestine nexus. In return for No-Dong ballistic missiles, which were renamed Ghauri, Pakistan had passed on to North Korea the know-how and technology for Uranium enrichment for making nuclear weapons. There is little doubt that China knew of this deal from the beginning. In hindsight, the deal was struck during the visit of Prime Minister Benazir Bhutto to North Korea in 1993—and was signed sometime in 1995—when Pakistan was looking around for long-range ballistic missiles to target large parts of India. China, at that time, was under the strict watch of the US for its blatant nuclear and missile proliferation, especially of about 34 complete M-11 missiles, to Pakistan. The road to Pyongyang was shown to Islamabad by China—it was not a coincidence that the first time Premier Bhutto went to North Korea was from Beijing.

What surprised the US officials about the North Korean admittance was the timing and their intractable behaviour. The timing could not have been worse: much against the wishes of the international community and the UN, the US was ready for a war with Iraq to overthrow Saddam Hussein. Even as the US has the military capability to fight two regional wars simultaneously, it cannot afford to annoy China, Russia, Japan and South Korea for the sake of North Korea. The answer lies in talking with North Korea. It is indeed ironic that the US has been forced to overlook the shabby proliferation record of China and Pakistan vis-à-vis North Korea so as to not open up new problem areas. It is in this context that Gen. Colin Powell's strange statement that Gen. Musharraf had assured him there was no proliferation to North Korea at present is to be understood. The US has decided to let bygones be bygones, as it was not under Musharraf that Pakistan passed nuclear know-how to North Korea. Implicit in the statement is a sense that as Pakistan's priority for stability in the region increases, the US may yet again condone its shenanigans.

Therefore, when President Bush called Musharraf a friend and a strategic ally, he was not referring to some short-term relationship. What he meant was that US-Pak relations had strengthened after the appointment of the interim President Hamid Karzai's regime in Afghanistan, and would continue into the future. Both the US and Hamid Karzai have sought close cooperation with Pakistan for bringing stability in Afghanistan. The US commander in Afghanistan, Lt. Gen. Dan McNeill, asked Pakistan in November 2002 to put more forces on its border to tighten the noose around Al Qaeda and Taliban cadres hiding in the mountainous ranges along the Pakistan-Afghanistan border. Based in Bagram, Gen. McNeill commanded about 8,000 US and 5,000 coalition troops. Pakistan said it could commit about 70,000 troops on its border with Afghanistan, provided the US ensured that its eastern front with India remained calm and tension-free. The US apparently took Pakistan's offer seriously, as it was under pressure to show more tangible results in its war against terror. A nagging criticism of the Bush administration, at home and abroad, was its seeking to open two new military fronts—against Iraq and, perhaps, North Korea at a later stage—even as the war in Afghanistan remained inconclusive.

For Hamid Karzai, who is on probation until the 2004 elections, the time to show results is running out. Incapable of controlling the warlords who run their fiefdoms outside the capital Kabul, Karzai's credibility depends upon gaining the support of the sizeable fellow Pashtuns in the south. This cannot be accomplished without Pakistan's support. Islamabad, which seeks strategic space in Afghanistan, would be willing to do so provided the Karzai government denies leverage to arch-enemy India in its nation building. Similarly, the US would hate to see its protégé Karzai fail in Afghanistan, especially since the Al Qaeda still remains a daunting challenge. This explains why, on Pakistan's urging, the US in November 2002 applied diplomatic pressure on India to go slow with its

Afghanistan involvement, an incident which embarrassed Delhi no ends.

The growing relationship between the US, Pakistan and Afghanistan has resulted in the Trans-Afghanistan natural gas pipeline deal. Turkmenistan, Afghanistan and Pakistan signed an agreement in December 2002 in Ashgabat, the capital of Turkmenistan, to build the 1,400 km line costing about $ 2.5 billion, designed to link the vast gas reserves of Turkmenistan with Pakistan—and possibly India, if it so desires—through Afghanistan. After the signing, a feasibility study funded by the Asian Development Bank has commenced, to be completed post-haste by June 2003. Once the project is cleared, it will run from the Davletbad gas field in southern Turkmenistan and Herat in western Afghanistan, before swinging across the country to Kandahar in the south. From there it will run to Multan in Pakistan, with one spur leading to the port of Gwadar—where a gas liquefaction plant would be set up—and another to Delhi, if the latter agreed. This pipeline would bring about $300 million annually as transit fee to Karzai's Afghanistan, in addition to catering for its energy needs. Moreover, the US would be back in the region's energy game after its giant Unocal Corporation was forced to shut shop in the wake of US attacks on Al Qaeda bases in eastern Afghanistan in 1998. If the Karzai government is able to ensure security of this gas pipeline deal, it would be a serious blow to the alternative Turkmenistan-Iran pipeline arrangement which the US opposes. Even while Iran has pledged to fight international terrorism, Washington remains adamant to include Teheran in its "axis of evil" nations.

Not to miss all available opportunities, Pakistan has sought to improve relations with Iran. Like India, Iran has been a powerful backer of the Northern Alliance against the Taliban regime, which viewed the theological Shia regime in Teheran as heretical. With the Taliban out of the way, it is easier for Islamabad and Teheran to mend relations, not to mention Karzai's interest in facilitating such a relationship. Karzai will be more than happy to see the traditional supporters of the Taliban and the Northern Alliance shake hands for stability in Afghanistan. For Pakistan, the biggest benefit of better relations with Iran will be the opportunity to scupper the warm ties between India and Iran. This explains the statement of the Pakistan Prime Minister, Mir Zafarullah Khan, to the visiting Iran President, Mohammed Khatami, in Islamabad in December

2002 that Iran must show greater concern with the Kashmir problem, just as Pakistan did towards Palestine. In the changed circumstances, Iran foresees enormous benefits in close ties with Pakistan:
an honourable settlement for the Northern Alliance in Afghanistan;
better relations between the two Islamic nations, with the added
hope of Pakistan helping Iran's clandestine nuclear weapons
programme as it did North Korea's; and, importantly, a possibility
that Pakistan provides the bridge between the US and Iran like it
did with the US and China in the seventies. The US, after all, is not
so much opposed to the moderate regime of President Khatami
in Iran as it is to the present regimes in Iraq and North Korea—
these being the three nations that comprise President Bush's "axis
of evil".

Strong possibilities, therefore, exist of Pakistan becoming an
important player, if not exactly the pivot of stability and energy
security in the region comprising Afghanistan, the Central Asian
Republics, Russia, China and Iran. The visit of President Musharraf
to Russia in February 2003 to discuss regional strategic stability
under the rubric of the newly formed strategic group is to be seen
in this context. The US, meanwhile, has many reasons to back
Musharraf: nukes are safe with him; he is unlikely to indulge in
nuclear proliferation as long as Washington keeps supporting him;
he is determined to fight the Al Qaeda brand of international terrorism and end Talibanisation within Pakistan; he is needed for
stability in Afghanistan; and he can help provide access to the vast
gas and oil reserves of the Central Asian Republics.

Unnerved by the growing clout of Musharraf, India has sought
to infuse more warmth into its relations with Iran. The gas pipeline project from Iran to India, planned to run overland through
Pakistan, has been revived. Despite refusing to talk with Pakistan,
India has indicated that it may not be averse to the proposed gas
pipeline running through the country. Feasibility studies done in
the nineties by India and Iran suggested that the pipeline would
run 1,000 km on Iran territory, and about 800 km in Pakistan before
entering India. During his December visit to Pakistan, President
Khatami had publicly spoken of the need for such a pipeline that
would not only enrich Iran, but also give Pakistan as much as $600
million annually as transit fee. Considering India imports around
two billion dollars of oil from Iran annually, its increased demand
would be met at a much lesser cost. While Musharraf silently

absorbed what Khatami had to say, India immediately took to Khatami's advice even if it meant giving $600 million to Pakistan every year. India, thus, is not entirely unaware of Musharraf's snow-balling importance. Similarly, President Karzai during his visit to Delhi in March 2003 urged India to consider the gas-pipeline which runs through Pakistan. Though Delhi has rejected the advice from both Khatami and Karzai, this is unlikely to be the last word from India.

Where does all this leave India? The coming together of the US, Pakistan, Iran and the Karzai regime for stability in Afghanistan would deny India the influence it had hoped for in the region. Once economic incentives like the gas pipeline deal show prom-ise of fruition, the US is likely to press India to go more than halfway to settle matters with Pakistan. Moreover, the US preoccupation with Iraq, North Korea and the Middle East leaves it little time to focus on Indo-Pak problems. India's continued refusal to talk with Pakistan would not find favour with the US. Russia, as a big regional player, would continue to pay some lip service to India's cause. As a non-permanent member of the UN Security Council, Pakistan would attempt to incessantly rake up the Kashmir issue at the world forum. India is indeed left with only two choices in dealing with Pakistan—either talk soon with Islamabad or not talk at all. Both options need to be considered carefully.

Need for Bilateral Talks

With Operation Parakram over, diplomacy should assume impor-tance. Even as the US and Pakistan want bilateral talks to com-mence, India's predicament has been that little was achieved by flexing military muscle for 10 long months. Infiltration continues unabated across the LoC, there is little respite from terrorist attacks in J&K, and the state and central government have no tangible initiatives for internal peace in the turbulent state. Worse, Pakistan has emerged more belligerent, and the US more supportive of its new-found ally. This was amply demonstrated when Gen. Musharraf recently congratulated his armed forces for having "earned the distinction of defeating the enemy without fighting a war". The US, meanwhile, recently told India to go slow with its involvement in Afghanistan as it was not to the liking of Pakistan.

For India, talking with Pakistan would mean conducting negotiations from a position of diplomatic and military weakness. Once
talks begin, the focus would necessarily be on the Kashmir problem. Pakistan has repeatedly said that for peace in the region, a
solution to the Kashmir problem would have to be found. The US
position is similar. Gen. Colin Powell, on a visit to India in June
2002, had emphasised that Kashmir was important, if not the
central issue for bilateral talks. And, the UN Security Council resolution 1172 of June 6, 1998, which was passed after the nuclear
tests, unambiguously states that Kashmir is the main cause of dispute between India and Pakistan.

What this means for India is that its agenda for talks would
assume a backseat. While Pakistan wants to discuss the Kashmir
issue, India wishes instead to focus on peace and security along
the LoC. These two issues constitute the "two" in the "two-plus-six"
formula which was agreed on for the composite dialogue between
the two nations in the nineties. During the failed July 2001 Agra summit, both sides had apparently agreed to elevate these two matters
to a political-level discussion from the earlier foreign-secretary-
level meets. Understandably, Pakistan would insist that threads
be picked up from the Agra summit, implying that the pressure to
show results would be enormous, especially after India accepted
the US in a facilitator's role. India clearly wants to avoid a difficult
situation.

Yet, India must talk with Pakistan at the earliest. The most important lesson of Operation Parakram for India was the need to have
a credible nuclear deterrent, and to establish an understanding
with Pakistan on nuclear and missile matters. After the 1998 nuclear tests, it was evident that India and Pakistan would need to evolve
confidence-building measures to tide over the destabilising factors—one created by the imminent nuclear weaponisation, and
the other pertaining to ballistic missiles. The process was started
with the signing of the Lahore declaration on February 21, 1999,
between Prime Ministers Atal Bihari Vajpayee and Nawaz Sharif.
Interestingly, the declaration had little to do with the problem of
J&K or other issues between the two countries. Its operative part
was the "Memorandum of Understanding", which broadly tack-
led four security related issues: to give advance notice in respect of
ballistic missile flight tests; to discuss respective nuclear doctrines
and security concepts for confidence building in nuclear and conventional fields aimed at conflict avoidance; to set up a nuclear

risk reduction centre to minimise risks of accidental or unauthorised use of nuclear weapons; and to better existing channels of communications.

Notwithstanding the operational report cards, the biggest challenge for both sides is to lay down mutually agreed ground rules, with preferably the US as the guarantor, to minimise nuclear alarms. Both sides have an asymmetrical nuclear doctrine—Pakistan prefers a first-use to India's no-first-use nuclear declaratory policy. Both sides have archaic and whimsical communication channels with one another. Both sides rely heavily on mutual friends for an early nuclear weapons warning. Considering the low mutual trust level, both sides would be tempted to misread ballistic missile warheads. The possibility exists of both sides getting overwhelmed by the high-pitch nuclear rhetoric during the war, which could lower planned nuclear threshold levels. For these reasons, both sides need to talk, even if a war between them is not ruled out.

However, if India decides not to talk with Pakistan, the nuclear and missile factors would remain a worrying concern, especially when the writing on the wall is clear: India does not rule out a war with Pakistan in the near future, and has decided to keep its powder dry. Consequently, the army's demobilisation has been termed "strategic relocation", implying that troops in J&K would stay put. These include the additional three divisions and Headquarters 33 Corps from the eastern front facing China. The holding formations would take up to four months to move back to the barracks completely—the heavy de-mining along the border is an excruciating process, and availability of railway carriages for the homeward journey of the troops would be a low priority. Even if the three strike corps leave their operational areas, a mobilisation, if needed, would be faster. The forward ammunition dumping will remain untouched, the drills for mobilisation have been well-rehearsed, and there is good coordination for strategic movement between the army and the railways. Even as the military is bracing itself for another Operation Parakram—it would be real this time— the political leadership should attempt to see the strategic imperatives as they are, and not as they ought to be.

Index

About the Authors

Lt. Gen. (Retd.) V.K. Sood is a former Vice-Chief of Army Staff. He is a graduate of the Royal College of Defence Studies, UK. During his career, Gen. Sood served as chief of staff of a strike corps, and held important command and staff appointments. He has worked in the Military Operations directorate at Army Headquarters, and was a member of the task force on Border Management, which was set up by the government after the 1999 Kargil conflict with Pakistan. Gen. Sood was awarded a Ph.D. for his dissertation on North-east India.

Pravin Sawhney is South Asia correspondent of *Jane's International Defense Review*, UK. A former major, he is the author of *The Defence Makeover: Ten Myths That Shape India's Image*. He has been a Visiting Fellow at the Royal United Services Institute, UK, and a Visiting Scholar at the Co-operative Monitoring Centre, Sandia National Laboratories, US. As a journalist he has worked with *The Times of India*, *The Indian Express* and *The Asian Age* and has written extensively on defence and strategic issues. He also writes a column for *The Pioneer* in New Delhi.